Praise for
Spiritually Intelligent Leadership

Yosi helps us dive deeper and reach higher to achieve new levels of effectiveness, growth & meaning as leaders. As a client who has experienced this firsthand, these modern integrative methods, along with the practical applications, will have a profound impact on all leaders, from aspiring managers to senior executives.
> **—Andy Byrne**, Cofounder and CEO, Clari

Yosi speaks from the heart and uses pragmatic, real-world examples to show how leading with authenticity and purpose is the best approach.
> **—Magdalena Yesil**, Entrepreneur, Venture Capitalist and Author,
> *Power Up: How Smart Women Win in the New Economy*

This extremely unique and important book offers a deeply holistic path for becoming a truly great leader.
> **—Eoghan McCabe**, CEO & Chairman, Intercom

It's a relief to finally find a complete account of what I've known to be true but had no words for—with research support and from a trustworthy source who has seen their practical application in real-world organizations. This is the book I've been looking for to offer my students in the wisdom-based leadership classes I teach.
> **—Neil Goldberg**, Author, Wise Design Leadership and Adjunct Professor
> at Pacific School of Religion

Working with Yosi and this book has helped me grow my repertoire of leadership behaviors and styles (e.g., leading from behind) while cultivating greater self-awareness. I've gained insights into my emotional responses and my ego, which has allowed me to tackle feelings of shame that previously influenced my perspectives and actions. Although I have yet to attain the level of spiritual intelligence I aspire to, the book provides a systematic approach and compelling case studies offering an enjoyable road map for the journey.
> **—Eli Chait**, CEO, Wholesail

Spiritually Intelligent Leadership *is a different type of leadership book. It offers refreshing mental models, examples, and exercises that can create lasting transformation for leaders to grow significantly and make a greater impact on their organizations and the world, while doing so with more fulfillment and joy.*
> **—Oswald Yeo**, Cofounder and CEO, Glints

This is a unique and powerful guide to knowing, integrating, and leading from the deepest, most brilliant, and essential parts of ourselves. The insights and practices will change the way we lead and live. If you want more aliveness, connectedness, and joy, dig in. This bold book has something profoundly important to teach us.
　　—**Jackie McGrath**, Executive Coaching and Leadership Development

Spiritually Intelligent Leadership *is good business: for your soul, your team, and the greater purpose of your organization. This is a readable and accessible book that helps us all grow and cultivate our sense of purpose, creativity, curiosity, resilience, and vision. All businesses experience adversity; this transformative book helps us develop and harness the inner wisdom that can come from that adversity.*
　　—**Chini Krishnan**, CEO Vimo

Yosi Amram's brave and visionary book is an important and fresh offering to the ecosystem of effective and transformative leadership. Yosi raises up the power of nonconceptual realization and dissolution of ego-clinging as essential components of becoming a changemaker—a great offering to the field.
　　—**Charles Lief, JD**, President Naropa University

Dr. Amram provides the essential, holistic map for developing your whole self. From the inside out Spiritually Intelligent Leadership *will help you reveal your gifts, heal your wounds, and develop inspired leadership wherever you lead in your life.*
　　—**Rabbi Zelig Golden**, Founder and
　　Executive Director, Wilderness Torah

Spiritually Intelligent Leadership *provides a powerful framework for how to ignite and sustainably fan the sparks of inspiration into a burning flame, illuminating our path and galvanizing our teams around a shared vision, which results in an organizational culture that is united and driven. Furthermore, it's a guide for shaping not just successful businesses, but vibrant communities that are aligned in their mission and values. The spiritual intelligence it advocates is more than a leadership strategy— it's a roadmap to authentic, purposeful, and profoundly impactful leadership. For any founder, startup, or other leader, this book is an essential read.*
　　—**Corey Reese**, President & COO, Wholesail

If you care deeply about building and leading high-performing teams with heart, put this book on your required reading list. Yosi encourages us to embrace the idea that, in its highest form, work is "love made visible" and he supports us in opening the door to incredible depth, meaning, and beauty in both our personal and professional lives.
　　—**Krista Bessinger**, Small Business Owner &
　　former VP, Twitter, Google, Oracle

SPIRITUALLY INTELLIGENT LEADERSHIP

How to Inspire by Being Inspired

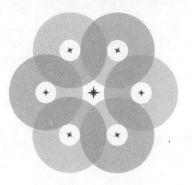

Yosi Amram, PhD

Waterside Productions
Cardiff-by-the-Sea, California

Printed in the United States of America

First Printing, 2023

ISBN-13: 978-1-123456-78-9 print edition

ISBN-13: 978-1-123456-78-9 e-book edition

Waterside Productions
2055 Oxford Ave
Cardiff, CA 92007

www.waterside.com

To all who lead the way

Who came before us

Who will follow us

Who are among us

and to

The creative spirit that inspires

He who knows others is wise;
He who knows himself
is enlightened,
He who conquers others is strong;
He who conquers himself is mighty.
—Lao Tzu

CONTENTS

PREFACE

SO, YOU WANT TO BECOME an inspirational leader. Or would you instead rather be an inspired leader? One, the other, or both?

Most of my clients look puzzled when I first ask them this question, wondering how the two might be different. When exploring how it feels to want to be an inspirational leader, it's as if it feels neutral to them—as a matter of fact. They say their attention is turned outward to look at the effect they have on others. On the other hand, while contemplating what it means to be an inspired leader, most report experiencing a higher level of energy, force, and vibrant aliveness; in which case their attention is turned inward, focused on how they feel about themselves.

Since we can't control how others feel, attempting to become "inspirational" in their eyes is putting our fate in their hands. Conversely, becoming "inspired" is within our own power. While we might want both, we must be clear on the relationship between the two: becoming inspired is the cause; others finding us inspirational is the effect.

Meaning you can only lead others after you lead yourself. You become an inspiring leader only when you are inspired yourself, when you're lit up by a vision that calls to you from your future. As your own spark is ignited, your cause, energy, and commitment spread like wildfire.

You might have tried all sorts of strategies in pursuit of becoming an inspirational leader. Maybe you took a workshop on public speaking or read articles about how to improve morale. Adding inspirational behaviors to your toolkit may come in handy for a presentation or a cocktail party, but they won't sustain you or your team over the long haul as you guide them toward accomplishing your mission.

So *how* do you ignite your spark and fan your flame enough to draw others in? The answer is through developing your spiritual intelligence (SI).

Spiritual intelligence is not a momentary epiphany of oneness, nor is it a belief in a higher power or God. Like emotional intelligence, a set of abilities that draws on emotional resources, spiritual intelligence is the ability to access inner spiritual resources and embody qualities like purpose, passion, compassion, integrity, presence, love, freedom, and joy. Spiritual intelligence helps these attributes permeate your life, lighting up your world and attracting others to you and your vision.

It has taken me more than half a lifetime to learn this. At eighteen, I was drafted into three years of mandatory service in the Israeli Air Force. Although I was very "successful" as a leader in the military, I chafed against the "command and control" military leadership model. I knew there had to be a more humane approach to leadership and resolved someday to build an organization that would inspire and support people's highest potential. Over the next few decades, I was fortunate enough to realize that dream, founding and leading two technology companies through initial public offerings (IPOs). But even with this success, blessed with health and wealth, I felt an ache in my heart for greater and deeper fulfillment. I didn't know then what it was, but I knew it could only be found through exploring my inner psyche. Eventually this yearning pulled me from my life as a CEO, sent me back to school for a PhD, and led to my current vocation as a clinical psychologist and executive coach.

In school, I focused my doctoral research on spiritual intelligence and its impact on leadership. I wanted to define and measure it, as much to contribute to the field as to understand its potential for my own development. The SI scale I created has since been translated into over a half dozen other languages. Many other researchers have demonstrated its predictive efficacy, showing that SI contributes to satisfaction and quality of life, work performance, and effective leadership. In fact, leaders with greater SI have been shown to produce not only better morale, commitment, and engagement in their teams, but also better financial results for their organizations than those with less SI. And throughout the entire organization, at all levels, people with greater SI are more productive and effective. Over a thousand papers have cited my SI research. As of today, two decades since its inception, SI has been established as a real and positive influence in our professional and personal lives.

Many things might motivate us to develop our spiritual intelligence, but no matter the impetus, we universally experience a similar divine kiss on our hearts; our souls are stirred up and our spirits are aroused. Naturally, we desire more. So, we begin by traveling inward—or more accurately, diving—to the depth of our being, into our essence, where we encounter the spark of our aliveness, our spirit (derived from the Latin *spiritus*, meaning the "animating force and breath of life"), where we are in-spired, where we are most *inner*-connected. Where we also find our *inter*-connectedness with all humanity, and ultimately all of life, sharing in its spark. It is there we are in alignment with the deepest truth of our nature.

And from that place, all our SI qualities naturally arise. Cultivating these qualities in our lives further fuels our spark and fans our flame, letting their light and energy radiate outward, drawing others in, and reinforcing each other in a positive feedback loop, thus uplifting ourselves and our world.

This is how we become Spiritually Intelligent Leaders (SILeaders), grounded in the core of our being. We become inner-directed with the courage to be our unique authentic selves. Inner-connected, we naturally stand our ground with confidence, and inter-connected, we listen to others with openness. Hence, we create and cultivate collaborative communities of people with common missions, visions, and values.

I have seen this happen in my own life and in my clients' lives. Now, as a therapist and coach, I have worked with numerous CEOs, many of whom have built successful businesses, leading organizations with thousands of employees and annual revenues in the billions. These individuals represent the entire spectrum of belief, from the spiritual-but-not-religious, to devout practitioners of a particular religion, to agnostics and atheists. Regardless of their orientation, they can connect with the sacred spark of their life force and use it to become more powerful, centered, and effective. They come to lead inspired lives that benefit themselves and inspire and impact all those around them, both personally and professionally.

Whether you're an aspiring leader or a seasoned veteran, you undoubtedly already embody many SI qualities. You hold some vision of your potential—the person and the leader you aspire to be. If you trace this aspiration to its source, you will find it arising from deep within your heart, your soul, and your sacred spark of life. This book is written to help you ignite that spark and fan your flame to lead an inspired life, so that your radiant light may shine through as you become more purposeful, graceful, joyful, powerful, and empowered.

Yosi Amram, PhD

Palo Alto, CA

A NOTE TO THE READER

THOUGH THE CASE STUDIES IN this book are taken from my client base, mostly consisting of privileged Silicon Valley CEOs and entrepreneurs, the spiritual intelligence leadership lessons are applicable in any industry, be it tech, health, retail, environmental, agricultural, or any other. Similarly, whatever the scale, from multinational organizations to small teams in family businesses, the human principles are the same. Besides my experience working with leaders in for-profit business, I have also had the opportunity to work with some in the nonprofit, government, or public sectors. Since the same psychological, spiritual, and leadership principles apply, I trust you will be able to apply them in your context.

INTRODUCTION

Tell me, what is it you plan to do with your one wild and precious life?
—Mary Oliver

IT IS THE SUMMER OF 1996, I am thirty-nine years old, and my life has become a complete nightmare. The headlines of the *Wall Street Journal* and the *New York Times* announce that Yosi Amram, founder, chairman, and CEO of Individual Inc., has commenced an immediate leave of absence. The day before, in an emergency session, the board passed a resolution putting me on this "voluntary" leave of absence due to my "emotional instability." By the end of the day, our stock price has fallen by half. Founding a company and guiding it through an IPO has been my lifelong dream. How has it come to this?

◎◎◎◎◎◎

It's 1974. I have just graduated from high school and, despite my pacifist leanings, am drafted for three years' mandatory service in the Israeli military. I start at the bottom of the ladder as a private. I've always been shy and introverted, so I'm surprised when my supervisors discover that I have latent leadership potential.

Over the course of my military service, I win awards and am promoted faster than anyone in the regiment's history, becoming the "commanding" sergeant major of my unit in eighteen months.

While I appreciate the recognition, I'm deeply conflicted. The rigid hierarchy that makes the military so effective chafes me. I feel that inspecting the socks and underwear of newly drafted privates and making sure they take showers to maintain the "military hardware"—their human bodies—is degrading for everyone involved.

I long for other ways to express my leadership. I think that one day I want to launch a company that's deeply humanizing. It would support the growth and unique expression of individuals above everything else. This dream begins to define my life.

Completing my tour of duty, I am eager to take charge of my life again. I conceive of using my aptitude for math and science to start a company based on technological innovation.

So, I move to the US and enroll at the Massachusetts Institute of Technology (MIT) where I earn bachelor's and master's degrees in electrical engineering and computer science. But soon I realize that I don't enjoy sitting in front of a computer day in, day out, so I pivot from technological development to business innovation. I enroll at Harvard Business School the following year.

In one of my first classes, the teacher assigns a classic *Harvard Business Review* article by Professor Abraham Zaleznik on the difference between managers and leaders. Zaleznik explains that a manager is someone who manages resources and makes decisions, but to be a leader, a person has to *inspire* those around them.

I look up the word *inspire* and discover that it has the same Latin root as *spirit*, which means "the animating breath of life." If inspiration means breathing life into something, then I figure leaders must be full of life, passion, and purpose, breathing that vitality into those they lead. I wonder how I can help everyone access that inspiration.

In the military, the call to serve often inspires heroic acts of self-sacrifice. People will volunteer to go to war, risking their lives to fight for freedom and defend their country. Soldiers will take a bullet to save a buddy. And ordinary civilians will also take extraordinary steps, jumping in front of an oncoming train or running into a burning building to save a stranger's life. So I begin to explore what I would later recognize as a foundation of spiritual intelligence, that we instinctively act to protect and serve life because we are intrinsically interconnected and interdependent with all life. With that sense of belonging, serving the larger whole feels natural and life-affirming.

We can also experience this sense of interconnectedness in a community, in business, or in a team with a shared sense of purpose. Feeling we are part of something bigger than ourselves makes us naturally want to serve it. So, the possibility of cultivating team spirit inspires me as well.

Following a several-year stint developing as a manager and leader at a tech start-up, I join a venture capital firm where I pay close attention to market trends, searching for a lead on a compelling business idea the firm would fund.

Within six months, the idea arrives. It's 1988, before the rise of the internet, and I observe that people need a way to filter an ever-exploding avalanche of information. The initial product I envision provides individualized newspapers delivered via fax machines. The company would be people's personal "knowledge bot," defining a unique profile for our clients' interests. Our sophisticated software runs against thousands of newswire stories and trade journal database articles, filtering for the person's specified interests to deliver customized results. It's a breakthrough in personalized news and promises to save people time while empowering them with much more timely information than would be readily accessible otherwise. I name the company Individual to reflect both the personalization of the news products we deliver, and an organization culture committed to supporting the development and growth of each employee.

Even as excited as I am, I soon hit some speed bumps. My venture capital partners decide not to fund the idea. Knocking on the doors of over 50 VC firms, I am discouraged when they all decide to pass as well, but I continue to pour all my energy into developing the idea, building a team, and raising money.

As my savings evaporate, I stop buying clothes or taking vacations. For the next two winters, my wife and I shop for our holiday gifts at the dollar store. Some days I can barely get out of bed, only to face yet another rejection. I nearly give up.

But, with my wife's encouragement, I manage to recruit three talented cofounders to join me without pay. Together, we convince an angel investor to take the first risk! With his financial and emotional backing, we sign on our first major customers. And with that, I am able to raise some institutional venture capital from other firms. Soon, more prestigious venture capital firms follow suit, and eventually my old VC firm joins the party as well. Finally, I can implement my vision! I pledge to create a humane workplace that fosters both individual growth and team spirit. Balancing individual autonomy with a sense of belonging turns out to be an important factor in our success.

By the end of 1994, I am thirty-eight. I've been working incessantly for about six years, often logging eighty hours a week. I frequently skip meals, exercise, and other renewing activities, and I can barely squeeze in time with my two young children. Even on date nights with my wife, my attention drifts to work. All my relationships begin to suffer.

Around this time, the internet begins its ascent, and it becomes clear that our traditional subscription-based, fax-based—and, by now, email-based—business will be threatened. I foresee that much of the information we sell will become available for free on an ad-supported basis.

But, as "info agents," we have access to our clients' unique interest profiles, a gold mine for advertisers. And, while attracting advertisers was part of my original vision, at this stage it presents an innovator's dilemma and a dangerous risk. To make the necessary changes to capture these still-nascent advertising revenue streams, we would have to secure a much larger audience that would appeal to advertisers—and that would require reducing our subscription prices. In other words, we would have to cannibalize our subscription revenues and slow our growth until advertising revenues could catch up. It's a perilous leap, one I'm terrified that we won't survive.

By this time, we've raised capital from some of Silicon Valley's top firms. Microsoft is a key investor, and we are the exclusive provider of their personalized news. My board consists of several high-profile members, CEOs of high-flying public companies themselves. I worry about what will happen to my reputation if we fail.

The pressure to maintain my standing while battling inner demons of doubt and insecurity throws me into a deep depression. With my wife's encouragement, I go to see a psychiatrist. In our first meeting, he prescribes Prozac.

I'm not yet ready to explore the root causes of my work compulsion and how I have come to tie my self-worth to my net worth. All I want is a quick fix. And Prozac provides it. Lo and behold, my mood improves. It's like a Band-Aid over a bullet hole, but it helps, and I begin riding the intoxicating new wave of the internet's promise. My fears miraculously disappear, and I move decisively, pushing my company into the future.

Emboldened as never before, I conceive of several new product offerings, which I call iAM and iCreate, that would enable people to connect and express themselves and their creativity on the World Wide Web, offerings that, while rudimentary, would resemble later social networks like Facebook and Pinterest. And I launch the first Dutch auction for selling advertising inventory on the internet, which mystifies my sales team and potential buyers at the time, but would become the standard several years later.

In this new state of manic intoxication, I undergo some profound realizations. While lying facedown getting a massage, I focus my attention and my breath on my aching tight muscles. As my body continues to relax and soften, my awareness and the sensation in my body become all one. What I normally have conceived of as three things: me, "an entity" who is the subject; the faculty of consciousnesses with which I am aware of my experience; and my sensations as objects in that awareness, are all but one thing. There is no longer a "me" that is some entity that is having this experience—there is only the experience made of consciousness. Suddenly I am in a state of nondual realization popularly called awakening, a state of oneness, in which all subject and object distinction disappear.

I had been for decades interested in what is called the mind-body problem and studying the intersection of information theory and physics—what the Nobel laureate physicist John Wheeler called the It-from-Bit. And I had been recently reading a book, *The Self-Aware Universe*[1] by a professor of theoretical physics. In that state of oneness on the massage table, I realize that all matter and energy I experience are made of consciousness taking on different forms, in-formation. As I open my eyes through the face cradle, looking at the floor, I am absorbed into it as it is absorbed into me. I perceive the interconnectedness of all things. I sense how the world is permeated by awareness and how all of time and space is linked into this seamless field of consciousness. I've never felt so alive, so whole, so connected in all my life. Over the coming days and weeks, I walk around in this state of euphoria, feeling connected to all of life and all reality. My life becomes full of synchronicities, and at times I even feel like I can communicate with animals.

I have no idea how to integrate these experiences and revelations into my life and work. My consciousness is stretching across the cosmos, but my behavior has become erratic. When I try to communicate my insights to others, they are confused and some even think I am mad. Consumed by my insights and vision, I have little interest in what others have to say. I can see the future. The internet, as the information network of networks that connects everything and everyone across time and space, takes on a mystical significance in my mind. I want Individual to be the engine that can realize that future. Overwhelmed by this vision, I am impatient. I ask for too much to happen too fast. I don't accept "It can't be done." I never compromise.

Years later, the very people who ousted me will confess that, had we executed my initiatives, we would have become major players in the explosive new internet-based world. But now, in 1996, everyone thinks I've lost my mind, which in a sense I have.

◎◎◎◎◎◎

Shortly after my board of directors decides to sideline me on a "voluntary" leave of absence, instead I resign, refusing to accept their determination. They in turn issue a press release saying that I've been fired.

A pariah, I feel like I have not only let down my investors, employees, and family, I've also lost what feels like my fundamental identity and value. I am shattered. I spend months dazed and depressed, wondering what it all means and who I am now. At night I drive to "my company's" office building. Sobbing, while remaining seated in my car in the dark parking lot because I am not allowed into the building, I feel humiliated. Dazed and confused, I periodically wonder if this is real or just a dreamed-up nightmare. Needing help beyond pills, I dive into therapy, aiming to understand, know, and heal myself.

As I begin to untangle my inner life and the various threads that led to my downfall, I reflect on the extraordinary states of oneness and nondual realizations I experienced as well. How can I discern between unhealthy clinical depression and mania and actual transformative spiritual revelations? The line seems very thin. Whatever imbalances might have induced those exalted states, the experiences I had still seem authentic and continue to resonate through my whole being. (Years later and with ongoing spiritual practice I learn how to readily reenter such nondual states of consciousness while remaining grounded.)

To understand my experiences better, I delve into spiritual literature. I am relieved to learn that visionaries throughout history experienced existential roller coaster rides too. Christian mystics, for example, describe a deep depression as a "dark night of the soul" that lasts for months or even years without a glimmer of hope, but which often precedes profound spiritual awakenings. Spiritual teachers, such as Saint John of the Cross of the Middle Ages and world-renowned modern authors, such as Eckhart Tolle who, deeply depressed, lived on a park bench for years, and Byron Katie, whose behavior led her to sleep on the floor of a cockroach-infested halfway house, all traveled similar pathways, waking from the depths of despair into the realization of encompassing unity. Furthermore, a number of powerful leaders, such as Abraham Lincoln and Winston Churchill, suffered from depression and mental illness,[2] and Mahatma Gandhi and Martin Luther King, Jr. both attempted suicide as teenagers.

Abraham Zaleznik, the professor who so inspired me in business school, observed that powerful leaders are often "twice born." They encounter major crises, only to emerge with a new, stronger sense of self and courage to express their authentic individuality.

And while, like you and me, all these leaders struggled with doubts and fears, they were connected enough to their larger sense of self and purpose not to indulge their insecurities. In that way, their lives became their teachings. And while I'm certainly no Gandhi or MLK, I am heartened knowing that I am in good company regarding the difficult experiences of which I have felt embarrassed and ashamed.

With a commitment to self-care and the aid of psychotherapy, I begin to stabilize and find my center. I get off my psychoactive meds for good and find the energy to return to work. However, I still feel compelled to prove myself in the business world. I join two other technical cofounders as the CEO of Valicert, an infrastructure for secure, trusted transactions and communications on the internet.

This time, however, I am far more grounded, and my identity is less defined by my role as CEO. Instead of working eighty hours a week, I make the most of a balanced fifty hours, which gives me more clarity and better judgment, rendering me more effective. Instead of micro-managing, I build a senior team and a support network and cultivate a collaborative relationship with my board.

I learn to delegate more and practice what is called "leading from behind," first conceptualized by Nelson Mandela, who equated a great leader with a shepherd who tends to his flock from behind (coincidently, the Bible tells of many great leaders who were shepherds, including Moses). In contrast to the conventional image of a leader as a bold visionary at the forefront directing others to follow their path, "leading from behind" facilitates others in setting their own course. Leading from behind is just as effective as leading from the front, but its impact comes from empowering others. At Valicert, I learn to alternate leading from the front and from behind as the situation demands, prioritizing self-care and keeping my ego in check.

With a less frantic work schedule, I develop a twenty-minute daily morning exercise and yoga practice routine. And being more present at home with my family, I make a point to walk or drive my kids to school on most days.

While developing my leadership style at Valicert, I am also drawn to investing and mentoring other entrepreneurs. Following Individual's IPO, I'm fortunate enough to have the financial means and experience to play the roles of an angel investor and board member helping other founders and CEOs in building their companies.

As I begin to work more intimately with these leaders, I see how profoundly their unconscious motivations drive their behavior. It becomes clear that to have the impact I want at deeper levels, I need more training. After six years at Valicert—and two years after the company's IPO—I cultivate my successor and hand him the baton.

I enroll in a PhD program to become a transpersonal clinical psychologist. Transpersonal psychology integrates spirituality into a comprehensive understanding of the human psyche. It addresses existential anxieties about suffering, illness, and death by transcending the ego-limited identity into a larger, more encompassing, and interconnected sense of self. An outgrowth of positive psychology, transpersonal psychology shifts the focus from healing mental pathologies to actualizing human potential and essential wholeness.

During my doctoral program, I begin to see more clearly that at the core of every ego is an unbearable existential sense of deficient emptiness and shame. Our ego grows around that painful shame, like an oyster putting layers around a grain of sand to help keep it hidden, even from ourselves, because it is so awful and painful. My ego, like all egos, had buried these insecurities rather than exploring and transforming them. And, as my ego pushed me to compensate for my feelings of inner deficiency, it also drove *me* into the ground.

The blessed irony is that the stress my ego generated actually catalyzed my dark night of the soul as well as my transcendent yet manic experiences, giving me a view of the reality beyond my ego. Yet, I am aware that unchecked, trying to compensate for its inherent insecurity, the ego will co-opt everything to enhance its sense of worth—be it money, sex, power, fame, or even experiences that only occur when we transcend the ego.

Its needs can never be met because it's based on a fundamental distortion, what Einstein called "an optical illusion of consciousness," that we are discrete entities, separate from the rest of existence. Failing to embrace our interconnectedness and interdependence, our hyper-individualistic culture holds "independence" as the ideal. Yet, as tribal social animals, humans are wired for connection and are interdependent with our families, friends, teams, and communities, needing them for our sense of safety, belonging, and love. And ecologically, we are interdependent, ultimately, with all of life, including the trees that provide the oxygen we breathe and consume carbon dioxide, and the trillions of bacteria within our bodies that enable us to digest our food.

The blessing that every struggle brings is the opportunity to awaken from the delusion of separation into the recognition of our true unbounded nature, our essence, or our spirit, which is already and always present and whole. And while the recognition can happen suddenly as an "emergency" or gradually as an emergence, it usually takes years or often decades of maturation to integrate it into daily life.

I learn, too, that this transformation of our essential identity is the foundational core for our emerging spiritual intelligence. Diving into this core of our essence, we discover the immense power and strength hidden in our depths while also realizing our interconnectedness with all of life sharing the same true nature, the same divine spark emanating from the same source.

I discover the term *spiritual intelligence* that introduces this concept in a book by Danah Zohar.[3] It grabs my attention because I am familiar with the powerful benefits of emotional intelligence (EI) for life and especially for leadership, a set of qualities popularized by Daniel Goleman in a book of that name. Could spiritual intelligence provide parallel benefits but also encompass the new realizations I am discovering?

But while there are numerous validated assessments for emotional intelligence and abundant research demonstrating how it contributes to well-being and effective leadership, I can't find any operational definition for spiritual intelligence that would make it measurable. And thus I set myself on a path to fill the gaps in SI research.

To start, I need to define spiritual intelligence in terms of behaviors. I initially conceptualize it as the capacity to draw on resources and embody qualities from the world's wisdom traditions in ways that enhance functioning and well-being. This definition emphasizes using resources and embodying certain qualities in daily life, which differentiates SI from spiritual beliefs, such as a belief in God or a belief that "we are all One." I also see SI as different from a spiritual or religious experience, such as hearing the voice of God or the realization of Oneness that might arise during meditation, prayer, or time in nature. SI relates to how we express our spiritual values, beliefs, and realizations in everyday life. It informs the way we experience life and function everywhere—at work, in our relationships, or while driving in traffic.

To develop a theory of SI, I need to find and interview "spiritually intelligent" people, those who already embody the qualities I'm wanting to know more about. I begin by interviewing spiritual teachers and leaders handpicked by their peers for enacting spiritual qualities. They include practitioners from most of the world's major wisdom traditions: Buddhism, Christianity, Earth-Based and Native American paths, Hinduism, Judaism, Islam, Advaita Vedanta, shamanism, Taoism, and yoga. In this way I can discover whether spiritual intelligence is the same for a Jew, a Hindu, a Christian, a Buddhist, Muslim, or a pantheist.

Through these interviews, I discover that every spiritually intelligent person embodies the same core qualities: a sense of purpose, service, compassion, trust, truth, and dis-identification from their ego. These qualities form the basis for a universal, ecumenical theory of spiritual intelligence, a theory that everyone, from an atheist to an evangelical Christian, can embody and apply to daily life.

This research leads to the development and publication of a grounded theory of spiritual intelligence.[4] And follow-up research produces the first validated SI scale, the Integrated Spiritual Intelligence Scale. Further research by others would demonstrate how SI contributes overwhelmingly to increases in well-being. One study even showed that leaders' SI predicted the financial performance of their organizations.[5]

My research continues with a focus on leadership. Controlling for established factors, such as EI and personality, I demonstrate how SI complements them in making a unique and significant contribution to leadership effectiveness. My study of 42 CEOs and 210 of their staff shows that the CEOs with greater SI cultivate teams that are more committed, work harder, have lower turnover, and exhibit greater team spirit and higher morale than CEOs with less SI.

After six years, my research is done. I graduate with my doctorate in transpersonal psychology and, after completing additional years of psychotherapy internships, receive my license to practice clinical psychology. At the age of fifty-four, I enter a new phase of life, dividing my time between practicing psychotherapy and coaching technology-oriented CEOs. Supporting these leaders, developing their spiritual intelligence, and empowering them and their organizations is the most gratifying work of my life. For the first time, my interests in psychology, spirituality, and leadership harmonize beautifully.

Since launching my practice, I have been honored to work with over a hundred CEOs, all of whom have successfully grown themselves, and often their teams and organizations have followed suit. I witnessed again and again how growing their SI enabled these leaders to energize their passion, purpose, and confidence. As they tapped into their source of power—an interconnected internal force field—they became Spiritually Intelligent Leaders (SILeaders™), naturally shining their light and activating a resonant energy in the people around them.

CHAPTER 1

IGNITING YOUR SPARK, FANNING YOUR FLAME, MAPPING YOUR JOURNEY

A mighty flame follows a tiny spark.
—Dante Alighieri

FOURTEEN BILLION YEARS INTO THE evolutionary history of the universe, a new singular expression of life has been produced: you, along with your unique gifts and talents. Never before and never after will this particular expression of life exist again.

Your gifts were given to you as an invitation from life. They're for you to actualize your potential and to express its possibilities to the fullest. The more you cultivate your gifts, the more you align with this evolutionary force of life, the more inspired and powerful you become.

Whether you're a CEO looking to elevate your organization, a manager aiming to energize your team, or an entrepreneur eager to align your values with your work, at the core of your being lies a beautiful spirit. Underneath all your conditioning, habits, personality structures, and limiting beliefs, at the center of your being is your essence—an inherently creative spark that is open, connected, and powerful.

You may have experienced your essential nature as a pure sense of vitality and aliveness, or as the feeling of flow when you're doing something you love. It could be a physical shining point of light in the center of your chest or a tender, sweet connection with someone you love. The brighter the spark of your spirit shines, the more fully your life reflects your unique gifts and deepest purpose. And you inevitably ignite a resonant flame in those around you—empowering them to actualize their potential too. You naturally draw others to you, thus creating a vibrant community of passionately engaged people working together toward your shared purpose.

However, it can also be that our mental and emotional states feel blocked. Preoccupied with our inner narratives, we miss information about our in-the-moment experiences until the stress we hold in our lower back, or the stiffness in our neck and shoulders, builds up. Pain is our body's way of letting us know it needs attention.

Over time, we can learn to better read our body's messages, which are the result of millennia of evolutionary intelligence, incorporating signals from billions of neurons in our head as well as millions of neurons in our gut and heart. Tuning into our body's messages not only gives us valuable information about our functioning, but also about the people and life around us, enabling us to assess situations more accurately, discern subtle cues, and make better decisions.

To help you tune into your inner source, my recommended exercises typically begin with physical injunctions to quiet your mind so that you can "hear" your body's voice. The more aspects of your living experience you can tap into—sensory impressions, emotions, energetic feelings, bodily cues—the more you can access multiple types of intelligence. For example, through visualization or guided imagery you can "flesh out" your experience, giving you more power to activate the transformation you seek.

Before each exercise, find a comfortable place where you can relax, and have an unlined notebook or sketchbook handy so you can take notes or draw impressions that come to you. Both are important; intuition most often speaks in images, so don't be afraid to sketch impressions that come to you. The message is far more important than your ability to draw well. You can read all the way through each exercise before commencing it, or you can read just one section at a time, following the instructions as you go. As you reflect and tune in, try closing your eyes. This frees up your brain's processing capacity from visual input, which typically occupies nearly two-thirds of our brainpower.

Lastly, some exercises suggest guided imagery. If visualization proves challenging for you, try stream-of-consciousness journaling, or another medium that suits your learning style.

However you do it, my point is clear: spiritual intelligence is not cognitive intelligence. The exercises are essential for you to begin to cultivate and embody the qualities of Spiritually Intelligent Leadership (SILeadership™) and set you on a course for ongoing practice.

YOUR TURN: MOTIVATING YOUR JOURNEY TOWARD SPIRITUALLY INTELLIGENT LEADERSHIP

Find a comfortable place, have your notebook ready, and take a few deep, slow breaths, feeling the expansion of your belly and rise and fall of your chest. Close your eyes. Gently let go of your other thoughts so that you can just be here with yourself, not thinking about anything else.

Once you feel settled, imagine it's ten years from now and you have become the leader you aspire to be. Without effort, invite a vivid image of your future self to appear in front of you in your mind's eye as a new, separate person. What do they look like? How are they holding themself? What do you notice in their eyes, and when they see you, how do they greet you? How does it feel to be around them? Allow yourself as much time as necessary to experience this future you fully.

Consider what you might want to know from them and silently ask. You might ask what enabled them to grow and mature into the confident, powerful, and inspired leader they are. Give them time to respond. Accept whatever comes without judgment, no matter how it may sound. Then imagine thanking them in a way that feels natural to you. Stay with your experience until you feel you have arrived at a natural closure.

Now open your eyes and capture your impressions in your journal through notes, drawings, or both. Once you've captured the feelings and messages, make a list of up to ten qualities you imagine your future self possessing. Review these characteristics, reflecting on what you appreciate about each one.

Then, consider your own life today. Where do you already demonstrate these qualities? Which qualities currently exist within you as seeds, or as potential? How do they show up at this time in your life? And contemplate how it would feel in your body, in your posture, and in your attitudes to embody these qualities more fully in the future.

If you aren't able to visualize your future self, don't worry. Simply focus on the qualities you listed about the leader you aspire to be: confidence, vision, power, purpose—whatever they may be. Then, consider the leaders you admire most, those you believe best exemplify these qualities. Imagine interviewing these role models, asking them what the keys are to developing and exhibiting such qualities. You can simply practice applying some of their insights to help you develop these nascent qualities within you. As philosopher Martin Buber wrote, "The future is waiting for you in order to be born."

BECOMING AN SI LEADER STARTS
WITH INNER-CONNECTION

In general, leadership is first and foremost an "inside job." It would be impossible for someone incapable of inspiring themselves to inspire others. Leaders need to first ignite their own spark and fan their own flame. Only then can they inspire others. And their spark, their fire, and power are all within. So, until leaders first uncover those by going within, they will go without their greater qualities being available.

That's because Spiritually Intelligent Leaders draw on their inner wisdom, align their purpose, behavior, and actions with their deepest values, and live in integrity and harmony with those values to fulfill their highest purpose: having a positive impact by uplifting themselves and the world around them. By transcending themselves, while also remaining immanent, connected, and embodied within themselves, they are more powerful than their individual selves.

No doubt you already embody these qualities to some extent. But you can cultivate them to an even greater degree. Because now, more than ever, we need leaders who inspire themselves and others to reach their highest potential for the good, the true, and the beautiful.

OUR INNER SPARK INSPIRES AND EMPOWERS US: THE CASE OF PAUL

Paul is the cofounder and CEO of a burgeoning company he started with his close college friend, Victor, who is now running its engineering organization. Having recently raised a large financing round, the business is poised for rapid growth. Yet, Paul is concerned about Victor's ability to scale with the company since the engineering department is encountering scheduling and quality-control problems. Though Paul and I have discussed this concern several times, he's been reluctant to confront the issue with his partner and friend.

In our session, Paul tells me how excited he feels about the company's growth prospects, and about expecting his firstborn due in two months. "My company has grown into its teen years, and now I'm expecting a new infant. Exciting time in my life."

Leaning slightly forward in his chair, he says the excitement feels like love and joy radiating out from his chest, from his heart. As I guide him in tuning into the source of those feelings, he reports the energy is now stronger and more palpable. I suggest he include an awareness of his feet on the ground, as well as the support of the chair behind his back. His posture shifts as he settles back. He says the energy is now permeating and streaming through his entire body. He describes it as white light.

I invite Paul to anchor himself in this inner energy and slowly open his eyes, adding the sound of my voice to his field of awareness. As we make eye contact, he says he feels connected—connected to himself and connected to me at the same time: "The connection feels like it's made of the same white energy, and we're both part of this one energy field."

I prompt him to describe how it would feel talking to his cofounder about the engineering scaling problems from this place and mindset. He says, "It's going to be a difficult conversation. Victor's feelings might get hurt. But I'm clear it's the right thing to do. I believe it's important for his own growth and happiness. And we might be able to shift his role to something he'd more likely enjoy and succeed at. It could be a win all around."

Resourcing himself with his excitement, realizing his love and joy, Paul finds his inner source of power and inspiration. Letting it pervade his body, he also becomes interconnected with me, the person in front of him. In that place he finds his clarity, confidence, and courage to implement what he has been hesitant to do before.

After practicing with me, Paul brings this same presence to his conversation with Victor. The conversation proves productive—Victor is happy and, in a way, relieved to consider giving up day-to-day responsibilities for engineering deliverables. Paul just had to find the power and inspiration inside himself first to pass them along to Victor.

THE POWER OF SPIRITUAL INTELLIGENCE

Over the past twenty years, I have coached more than a hundred CEOs. As I watched them and their companies grow, I observed the characteristics that made them the most inspired and the most inspirational. In addition, I have studied the lives of some of the world's greatest leaders, including Moses, Malala Yousafzai, Jesus, Mohammad, the Buddha, Mother Teresa, Ruth Bader Ginsberg, Gandhi, Martin Luther King, Jr., Wangari Maathai, Helen Keller, Rosa Parks, and Nelson Mandela. Each lived a life rooted in spiritual values, such as love, service, selfless devotion to a cause, and a positive vision of the world.

Though having a larger-than-life impact, these historic figures had the same doubts and fears we all face, and they made the same kinds of mistakes we all do. Jesus on the cross cried out "My God, my God, why have you forsaken me?" Mother Teresa suffered a complete loss of faith, documented in her journals. And Moses, the greatest prophet and leader in the Jewish tradition, in his despair pleaded with God, "The burden *is* too heavy for me. If You treat me like this, please kill me here and now—if I have found favor in Your sight—and do not let me see my wretchedness" (Numbers 11:15). Yet, each found the courage and capacity to move forward in the face of their difficulties. Inner-directed, connected to their purpose, and following their inner wisdom, these people were inspired to act and devote their lives to their deepest values. In that way, their lives fulfilled their teachings. And they have touched, inspired, and affected billions of people.

THE SEVEN DIMENSIONS OF SPIRITUALLY INTELLIGENT LEADERSHIP

Through research and coaching work, I have discovered seven primary dimensions of Spiritually Intelligent Leadership in individuals and in their organizations:

1. *Meaning*: Articulate a vision for service and instill a sense of purpose

2. *Grace*: Lead with dignity, joy, trust, and gratitude

3. *Inner-Directed*: Align with and inspire others from an inner core of authenticity

4. *Community*: Foster cohesion, connectedness, and collaboration

5. *Presence*: Bring full attention, focus, and clarity to every moment

6. *Truth*: Motivate oneself and others based on truthfulness

7. *Wisdom*: Tap into intuition

These dimensions dovetail with several modern leadership theories that highlight the importance of mobilizing meaning and cultivating trust,[1] authenticity,[2] humility,[3,4] emotional intelligence,[5] conscious leadership,[6] and servant leadership,[7] to name a few. My work also illustrates how many of the characteristics of inspired and inspirational leadership arise organically in those with high spiritual intelligence. Furthermore, a study by the international consulting firm Bain & Company identified thirty-three characteristics of inspirational leaders and found that "inspired" employees are twice as productive as merely "satisfied" employees.[8]

Each of the seven dimensions is made of several building-block *competencies*. For example, mobilizing a shared sense of Meaning takes a strong sense of Purpose, a call for Service, and involves a compelling Vision of the future as well as abilities at reframing Difficulties into Opportunities.

If you feel daunted about developing all seven dimensions and their competencies, don't worry. I've never met or studied a leader who excels in every area. This model is not a standard by which to judge yourself. Every leader has a unique set of talents and gifts. Some excel at leading from the front, inspiring others with their bold vision and fierce sense of purpose. Others find their effectiveness leading from behind, empowering people, engendering their creative potential, and fostering a strong and collaborative team. Regardless of where your strengths lie, you still have plenty of opportunities to leverage them more fully and for further growth.

Which of these are your strengths? What can you do to leverage them? Which competencies in the chart do you want to cultivate and apply further? You're free to use this book as a guide and work with the material any way you want, even skipping straight to the chapters covering the competencies you'd most like to develop first.

WITHIN THE PAIN IS THE REMEDY: THE CASE OF KEVIN

Kevin is an entrepreneur with an engineering background whose wife tragically died two years prior due to a misdiagnosis by her doctors. A single father of two teenage kids, he is also fighting to keep his company afloat. In our session he reports how his mood is somewhat improved, but he still struggles to get out of bed in the morning, hitting the snooze button over and over again. I ask him to put himself in the mindset of his morning wakeup scene and then compare the feeling of these two statements: "I want to go back to sleep" and "I need some comfort." As Kevin expresses his need for comfort, he tears up. The need for comfort resonates much more with him than the need for sleep. Since his wife died, he hasn't had much support or someone to lean on at work and at home.

I ask if this feeling is familiar to him, and he recalls that as a young teen he was terrified of losing his single mom, who was battling cancer. No one was there to hold, comfort, or support him as he anxiously waited for hours on end at the hospital.

I direct Kevin to visualize talking with his teenage self and asking that young man what he needs. He tells me his teenage self says, "A hug." He imagines embracing his teen self and saying, "I understand this is scary. I'm here with you, and we'll get through this together." Afterward, Kevin reports that both his younger and adult selves feel lighter, more relaxed, and more open. He says the flow of love between them is palpable. He describes it as warm energy with white, yellowish, and purple tones around his chest, arising from the base of his spine. Focusing on its source, he feels a warm glow filling his entire body and an expansion in his chest.

After he is anchored in his inner source, I invite Kevin to slowly open his eyes and look into mine. He reports an energetic connection between us, that it feels like it is made of the same energy—love, and that he feels inner- and inter-connected.

For the rest of the session, he looks vibrant. Tapping into his self-compassion has helped him recover his energy and motivation. He feels much more ready to handle life's challenges. And though Kevin happens to be an atheist, the tangible effect of spiritual intelligence on his being is apparent to him and to me.

SPIRITUALLY INTELLIGENT LEADERSHIP
DOMAINS AND COMPETENCIES

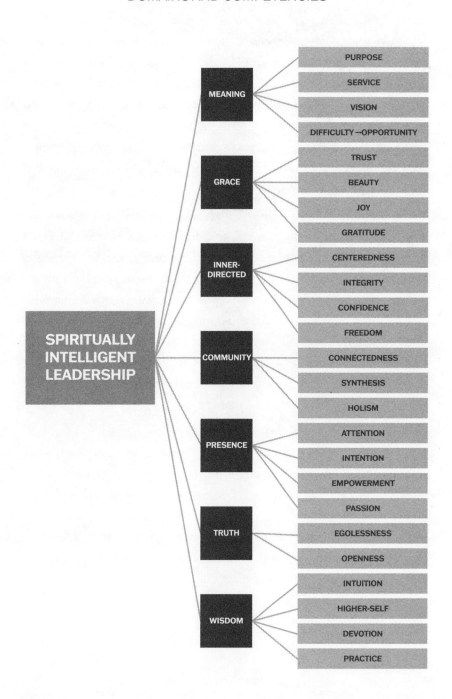

INNER-WHOLENESS: THE POWER OF
INTEGRATING PSYCHE AND SOMA

Kevin stands as an excellent example of what happens when we culti-vate the spiritual intelligence capacity of our inner-wholeness. For him, this meant embracing the younger, scared self still within him. He also utilized mindfulness, another SI capacity, by recognizing his need for comfort and remaining aware of his associated thoughts, feelings, and bodily sensations. Accepting, embracing, and working through his so-called negative emotions, he uncovered the "positive ones" of energy, compassion, and love. As they arose within him, he was able to tap into them with somatic awareness.

While deep insights and breakthroughs can happen in a single session, the insights usually build on months, and sometimes years, of culti-vating greater somatic awareness and inner attunement. And the shifts that stick most often require significant integration time through re-peated reminders and practices in a process of rewiring the brain with new habits in thinking, feeling, and doing. It's important to keep this in mind so you are not discouraged; such transformational processes often take significant time for all of us. (For a realistic view of the process, the epilogue describes Ted's journey using leadership as a crucible for healing and growth over several years.)

As a transpersonal psychologist, I look at our human condition and evo-lution through a holistic lens that integrates the whole person: mind, body, emotion, and spirit. Today *psyche* is usually associated with psy-chology, but in the original Greek it means "soul." And our soul—our essence—is affected by both our psychology and our spirituality. Our psychology—thoughts, feelings, emotions, and mind states—are all af-fected by our soma, our body as well as our actions. Conversely, our thoughts, feelings, and actions affect our mood, which affects our phys-iology, hormones, and the flow of neurotransmitters in our brain. It's an interconnected, all-pervading web.

While at times it may be useful to think of the mind and body as separate, in fact they are inextricably interwoven and interdependent. For example, research points to the link between our immune system and brain, demonstrating causal connections between illness, stress, mood, and thought. Research has also documented our brain's neuroplasticity such that it can be physically altered and "rewired" through prayer and meditation, as well as other methods that change our thought patterns, attention, and practices.

Research has also documented how traumas are held in our body, limiting our capacity to regulate our nervous system or access certain emotional and spiritual states. Modern spiritual teacher, trauma specialist, and author of *Healing Collective Trauma* Thomas Hübl says, "I have witnessed what science has revealed as I listened to hundreds of thousands of people over the years: the most significant disruption in the flow of information within a human system is trauma." Trauma, in fact, is "mysteriously" inherited from our ancestors and passed on to our offspring—even third-generation mice will have similar traumatic responses as their traumatized forebears. Furthermore, through epigenetic research, we now know that even our gene expression is influenced by our environment, beliefs, and behaviors. The bottom line is that mind and body are intimately interwoven, with no clear demarcation separating them.

Thus, full access to our spiritual intelligence requires the holistic integration of our psychology, spirituality, and trauma healing. My work with clients draws on all three domains, including a wide variety of approaches and modalities from different traditions, psychology and therapy schools, religions, and wisdom lineages, each uniquely beautiful.[9, 10] Paraphrasing Newton, however far I may have seen, it is because I stood on the shoulders of many giants who came before me.

YOUR TURN: GETTING INSPIRED

Since spiritual intelligence—the foundation of SILeadership—is not the same as cognitive intelligence, it can't be developed through

reading and cognitive understanding alone. While mental understanding is important and helpful, experiential exercises and practices are crucial for the development of SI and SILeadership.

To support the cultivation of your capacities, throughout the book
I will be suggesting various exercises. Often the exercises begin
with techniques to bring you into the present moment in a state
of wholeness by enlivening your being with breath and awareness,
heart and emotion, and mind, thought, and spirit.

One particularly effective way I have discovered is the **INSPIRED**
protocol outlined below. It involves becoming present to the dignity of your essential being as you open to receiving inspiration. It
begins with tuning in, allowing your spirit to soar, while remaining
grounded and connected to the core of Mother Earth. Some of the
words and instructions may not make sense to your rational mind,
but I invite you to trust your intuition and experiment in directing
your attention by following the words below:

Inward gazing

Nostril breathing

Spine supporting, spirit soaring

Posture aligning

Inhaling, exhaling

Relaxing, receiving, resting feet flat on the ground connected
to the core of Mother Earth

Expanding awareness: pelvis, belly, diaphragm, heart, chest,
shoulders, arms, legs, entire body, and the space all around

Deepening into essence

Now take a moment to simply abide in being as you are, noticing
what it's like.

For a shorter, potentially easier acronym to recall, you can use the **SPIRIT** protocol.

Spine supporting, spirit soaring

Posture aligning

Inhaling, exhaling

Relaxing, receiving, resting feet flat on the ground connected to the core of Mother Earth

Inward gazing

Total expanding awareness: pelvis, belly, heart, chest, shoulders, arms, legs, entire body, and the space all around

Again, simply take a moment to rest in being as you are and notice the effect.

If either of these protocols seem too long or difficult to remember even after several practices, simply substitute the following:

Relax, resting your feet flat on the ground feeling your connection to the core of Mother Earth

Bring awareness to your spine and posture alignment

Let your heart and spirit float up and soar

Take a few deep breaths inhaling through the nose and exhaling through the mouth

Sense your entire body and the space all around you

And if none of these approaches work for you, use any other method that helps quiet your mind, deepen your breathing, relax your body, recenter, and bring you into presence.

SPIRITUAL INTELLIGENCE PARALLELS EMOTIONAL INTELLIGENCE

My doctoral research revealed that spiritual intelligence is the true foundation for powerful, effective inspired leadership. As Stephen Covey writes, "Spiritual intelligence is the central and most fundamental of all the intelligences, because it becomes the source of guidance for the others."[11] SI is our capacity to draw on resources and embody qualities from the world's wisdom in ways that enhance functioning and well-being. It parallels emotional intelligence (EI)—our ability to draw on emotional resources, be aware of and regulate our emotions, and accurately perceive and modulate the effect we have on others.

When I assessed both EI and SI, controlling for personality (which also contributes to leadership effectiveness), I employed established outcome measures of commitment, loyalty, diligence, morale, and team spirit/ sense of belonging. I examined how the CEOs rated themselves on EI, SI, and personality, and how their employees rated them on those same measures, including how those scores predicted leadership effectiveness as rated by employees. While EI and SI were correlated, each explained leadership effectiveness on their own terms. In analyzing the employee-assessment scores, EI explained 41 percent of a leader's effectiveness and SI explained 46 percent of leader's effectiveness. Combined, they explained 67 percent of leadership effectiveness. These results suggest that EI and SI complement each other, yet SI makes a larger contribution. (See appendix A for more on the relationship between EI and SI.)

Furthermore, the leaders' self-assessment of their SI predicted their effectiveness as rated by employees, but the leaders' self-assessment of their EI did not. This cross-method predictive validity further reinforced the power of SI for leadership effectiveness.[12]

Studies by researchers who used the SI assessment in other applications, some of whom translated it into other languages and validated it across different countries and cultural contexts,[13, 14] found that it contributes to a variety of positive outcomes, such as mental health,[15] job and work satisfaction,[16, 17] work performance,[18] resilience,[19] life satisfaction, and experiences of awe.[20]

Furthermore, banks where employees reported higher spiritual intelligence showed higher performance as measured by return on assets and other financial outcomes.[21] Similarly, in another study with nonfinancial institutions, the leader's self-assessment of their SI also predicted their organization's financial performance while the leaders' self-assessment of EI did not.[22] Now with nearly two decades of research on SI, without a doubt, SI is real, measurable, and positively impactful.[23]

(See appendix B for a breakdown of SI and appendix C for how SI capacities are the foundation for SILeadership competencies and their interrelations.)

YOUR TURN: GETTING INSPIRED, CONNECTING WITH YOUR SACRED SPARK

To begin, take a moment to relax, open up, and become present and INSPIRED with spirit practicing the above protocol (see page 14). Take a moment to simply hang out and marinate in this quiet state of presence while tuned in.

Then, rest your attention at the center of your chest around your heart. Place the palm of your right hand on the center of your chest and your left hand flat on top of the right. Continue to breathe, feeling the rise and fall of your chest as it touches your hand. Do this for a few breaths. Now focus on the center of the space inside your chest and complete the following sentence stem silently to yourself:

My heart's deep desire is . . .

Do not judge whether your statement is true or not, just notice. Repeat completing the sentence several times to get more information. After you have come up with five to ten completions, pause and write down the ones that have the greatest energy and resonance for you.

Now return your right hand to the center of your chest, and this time place your left hand flat on your lower belly, just under your navel. Take a few breaths, feeling the expansion and contraction of your belly and chest. Now repeat and complete the following sentence stem silently to yourself:

A high aspiration of mine is . . .

Again, repeat the process, letting five to ten completions come to mind without judging their truth and writing down the few that have the greatest resonant energy.

Now, reflect on these two lists and see how they relate to one another. Notice which desires or aspirations hold the deepest meaning for you. Now pick the one item from each list that draws you the most. If you can't decide between two, just pick either. It's not about choosing the "best one," just one that's true and essential to *you* at this point in your life.

Whichever you chose, let it touch you. Let yourself FULLY AND COMPLETELY feel this deep desire, this high aspiration, whether you think it might be achievable or realistic. Don't judge its practicality. Treat this deep desire or high aspiration of yours as sacred.

Do you feel more or less alive? Energized? Whole? Expanded? Inspired?

Are the feelings associated with certain parts of your body or location in space, or are they untethered as if permeating your being?

Now, just for a moment, imagine your deep heart's desire or high aspiration being fulfilled. What is your experience now as you, just for a moment, imagine its fulfillment?

Take some notes about your experience. For the coming week, make it a practice to repeat recalling your deepest desire and highest aspiration daily, taking inner snapshots each time. As you do this, your inspiration and aspiration will guide you to your destination. Keep in mind that your desires may change each time you do this exercise.

Now let's explore all aspects of SILeadership or spiritual intelligence that interest you as you go through the book. Notice which dimensions resonate most with you. Just follow your intuition. You can't go wrong. Each chapter provides case studies and experiential exercises. And while the case studies are drawn from my client base, predominantly tech CEOs, the human dilemmas and leadership challenges are universal across any industry, sector, and scale. Along with the experiential exercises, which are integral to this book, you should be able to apply them in your own environment.

For your spiritual intelligence to develop and shine through, as in the earlier cases of Paul and Kevin, you will need a transformative experiential process, not just a cognitive understanding. When I meet a client in this transformational process, aware of the moment as they are experiencing it—whether it is "positive" or "negative"—I help them slow down and shine the light of their awareness into their experience, including their bodily sensations, thoughts, feelings, images, and action impulses. Opening to the truth of their experience in the moment, plumbing its depths, uncovers its hidden treasures, its beauty. Here, in the profundity of their actual lived experience, wisdom and insights are revealed. Unconstricted and without resistance to the truth of what is real, within and without, their life force naturally begins to flow and reveal more of their true nature's innate spiritual intelligence. And, on the other end of these transformative experiential processes, my clients usually find the solution to their problems right there inside themselves.

These cases may seem similar to each other or repetitive at times, but it's because the formula (and practicing it) works. Learning how to turn inward and navigate their inner landscape, my clients uncover the necessary hidden resources to more effectively deal with the outer world.

And it can happen to you too. You'll see for yourself as you read and do the practice exercises.

You may also be interested in looking at the complete set of spiritual intelligence and/or SILeadership assessment questions, all of which are available on the intelligensi.com website (a basic SI assessment is available free, and you can use the voucher code SILeadershipBook for a 25 percent discount on any of the paid assessments). These assessments provide you with a personalized report to help you uncover and leverage your strengths and opportunities for growth, including developmental tips and practice suggestions. I further suggest engaging with a mentor, therapist, or coach to support your development. I also highly recommend learning to practice meditation, which, in addition to its widely researched health benefits, can help develop your capacity for presence and sensitize your awareness to the subtlety and richness of your life's experiences.

CHAPTER 2

MOBILIZING MEANING

*There are two great days in a
person's life—the day we are born
and the day we discover why.*
                        —Mark Twain

THE FIRST DIMENSION OF SPIRITUALLY Intelligent Leadership is the ability to mobilize a sense of Meaning for yourself and those you lead. This ability rests on four essential competencies:

- *Awakening Purpose*: Identify and maintain focus on the deeper values and mission that drive you and your organization.

- *Inspiring Service*: Answer the question, "Why are we here?" Articulate how your work and organization serve needs and add value to those around you and to the world.

- *Articulating Vision*: Painting a detailed and compelling picture of the future.

- *Reframing Difficulties into Opportunities*: Finding meaning in adversity and setbacks. Relating to them as opportunities for growth and learning.

AWAKENING PURPOSE

Humans are meaning-making creatures. And as philosopher, psychologist, and Holocaust survivor Victor Frankl said of those who lived in concentration camps, "everything can be taken from a man but one thing: the last of the human freedoms—to choose one's attitude in any given set of circumstances, to choose one's own way." We can create meaning under almost any circumstance, and that meaning we make can even keep us alive.

To choose our attitude is to choose the meaning we make of our lives. Frankl saw how the meaning these people drew on under the most horrific of circumstances enabled them to express their greatest humanity and, perhaps, even motivated them to live—or conversely, enabled them to sacrifice themselves to demonstrate that altruism was a higher value to them than their personal survival—an affirmation of the goodness of the human spirit. As Frankl put it, "In times of crisis, people reach for meaning. Meaning is strength. Our survival may depend on our seeking and finding it."

Research conducted since Frankl's initial insights confirms that maintaining a sense of meaning is central to our well-being, more central than momentary pleasure and enjoyment. Aristotle was the first to make the distinction between *eudaimonic* well-being, which comes from meaning and purpose, and *hedonic* well-being, which comes from pleasure and enjoyment. Pursuing pleasure can lead to what psychologists call the hedonic treadmill, because no momentary pleasure leads to lasting satisfaction. While the pursuit of meaning may involve great sacrifice, such as training for a marathon or raising children, the contentment it generates is far deeper and longer lasting.

PURPOSE ENERGIZES AND MOTIVATES: THE CASE OF STEPHEN

Stephen is an Australian-born entrepreneur and CEO in his mid-forties with a PhD in mathematics. After serving as the Chief

Technology Officer of a few well-regarded Silicon Valley companies, he developed a revolutionary technology for database security at a start-up of his own. Though this technology has great promise, he has been having difficulty getting his company funded. In fact, Stephen and his team of seven full-time engineers and a half dozen part-time employees have been working out of his home without salaries for over a year now. He hasn't been able to pay his mortgage for over six months, and the bank is about to foreclose.

When Stephen and I meet for his session, none of that is apparent to me. He sounds easygoing as he tells me about a new lead on a customer who may fund the company. When I finally ask about his financial situation directly, he acknowledges that, indeed, his house is on the verge of foreclosure. Even so, he is determined not to give up. "The company is my destiny," he declares. "It's an expression of what's important to my life's purpose to help in sharing human knowledge." He pauses, takes a deep breath, then continues combatively: "I refuse to be just a carbon footprint on the planet."

I'm struck by the contrast between those last two statements. When he affirms, "This is my destiny," he exudes relaxed confidence and radiance. I feel the love that fuels his commitment and devotion to his cause. While at the thought of being a mere "carbon footprint," he deflates, as if a terrible fate looms over him. God forbid his existence could be reduced to something so meaningless.

I suggest that he repeat his energizing statement, "I am living my destiny." As he does, a smile spreads across his face, and his breathing deepens. He tells me he feels bigger than the room, as large as Palo Alto. Following our session, he writes "I am living my destiny" on the whiteboard above his desk, where he can readily turn to it as a source of strength. He does whatever it takes to keep the bank at bay and manages to continue building his company, exemplifying the words of Nietzsche, "He who has a why to live for can bear with almost any how."

His enthusiasm is infectious. His team of talented engineers could easily have "walked across the street" in a hungry Silicon Valley market and into high-paying positions elsewhere but didn't. I myself agreed to work with Stephen for over eighteen months for deferred pay, turning away other potential paying clients, because his passion and sense of purpose inspired me to support him.

Stephen was able to sustain his efforts—recruiting, building, and preserving his team for deferred pay—not just because of his personal sense of purpose and destiny, but because he enrolled others in a mission they found meaningful as well. For them, and for me, it wasn't about the money. As the research shows, once basic financial needs are met, we are much more motivated by the sense of meaning our work provides.

The ability to mobilize a sense of meaning is not only central to well-being, quality of life, and long-term fulfillment, it's also a cornerstone for spiritual intelligence. When I was interviewing the exemplars nominated for the ways they embodied spirituality in daily life as part of developing the construct of spiritual intelligence, I asked what held meaning for them. Nearly all of them emphasized the importance of acting from a sense of purpose, specifically one tied to service, be it to others, a larger whole, or to the divine.

The form their service took ranged widely, from coaching to founding a private university to teaching in a spiritual community. But perceiving a calling to serve need not involve what may appear to be some lofty goal. It can be as simple as helping clients find just the right house or reliably delivering packages overnight or serving food attractively and efficiently so that customers (or family members) have a pleasant evening.

Opportunities for service are all around us at work, at home, and in our community. It only takes the discerning heart and a meaning-making attitude to see the beauty of service in almost everything we undertake to elevate our concerns beyond our individual boundaries. Beyond an identity that breaks from our conception of the isolated, separate self and expands to include a more interconnected sense of our being and wholeness.

The Integrated Spiritual Intelligence Scale is used to explore how SI qualities correlate with effective leadership in business settings. I found that CEOs who scored high on the purpose dimension tended to lead teams who were more committed, worked harder, exhibited higher morale, possessed greater team spirit, and stayed longer on the job. This suggests that the ability to mobilize a sense of meaning through shared purpose based on service inspires greater commitment and passion in others. Igniting that sense of meaning in a team, community, organization, and beyond is at the heart of inspired and inspirational leadership.

OUR INDIVIDUAL AND COLLECTIVE STORIES REFLECT MEANING

Since igniting a sense of meaning is central to SI and SILeadership, it's worth taking a little detour to understand that our sense of meaning and purpose comes from the stories we tell ourselves.

Since our earliest ancestors first developed language, we have sat around fires and shared our stories. The narratives we tell each other and ourselves have enormous power. They enable us to form communities, make sense of the world, and transmit meaning to ourselves and to those we lead.

As we recognize these stories consciously, we can choose to alter their narrative. However, they often represent unconscious worldviews based on existential assumptions about who we are, why we are here, what we can expect from life, what kind of world we live in, and even what our place is in the universe. In fact, we don't make up our personal stories entirely on our own. Some stories are unconsciously absorbed and accepted from our culture and environment. For example, people who grow up in individualized cultures, such as the United States, tend to value personal freedom and independent self-expression, and their stories often hold such messages, whereas people who grow up in collectivist cultures, such as Japan, tend to value the group and belonging, and their stories hold messages about fitting in. Other stories are created in response to our unique life circumstances: life presents us with all sorts of situations, and we usually unconsciously adopt narratives and assign meaning to make sense of what is happening, such as, "I'm good when I'm obedient."

Shared stories, tales about origins and destinies, establish the paradigms within which whole civilizations live—the unconscious lenses through which we see our world, our worth, and our identities. These collective stories, the most powerful of which are conveyed by science, politics, and religion, and more specific ones, such as family stories that tell us what it means to be a "Jones" or a "Smith," form the intimate context of our lives.

These stories don't have to be true to hold power, yet they are self-fulfilling prophecies. For example, if we did not receive the love and nourishment we needed growing up, we may erroneously and unconsciously assume that it is our fault, or that we are bad, or that something is fundamentally wrong or lacking within us. Such stories will invariably affect our self-esteem and mood as we may conclude that we must suffer or perform heroic acts to be deserving of happiness, belonging, and love.

If our story is that life is an endless struggle, we are more likely to remain in jobs that are unfulfilling. On the other hand, if our story is one of struggle toward ultimate triumph, like the hero's journey, we are more likely to look inward and find resilience and perseverance. As Henry Ford said, "If you believe you can, or believe you can't, you are right." And the father of the self-esteem movement, Nathaniel Branden, summed up the idea with the phrase, "Self-concept is destiny."

INTENTIONAL VALUES: THE CASE OF GEORGE

Like many kids who suffer from attention deficit hyperactivity disorder (ADHD), George had difficulty sitting still, received lots of negative feedback about his behavior, and got into trouble with his teachers in elementary school. And to make matters worse, he was mocked and continuously shunned by his peers on the playground. As often is the case in these situations, he unfortunately internalized an unconscious story that he was weak and deficient.

Now as an adult, and with a chip on his shoulder, he resolved to build a successful company. He dreamt that someday the people who had shamed him would all read about his success and regret their behavior. Indeed, George had successfully started and built his multiplayer mobile gaming company from a start-up to an organization of eight hundred employees and $200 million in annual revenues, achieving a valuation of over $3 billion. He never had to work again. Still, after eight years of hard work and relentless drive, George felt burned out.

What had provided motivation and energy once had suddenly lost its meaning. He was beginning to feel depressed. I was curious as to what we'd uncover together during a visualization exercise in which he visited his elder self on his deathbed. To his and my surprise, George's elder self told him that sharing the magic of life with family, friends, and colleagues was what he treasured most.

Until that point, he had approached his work as if it were a battle, which squeezed out all the joy and left him feeling isolated, exhausted, and depleted. His new mission gave him new levels of motivation and transformed his leadership. He revised the company's mission and values statement, relied less on fear as a motivator, and connected with his employees more personally as human beings, not as foot soldiers to be commanded in battle. As he slowly healed and let go of the chip on his shoulder, he became more inspired and motivated by the beauty and creativity that was expressed through his work. It set the tone for a profound shift in the company culture that energized him and his staff and rekindled their passion for mission and work.

STORIES ABOUT OUR WORK CREATE
OUR PURPOSE

Here's a little story from a classic folktale. A man is walking down the street in a village and comes across three men laying bricks. He asks the first one, "What're you doing?" The man responds grimly, "I take the bricks from a pile over there and bring them here. I lay them on top of each other, putting some wet cement between them." He asks the second man the same question. He answers matter-of-factly, "I work in construction. I build stuff. It's my job and how I support my family." He then asks the third person the same question. The man holds up the brick and, with a sparkle in his eye, answers enthusiastically, "I'm helping to build a new hospital for our community, so people don't have to be rushed to the one in the next town."

While the three men are engaging in the same exact activity, each has a very different story about his work and finds vastly different meaning in it. The first one has a job, the second has a career, and the third has a vocation. Their sense of satisfaction and, therefore, the quality of their work, reflects these varying levels of meaning and purpose. Which of these workers would you rather have on your team?

When the story we tell ourselves about our work endows it with a rich sense of purpose and meaning, we bring more passion and commitment and, in the process, also inspire others to do the same. We become an undeniable asset to any team.

The task of SILeaders is to inspire answers to existential questions such as "Who are we?" "Why are we here?" "How shall we act?" The SILeader must help uncover the unconscious, disempowering stories in the community and instead emphasize the most empowering and inspiring ones for all to follow.

We saw how Stephen's choice—to shift from the narrative of insignificance (being a mere "carbon footprint") to living his destiny—brought forth new levels of energy and confidence in him. It's possible for us to follow suit; to detect the stories we unconsciously tell ourselves that shape our lives and choose more life-affirming ones.

One day during a session with a client I'll call Robert, who was suffering from low-motivation symptoms of depression, I asked him, "If someone made your life into a movie, how would you sum it up in one line?" After some reflection, he answered, "Boy grows to be a powerful man, proving others wrong." This revealed how Robert was still living his life as a reaction to the painful childhood experiences of having been told by his father that he would fail and having been clobbered by bullies. His adopted narrative was that more than anything, he would need sharp elbows to fight his way through life.

Robert could see how this story kept him beholden to his father and the bullies, and how they were still controlling his life. And while initially this story was motivating him to work hard to prove them wrong, eventually it lost its meaning. This new awareness was the first step in the transformative process of letting this dispiriting story go and deciding on a more inspiring one.

We tried on a few stories to find which energized him the most. In the one we selected, Robert was on a journey of healing and transformation, sharing creativity, love, and joy along the way. As he affirmed this for himself and felt the truth of it resonate, his armor began to melt away, his posture visibly opened, and he was able to access more of his loving and joyful nature. Robert's new narrative had an enormous impact on every area of his life. Inspired, he organized an executive team off-site retreat to redefine the company culture from one based on purely hard work and financial rewards to one focused on creativity and community. He found, in the words of Kahlil Gibran, "Work is love made visible."

YOUR TURN: WHAT'S YOUR STORY?

If your life's story were made into a movie, what would the title be? What single sentence would summarize it? How would the movie end?

How might this story support you in becoming your best self and most effective leader? How might it be limiting you?

What could potentially be a more inspiring story that reframes the past and energizes your future?

What is the new title of this movie? What single sentence summarizes it? How would your life be different if you lived it from this story? What greater life might all your most challenging experiences be preparing you for?

PURPOSE SHAPES YOUR FUTURE

The participants in my research into spiritual intelligence all live with empowering stories that, most notably, frame their lives as *inseparable* from those around them. From a story of interconnection comes a life of purpose and service which in turn provides the greatest levels of meaning. The task of the SILeader is to live in those stories that are most motivational, not only for themselves, but also for their communities to follow.

While many psychological theories suggest that we are defined by our history, other research shows our orientation to the future also plays a considerable role in shaping our lives. When we connect to a vision of the future that pulls us toward it—a future in which our values and vision are realized—it becomes our North Star, guiding our life toward more meaning. We're suddenly capable of devoting time and energy to it. Our passion and devotion make that future possible. As SILeaders we have an intimate relationship with that future, and when we share it, others feel it calling them too. However you experience purpose in your life, it ultimately draws forth your unique gifts in service to a future that is waiting to be born through you.

In the words of Pablo Picasso, "The meaning of life is to find your gift. The purpose of life is to give it away." Picasso is commonly referred to as a genius, from the Latin meaning "guardian spirit for one's great naturally endowed ability." Accordingly, we need not be Einsteins to be geniuses. We develop and express our genius by contributing our unique talents to, and aligning them with, our purpose. When we do, it feels like we have mastered our divinely given instrument and are playing it in harmony with the greater symphony of life.

MISSION AND VALUES STATEMENTS
MOBILIZE MEANING

Powerfully articulated mission and value statements help SILeaders mobilize a sense of meaning. While much has already been written about the importance of mission and values statements, I'll briefly summarize what I've learned about each as it relates to spiritual intelligence and inspired and inspirational leadership.

An effective mission statement articulates the highest purpose of the organization, and the core human needs it addresses. It is not enough to express a mission that will cause the company to grow and make the shareholders rich. It must be based on deep values to inspire people's desire to engage, commit, and contribute.

Google's mission is to organize the world's information and make it universally accessible and useful. The TED organization's mission is to spread "ideas worth sharing," while Water, a nonprofit charity, aspires to "bring clean and safe drinking water to people in developing countries." The more the mission addresses universal, relatable, and fundamental needs, the more inspiring it is likely to be.

While leaders facilitate or articulate the mission statement for the organization as a whole, it can be powerful to set forth one at any scale for departments, teams, or individuals. For example, a finance team might declare the mission of enabling better decision-making by empowering stakeholders with accurate, organized, timely information and insightful analysis. Similarly, a customer service team may define its mission as giving customers the best and easiest experience of their product through friendly and knowledgeable service. A doctor may have a personal mission of facilitating health, and an artist may seek to express and share beauty. Your personal mission is what gets you out of bed every morning, energized to meet life, no matter how difficult it may seem.

My personal mission is to awaken and support greater levels of spiritual intelligence and SILeadership on our planet.

Have you thought about your own personal mission statement? How might it relate to and energize your work as an SILeader to help articulate your personal and your organization's mission?

As with mission statements, a departmental values statement can complement and live within the context of the overall organizational values statement. With any luck, your own values align with those of the larger entity in which you are embedded, even though some may be more specific to your team. For example, you may be leading a team of repair mechanics working for an airline that upholds friendly service as its highest value. Yet, you and your team might want to define your own departmental values emphasizing precision and craftsmanship. Your team's mission and value statement create a sense of purpose and culture unique to your department.

Whether we're sharing scientific knowledge or landscaping a community, we find meaning when our actions align with our most deeply held values. Values are at the heart of our purpose and mission. Accordingly, they inspire others to the extent that they share our same values. The mission and corresponding cultural principles at my first start-up, Individual Inc., expressed the value of individuality and uniqueness, self-responsibility, community, creativity, fun, and lifelong development.

YOUR TURN: REALIZE AND HUMANIZE

Articulating a powerful mission starts with clarifying our own values. With your notebook, find a quiet place and take your time to pause and reflect intentionally on your values and the role they play in your life and work.

Reflect on the people who inspire you the most. What qualities do their lives express?

Reflect on some of your pivotal life decisions—falling in love, failing at something, or succeeding at something. What were those decisions based on? What do they reveal about what really matters to you? Why did they matter to you? Do they still matter? What values were honored at the high points? Which were missing at the low points?

Have you seen other people embody those same values? What effect did those people have on others in their own lives?

What keeps you feeling connected to your highest values? How can you make sure you nurture that connection so that it continues to inspire you and those around you?

Take some time to consider how it would feel for your life to be a full expression of your highest and truest values. How would your life be different right now, next week, next year, in five years, or fifteen years? As you imagine yourself living and embodying those values in the future, how do you feel in the present? What sensations do you notice in your body? What happens to your posture? To your breathing?

MISSIONING AND VALUING

Missions and values aren't static nouns, they're dynamic verbs in a state of constant refinement and evolution. During my tenure at Individual, the mission and values statement grew from one to seven pages, as my senior management team, and then eventually the entire company, continually contributed to its evolution. In fact, the process of including people's input reflected the very values our mission stood for—personal expression and collaboration. This helped create our culture's very foundation.

Continually reinforcing an organization's mission and values, both in words and in action, is one of the central tasks of SILeadership. That doesn't mean we have to do it alone. In fact, involving others is essential to ensuring their buy-in to support the dynamic life of the organization.

At Individual, we also shared our mission and values with prospective employees early in their recruitment process so they would have a sense of our culture and could ask any questions they had about the organization. Having this conversation early was an effective tool to discern whether the company and prospective employee were a good fit. In fact, prospective employees often self-selected based on their response to our values, so the ones who joined us resonated with our culture from the start and contributed to creating a cohesive, passionately engaged community to make a lasting, positive impact on the world.

INSPIRING SERVICE

MOBILIZING SERVICE VALUES: THE CASE OF MENG

Meng was born and raised in Beijing. At eighteen, he was awarded a scholarship to study computer science in America. After graduating and working at several start-ups, he started his own software company, which he built into a $60 million business with hundreds of employees within ten years. He did what others only dream of.

Although Meng initially poured all his time and energy into the company, over the last couple of years he has started showing interest in other pursuits. He has begun taking online courses in advanced physics and personal voice lessons. Recently, Meng has been contemplating what his next chapter will be after he sells his company—its value is estimated to be $400 million and he would walk away with over $40 million personally, more than he'd ever dreamt of having in his entire life.

Meng arrives at our meeting with an unexpected dilemma: a new opportunity has opened up that could easily double the value of his company. The only issue is that pursuing it would take three long years. I ask him what doubling his net worth would mean for him. He reflects for a while, then answers, "Actually, not very much in terms of my lifestyle. I don't need multiple homes, a private yacht, or any such things. Sure," he admits, "it would be a nice ego boost," but he isn't certain it would be worth all the extra time and effort. He pauses again, then leans forward and, with renewed vigor, says, "But what would be really great would be the opportunity to double our user base and continue growing our team."

Currently, his company provides US government agencies with a software platform to reach over three million citizens in a prompt and friendly manner. Coming from China, where government services aren't as readily accessible, helping people receive better service is very meaningful to him.

Meng continues to reflect on the satisfaction he receives through service. Having sold some of his company's shares earlier in the year, he has been sending $2,000 each month to an organization that feeds children in Beijing. He is fulfilled knowing that his donation has funded over ten thousand meals a month, and he relishes how, for the past six months, he has awakened every morning to an email from China with photos of the children he feeds. Seeing their happy faces brightens his mood for the entire day.

He considers how expanding the company will enable him to contribute even more to philanthropic causes like this one, while also serving more of his client base users. With more reflection, he decides that working for a few more years is well worth it. With this new inner resolution and direction, Meng reports feeling clearer and more energized already.

He may not necessarily consider his process to demonstrate Spiritually Intelligent Leadership, but, given his motivations, he's a perfect example of how to use those building blocks to inspire oneself and an entire organization.

Nearly all the participants in my research into spiritual intelligence described how their senses of purpose sprang from the simple desire to serve. They saw this impulse as a natural expression of being part of an interconnected whole. From that sense of connection, the desire to serve naturally emerges, and with it comes love, meaning, and purpose. To quote Lazer Gurkow, "By serving a cause greater than ourselves we in fact *become* greater than ourselves."

In my follow-up research with CEOs and their staff, the same five qualities (commitment, diligence, morale, team spirit/sense of community and belonging, and loyalty) appeared to be positively correlated with the leader's Service score. CEOs who score high on the Service dimension of spiritual intelligence lead teams who are more committed and harder working, and possess higher morale, greater team spirit, and lower turnover than those who don't.

The effect was particularly pronounced when looking at the 360-feedback scores in which the team rates their leader using the same questions (for example, "In her/his daily life, s/he feels their work is in service of the larger whole"). When the leader's call to service was robust, everyone on their team felt it. Their own purposes were more strongly aligned, and their engagement levels increased overall.

There are countless ways to be of service. You can offer a simple thank you to the cashier at the grocery store, let someone merge into your lane on the freeway, or cook a meal for someone in your life who needs support. I've experienced the rewarding aspects of service as a volunteer counseling incarcerated teens and attending to people in hospice. Through my work with the teenagers, I rediscovered what it means to find hope, and through my time with patients in hospice, I fostered profound connections with people of widely varying religious and spiritual beliefs.

Service on any scale can bring joy. For instance, one of my favorite practices is paying for the driver behind me at the toll booth, watching their surprise and delight in my rearview mirror. Sometimes, they speed up to reach me and wave a thank you. It transforms my driving experience from one of disconnection—boxed-in in a metal tank—to one of connection.

And as fulfilling and rewarding as serving strangers can be, how much more so with those we love. When my children were young and I would bring greater presence and mindfulness to being with them and the motivation behind my actions, I would find a heart-warming delight in performing the simple, mundane tasks of feeding them, clothing them, or cleaning up after them. Folding laundry, spreading peanut butter over lunch sandwiches, and driving my kids to school slowed me down. It pulled me out of my self-importance as a CEO and grounded me in my humanity. Most of all, it connected me to my heart and my love for our family.

YOUR TURN: REALIZE AND HUMANIZE

Bringing in your notebook to capture your reflections, begin by slowing down and tuning in to get INSPIRED (see page 14).

With your mind quiet and relaxed, recall what moments of joy or satisfaction you have experienced doing something in service of others. Did the decision to extend yourself take any deliberation or did it arise spontaneously? How do you imagine it felt to be the recipient of that kindness?

How does it feel to recall the moment now? Notice how doing so affects your body and energy. What happens to your breath? Your tension levels? Your general sense of well-being?

Think of a time when you were the beneficiary of an act of kindness. How did that feel? What do you notice in your body and energy when you recall receiving kindness? What happens to your breath? Your tension levels? Your general sense of well-being?

Comparing the two, what is the difference in your experience between being the giver versus the receiver of service?

Is there a difference between doing something for others out of a sense of "should" versus out of generosity? What's the difference for both the giver and the receiver?

When Meng opens his email each morning, he not only feels good, but also his health improves measurably. Science and modern psychology are now confirming that "it is in the giving that we receive." In the words of Gaur Gopal Das, "Takers can eat well, but givers can sleep well." Helping others lowers our blood pressure, reduces stress, and improves our overall health.[1] For example, research shows that volunteering has proven to be beneficial for our health.[2] In fact, even watching others engaged in altruistic acts can boost our immune system.

One particularly interesting study had people participate in a lottery, and the group of winners was divided in half. One half was instructed to spend the money on themselves, and the other half was told to spend it in ways that would benefit others. While everyone who won money experienced joy initially, at the end of the day only those who gave away their winnings enjoyed a sustained elevated mood.

As social animals, we are hardwired to care for each other. Our brains possess what scientists call "mirror neurons" that reflect other people's emotional states and enable us to feel their joy and pain. Mirror neurons help engender empathy and compassion, as do the thousand joys and sorrows every human life entails. Even ten-month-old babies express sympathy and care when observing someone in distress.[3]

Humanity did not evolve only through social Darwinism, competition, and "selfish genes." We are also biologically inclined toward prosocial, altruistic behavior in a virtuous cycle.[4] Feeling happy and healthy increases our inclination to give to others, which makes us happy, healthy, and generous.

Meng's choice to provide citizens with friendly software and to fund meals for hungry children reflects his personal values, talents, and history. Another client who had battled a frightening disease dedicated herself to providing biotechnologies to help those suffering similar medical conditions. Often, the desire to serve arises from the specific difficulties and pain we've endured. It is natural to want to support others going through the same experience.

In fact, in a survey of over a hundred experts in human behavior, altruism was ranked among the top traits of psychologically healthy individuals. Altruism, from the Latin root meaning "other," involves taking action to promote others' welfare. Buddhist scholar and monk Matthieu Ricard explains in his book, *Altruism: The Power of Compassion to Change Yourself and the World*, that altruism does not require self-sacrifice. It simply means that our actions are rooted in compassionate care for others. Better yet, they're rooted in love.

For us humans, love isn't just a nicety, it's essential. Children can be well-fed in orphanages but will still stop growing physically and emotionally if deprived of emotional warmth and affection. In a study on rhesus monkeys, the babies preferred cuddling with a stuffed-animal surrogate mother over a cold and metallic surrogate, even though the latter gave an extra bonus of dispensing sweet milk.

Almost all acts of kindness occur when we're feeling open and connected, internally and interpersonally through our hearts. It is, after all, through our hearts that we sense our interconnection. It seldom happens when we're feeling pressured, rushed, or guarded.

Through our service we radiate love, and like the sun, our love naturally supports others to grow and bloom. Love is the engine of service. Whatever we love, we are drawn to serve. And though we may not explicitly think in terms of practicing love in a work environment, every time we as leaders engage in service, we are love in action.

Service is beneficial at any scale, for both the giver and the receiver. As Mother Teresa put it, "Not all of us can do great things, but we can do small things with great love. . . . We shall never know all the good that a simple smile can do."

Large visions, important and inspiring as they are, risk becoming traps for our egos. When ego is on the line, the ends can seem to justify the means, obfuscating and corrupting our true motivations, and any benefits—physical, emotional, or spiritual—may be foregone.

However, it is not only lofty visions of service that can be co-opted by our egos. So can the identities we form around being a helper or rescuer of people in need, of people with whom we might foster codependence, all with the underlying motivation of boosting our egos and deficient sense of value.

As Adyashanti, a modern spiritual teacher, says: "A lot of people do not want to be bothered with taking part in service to something unless they can create a public, visible effect or unless their actions can have cosmic significance. That is not service; it is egotistical self-aggrandizement. Real service is humble energy. It is looking for where you can serve the things you love."

In my own life, I have fallen into those kinds of ego traps, and from time to time still do. It is difficult to completely dissolve or transcend the ego. Yet, in becoming aware of it, dis-identifying from it, we can check those impulses to build our self-image up by serving others and staying true to our purer motivations to serve. Because the richest satisfaction comes from bringing together our natural blessings, personal history, and the love that calls us to serve something meaningful.

YOUR TURN: YOUR CALL TO SERVE

Sit in a comfortable chair with your spine straight, yet relaxed, and your feet flat on the ground.

Take a few deep breaths and exhale, letting go of tensions.

As you relax, imagine breathing from the earth up through your feet, then your legs, torso, and all the way up through your head, pausing, sensing, and touching each part of your body from the inside with your breath and your awareness.

Next, spend a moment or two resting your attention at the center of your chest cavity, noticing any sensations, feelings, or images that come up. After a while, ask your heart, "What do I care about that calls me to serve?" Dwell in the question while staying aware of your chest.

Take your notepad and write on the top of the page: "What calls me to serve others is . . ."

Without editing yourself, write down five to ten answers to the prompt.

Review what you've written and notice what resonates with you most deeply—what holds the most meaning.

Consider what unique background, talents, and gifts you can align with your call to serve. You can refer to the gifts you've explored in the Purpose Chapter.

Any organization—for-profit or nonprofit—exists to serve its constituencies, be they customers, internal or external users, employees, vendors, stockholders, communities, donors, or other beneficiaries. The SILeader's job is to mobilize meaning by communicating clearly why people are involved in the organization and show how what they're doing contributes to the world. This call to serve has no doubt influenced their mission and values statements.

We recognize how successful companies, from Southwest Airlines to Ben & Jerry's to Patagonia, have built brands emphasizing exceptional customer service and product quality. What is less widely understood is the importance of applying the same service ethic to their other stakeholders—employees, stockholders, partners, and communities-at-large. For example, Patagonia's mission and culture statements emphasize their commitment to "fighting the environmental crisis and defending nature." Southwest's website states, "Our Culture is woven into all aspects of our business and our Employees' lives, from the way Employees treat each other to the way that our Company puts our Employees first." In an environment that attends to their needs and encourages fun, Southwest employees are motivated and able to transmit high-quality service to their customers in an enjoyable environment. And the result is that they have built a powerful brand.

A similar philosophy is advocated by Hal Rosenbluth, CEO of Rosenbluth International, a corporate travel management company. In his book *The Customer Comes Second*, he reveals his controversial belief that companies must put their people, not their customers, first. He reasons that happy employees do their best to make customers happy. Based on this philosophy, Hal's company has grown and thrived in a challenging travel services industry.

Whichever comes first, the customer or the employee, research shows companies that serve the needs of all *stakeholders* produce better shareholder returns than those that focus exclusively on maximizing profit.[5]

It is on you to deliver and model good service to the people you lead. If you serve them well, you will engender their trust, loyalty, and commitment, while inspiring them to be of greater service to your end customers and constituents. Recognizing this flips the traditional organizational chart on its head. Instead of using your power as the chief to direct others who serve you, you serve your team, activating their highest potential to serve others, and ultimately to serve your shared mission. You are not serving a master or diminishing your power or sovereignty, you are serving your purpose, and you are serving life through love. There is no higher honor and satisfaction than to serve that which we love.

This orientation to leadership was advanced by Robert Greenleaf in his book *Servant Leadership: A Journey into the Nature of Legitimate Power and Greatness*. To practice servant leadership, Greenleaf suggests asking yourself, "Do those served grow as persons? Do they, while being served, become healthier, wiser, freer, more autonomous, more likely themselves to become servants?"

Unsurprisingly, the Bain study cited earlier found Unselfishness and Servanthood to be among the key characteristics of an inspiring leader. Servant leadership does not feed or engage the ego, nor does it require eliminating the ego. As the Dalai Lama says, "We cannot and need not eradicate our ego; rather, we must make sure it is a *serving* ego not a *deserving* ego."

YOUR TURN: BECOMING A SERVANT LEADER

Take a moment to journal about the relationship between your service and your leadership. Feel free to use the questions below to prompt your writing.

What does being a servant leader mean to you? How does it feel to consider yourself one? What, if any, part of you is resistant? In what ways does this challenge your current ideas about leadership? What do you like about it?

In what ways are you already a servant leader? Have you seen others practicing leadership in this spirit? If so, what effect do they have on you?

What small step could you take toward becoming a service-oriented leader? What impact do you imagine it might have on you and on those you lead?

Actualize through Practice

Expand your heart by exercising your service muscles, performing one simple act of kindness, generosity, or care that you can do each day. After practicing the acts you decide on for a week, notice what impact they have had on you and on your relationships.

Some suggestions for actions include:

At the beginning of a meeting, become fully present. Take a couple of breaths into the center of your chest, connecting with your heart as you make eye contact and show a personal interest in the other person and how they are feeling.

Look into your heart, and in-person or via email, express appreciation and gratitude to someone on a job well done or for some support they provided and how it impacted you.

With vulnerability and kindness, ask for a person's help on something. Inviting others to help can be of service to both parties by communicating to them that they have value and their contribution matters. And in recognizing our own need for help, we can feel some relief in not having to carry the weight all by ourselves. The key is to make the request from a place of humbleness rather than as a demand.

ARTICULATING VISION

A COMPELLING VISION ACTIVATES PASSIONATE ENGAGEMENT: THE CASE OF SARAH

Sarah is practically shaking as she describes her company's perilous position. The development of its product and technology has taken much longer than she anticipated. This has forced her to raise money during the pandemic's market crash and accept very onerous terms from new investors. She has tried to get her team to map out a plan for completing the project, but, with this fresh infusion of money in the bank, she feels they lack any sense of urgency. She insists, "We don't have time to mess around."

I empathize with her frustration, then surprise her with a question, "Would you prefer a sense of urgency or one of passionate engagement from your team right now?" Puzzled, she's not sure what the difference is, nor what "passionate engagement" really means.

I invite her to reflect on times she's experienced or witnessed a sense of urgency and share what that concept brings to mind. She describes the need to move and act fast, as well as feelings of extra-sharp focus, difficult trade-offs, hard work, and the fight-or-flight response. "It feels like a sprint," she says. Next, I ask her to remember times when she experienced or witnessed "passionate engagement." This time she recalls excitement and enthusiasm from her team as they pulled together, enjoying the hard work and caring about the outcome over the long haul. She says, "It feels more like a measured and sustainable pace for running a marathon."

Then she breaks into a smile. "I guess I really want passionate engagement, not a bunch of people running around frantically without a shared vision and no strategic focus, with lots of activity but no real progress. Urgency and sprinting are needed sometimes, but that's not what we need right now."

I suggest that this might be the time for her team to have a visioning session to identify their "Mt. Everest," a.k.a. the peak they're inspired to reach in the next three or five years. Only then can they chart the best path to reach the summit.

In our next session, Sarah is visibly calmer. She is eager to share her team's mission statement: "To enable people to express and share their creative artistic talents, while connecting with like-minded others." As she speaks, I can feel bright energy, enthusiasm, and vibrancy radiating from her.

But now she wants some guidance for developing her vision statement further, so we begin an exercise in which I ask her to close her eyes and imagine her company's product and community of users one, three, and five years in the future. Sarah describes a product that adults and children could use to create, express, share, and receive feedback on their digital drawings, poetry, musical compositions, or other creative projects. She envisions a rich, nourishing community of creators with increased access to potential funding, collaborators, and awards and then tells me, "There's a lot of excitement and energy flowing like electricity through my body."

We take a moment to enjoy the experience before I invite her to imagine herself five years from now, standing in front of her employees announcing the milestones they've reached since. She smiles, "I can see it all very clearly—like it's projected on a screen behind my eyes and between my ears." Focusing her attention on that spot, she describes "an immense light source shining, and shimmering points of light bouncing off the ocean on a clear sunny day." The whole room feels brighter.

Sarah then led her team in the same visioning process so they could experience how millions of people would feel enlivened, seen, and connected using the platform. Using the clarity of their mission and the image of the summit they long to conquer, the team can now more easily reach consensus on the best path forward.

Seeing the future, Sarah and her team feel called toward it. They have harnessed the three pillars for mobilizing meaning: a clear sense of purpose, a call for service, and a detailed and compelling vision of their mission and purpose being realized. It manifests as a reality in their minds' eye, naturally calling and pulling them toward it and uniting their passionate efforts.

While a mission statement is intentionally broad and vague, leaving open many possibilities for fulfilling it, the vision statement puts flesh on the mission's bones. Without the specificity of the vision, the mission remains abstract. The vision actualizes both the organization's mission and purpose. As Rachel Copelan says, "Remember that all reality was once a figment of someone's imagination."

At Individual, our mission was to "spread the power of knowledge." Our vision was a world in which hundreds of millions of people would receive daily personalized and interactive newspapers selected through artificial intelligence, and through what later would be termed machine learning software. As often is the case, our vision evolved over time, from fax, to email, to ad-supported web pages, in response to shifting technologies and market needs. The mission, however, remained the same. This is intended to hold true at any level in an organization.

The more detailed and compelling our vision of the future is, the more energy it activates in us and the greater the force that pulls us toward it. Our brains don't differentiate between what we see with our eyes in the present moment, what we remember from the past, and what we imagine about the future. Each state produces a similar physiological response, activating the same neural pathways,[1] thus producing similar inner experiences, whether it be anxiety, sensual arousal, or awe.

Envisioning a dream as if it has already come true reinforces our belief that anything we imagine is possible. And it literally carves the neural pathways for us to make it so. It is not only that our own brain pathways have been laid down for us to traverse, but also that the universe's pathways have cleared our way.

That's why many athletes use visualization in their training. Al Oerter, a four-time Olympic discus champion, and tennis star Billie Jean King were among those who began popularizing the practice in the 1960s, and more recently used by twenty-three-time gold medalist Michael Phelps. Nowadays, a gymnast imagines a perfect routine, a golfer sees the future arc of the ball as they take their swing, and a martial artist visualizes their hand cutting through a cement block like a hot knife through butter. When each of these individuals does this, they reinforce the right neural pathways without ever even physically moving.

Many people think vision only applies to larger long-term undertakings, such as competing as a professional athlete, building a company, or transforming the world. But we don't all have to be a Martin Luther King, Jr. Envisioning a specific future of any kind at any scale helps bring it to fruition.

VISUALIZING AT ANY SCALE: THE CASE OF TED

Ted had gone through a difficult year in which he had to lay off a number of employees. He looked at the coming year and articulated clear goals for recovering from this low point but was nervous about reaching his targets.

So, I guided him to visualize how it would look and feel to achieve those goals. Then I had him imagine reporting this success to his employees in a company-wide celebration and in a board meeting. As he relaxed and began to smile, I invited him to notice the reactions on people's faces and imagine what it would feel like to go home and tell his spouse about how those events had gone, noticing her reaction as well. His breath deepened and when he opened his eyes he shared how the vision touched and uplifted him out of his funk, out of the negative outlook that had set in after a year of disappointing his employees and board. In its place, he found his confidence and optimism.

With renewed vigor, he used the same process with his staff, inviting everyone to imagine both their own department and the overall company's success one, three, and five years in the future—to experience it as a felt reality.

The following year, Ted reported that the company had met most of their objectives. As he had imagined one year earlier, they found themselves celebrating. In fact, just by visualizing the turnaround with the full force of their hearts and a detailed picture in their minds, they planted the seeds for it to manifest.

Filled with excitement about this magical process, Ted decided to try it in other contexts. As the father of two rambunctious teenagers, he set his next goal of making their family dinner emotionally nourishing and relaxing. I invited him to visualize himself being present and attentive while connecting with his sons and wife, sharing each day the moments they felt grateful for and those they found challenging. Before he knew it, his vision was a reality. For every significant endeavor since, Ted has consistently turned to his new power: envisioning his intended outcome and bringing his best self to make it a reality.

It's important to note that visualization, whether it's for the perfect drive on the golf course or a successful presentation to the board of directors, works best when it is as complete and vivid as possible. The more you can become aware of the multimodal experience of your body in the moment, and in the times when you are visualizing past, present, or future states, the more powerfully you function and the more sources of intelligence you can access.

YOUR TURN: VISUALIZE YOUR FUTURE

Find a quiet spot and sit in a comfortable position where you can get INSPIRED (see page 14). After a moment of rest, bring to mind a goal you have for yourself or your team that might seem to be a bit lofty but still doable. Write down a description of the overall outcome you would like to see occur.

Take a few more deep breaths, and now closing your eyes, imagine this future outcome as if it were happening in this very moment. Watch it play out like a movie and add more vivid details. Who is there, what are they doing, and how are they feeling?

Now include an image of yourself in the scene. How are you holding yourself? What attitude are you exuding? How are people responding to you? Holding this scene in your mind, sense and bring your awareness to your body. How alive do you feel? What emotions do you feel? Where do you feel closed or opened, contracted or expanded?

Take a snapshot of your experience, an "inner-selfie," in its full color and detail. Then save it in a "long-term memory album" where you can access it in the future to refresh your state of mind and nervous system.

Now recall that snapshot. Hold it in your imagination. Ask your future self what were the important factors that enabled you to get there? What was the path you traveled? What were the obstacles, and how did you overcome them?

When you finish, notice how you feel. What have you learned about and from your future self? Does your dream seem more or less achievable? What is your level of vitality and confidence?

Write down notes to refer to again.

The visioning process's power extends to include the future of teams and individuals as well. Seeing the highest potential in others is a powerful lever for their development and an important mentoring skill for leaders to utilize.

When I was in the Israeli military, the person who had the most positive impact on my leadership development was our regiment commander. Though over four decades have passed, his modest build, the brilliant clarity of his penetrating blue eyes, and air of dignity and confidence remain firmly in my memory. He seemed to see the best in everybody and believed in us more than we believed in ourselves.

Although I only had a few occasions to meet with him one-on-one, I felt a personal connection from the way he looked at me. His public expression conveyed his high regard for me and for my leadership potential, which was confirmed in our rare private exchanges too. His encouragement boosted my confidence and emboldened me to take initiative when it was needed, even when I didn't have a formal position of authority.

HOLDING A POSITIVE VISION: THE CASE OF SAM

Sam's company has grown rapidly, reaching hundreds of millions of dollars in annual revenues. As a visionary and manager who could both see the big picture as well as drill into any level of detail, he is having difficulty stepping back from the minutiae and is getting mired in auditing and quality assurance. Despite his aspiration to assume the role of leading from behind by mentoring his employees, instead he often reverts to being argumentative and controlling. His team finds it disempowering, and he finds it exhausting and isolating.

I invite Sam to visualize himself and his employees at an off-site retreat a year from now, having reached his desired team dynamics and personal goals.

He pictures his team of directors, feeling and taking responsibility to ensure their product releases were of high quality, fully aware of their authority to decide on and secure resources to ensure such quality, having autonomy within their scope, and working collaboratively with each other. He sees a culture of blameless accountability where people could challenge one another, including him, while owning and learning from their mistakes. A place where people are feeling energized, leaning forward, participating, and contributing. I guide him to notice what it feels like for his future self to be leading such a group. He describes it as a sense of belonging and camaraderie, satisfying, and lightening the load of his responsibilities as CEO.

I then ask Sam to interview his future self to find out what key ingredients had made this future come about. Sam talks about creating an environment of psychological safety where mistakes are not only tolerated, but are, in fact, expected and viewed as opportunities for learning and growth, thus minimizing the chances they are repeated. He also sees himself setting an example by being more vulnerable and forthcoming in admitting his own mistakes. Last, Sam sees his future self patiently sitting back in meetings, letting others speak more, and allowing conflicting viewpoints to be debated thoroughly before decisions are made.

In the coming months, Sam continues returning to his desire to practice leading from behind and continues to refresh his state of mind before important meetings to open himself to different perspectives. With clear commitment and practice, over time, he gradually becomes more able to shift his habit away from being controlling to being empowering.

People often act in accordance with how we see them, so seeing their best brings out their best.

YOUR TURN: BRINGING OUT THE BEST

Sit comfortably in a quiet place and take some deep, centering breaths until you begin to feel settled.

Close your eyes and bring to mind someone on your team. See them vividly and reflect on their strengths. What do you admire and appreciate about them? What are their superpowers? Consider how good it would be for them and your organization if these qualities, and maybe even ones they're not yet aware of, could emerge and blossom.

Now imagine it's a year later and these qualities are more developed. What new capacities emerge? What new responsibilities are they assuming? Let the image of them thriving become more vivid. How are they holding themselves and affecting others?

Write down notes to refer to again.

We are each ultimately sovereign over our individual selves. So, when it comes to visioning others, take care not to impose your vision for their future onto them. Honor them by creating the conditions in which their inherent gifts can be aligned with their aspirations. Ask them where they want to see themselves in the future. Enter a dialogue with them on what you each see as their growth potential and how you might help them realize it. Notice the effect of the conversation on their behavior in the days and weeks to follow. Notice if you feel more energized and motivated having a shared vision for their potential growth. Do you feel intrinsically rewarded knowing you facilitated someone's growth?

Can you sense a future wanting to be born through you? If so, treat it as a vital seed in the soil of your soul. Water it by feeling all that it evokes in you. As you do, your dream will naturally energize, mobilize, and draw you toward it. In time, it will germinate, come to life, and blossom through you. And remember, in the words of the poet Rilke, "Have patience with everything unresolved in your heart and try to love the questions themselves."

As you continue to reflect on your unique gifts and what calls you to serve, evaluating and thinking through your options, trust that in time the right vision for your future will reveal itself. And till then, simply rest assured that bringing your authentic presence to life is its own gift.

REFRAMING DIFFICULTIES INTO OPPORTUNITIES

THROUGH THE HEAT OF FIRE, STEEL IS FORGED: THE CASE OF MEI

"I'm a serial entrepreneur. Or, more like a serial failure," Mei tells me in our first meeting. The daughter of Vietnamese refugees, she spent her teenage years working in the family's small beauty salon where she learned about the operational challenges. Now, the larger beauty business Mei most recently founded has similar challenges, just on a different scale.

With her organization gaining traction, she has been able to raise several rounds of financing and create a culture of growth she is proud of. Unfortunately, just as she and her team were becoming confident about their future, the COVID pandemic hit and her company lost over 50 percent of their revenue forcing her to implement three rounds of layoffs.

Not only were the layoffs demoralizing for the remaining employees, but they were also excruciatingly painful for Mei—disappointing her employees and investors felt nearly intolerable. Falling into a depression, she could only work at half her capacity. But despite these difficulties, she and her team persisted for months exploring ways to reinvent the business. Finally, exhausted and with no solution in sight, she has begun speaking with a bankruptcy lawyer.

During our session, Mei describes the two companies she started prior and how they also failed. She tells me she feels stuck in a loop of failures, moving from crisis to crisis in her life. She says she's embarrassed by how long it took her last time to pick herself back up.

I ask her how she overcame her depression after the first loss. She recounts how one day she woke up somehow inspired, suddenly motivated to go travel around the world for several months.

I invite Mei to connect with the place in herself from which the inspiration to travel came. She closes her eyes and draws her attention inward. Her face begins to lighten up, and she says she feels a spring of energy around her solar plexus.

Her face softens and her smile begins to shine. I invite her to stay with this fountain of energy while also staying aware of her feet resting on the ground. Her posture straightens, and I sense her energy radiating outwardly and occupying a larger space around her body—her field of presence grows larger. Scanning her body, she describes a growing feeling in her lower belly as "full, and warm—like glowing red fiery lava," pointing to the area martial artists and a number of healing modalities focus on called the *hara*.

Having found her inner sources of power, we reflect on her journey. Feeling and leaning into her earlier impulse to go traveling had reconnected Mei with her spark of life, which in turn gave her the energy to see, forged in the fire of her previous failures, having fallen and risen again and again, how much she has grown in resilience. Though changing our habitual narrative can take time and practice, Mei is now able to reframe her life story from one of a serial failure to that of a continual learner. And what had seemed like disaster has turned into an exciting opportunity.

It is not uncommon for great businesses to emerge from what have seemed like setbacks. In fact, I challenge you to find someone highly accomplished in any field—business, science, art—who has not faced and been forged by adversity. In his famous commencement address at Stanford, Steve Jobs told of the three defining moments in his life: dropping out of college, being fired from Apple, and receiving a cancer diagnosis. He used each of these disruptions as an opportunity to reinvent himself.

In my coaching practice, three of the four clients of mine who have become billionaires, all, like the phoenix, have risen from the ashes of failure. One's company hit a dead end and his investors all bailed out, yet he along with his team reinvented themselves. They set their company in a new direction and it became a runaway success as a global brand with hundreds of millions of users. And because their investors all had walked away, he ended up owning a larger percentage of the company than before. Another was fired as CEO but went on to run an even more successful company. And the third person, well, his business was slow to grow, low on cash, and running on fumes. Yet, only when all potential fire-sale buyers turned him down and the company's escape hatches were closed, was he forced to find a way forward and recommit to his vision. He and his team soon hit an inflection point in their growth and eventually became a high-flying public company.

True, not everybody prevails over adversity. Some people are beaten down, succumbing to the difficulties and unable to see a way forward. So, what makes the difference? For Mei, it was finding a resource, a moment of inspiration hidden in a story of defeat, that not only revealed the gifts she had received from her past failures, but also tapped into her not-yet-extinguished spark of life force. Thomas Edison, one of the most renowned inventors in history, tells us, "I have not failed. I've just found ten thousand ways that won't work." It is no coincidence that stories of people's persistence in the face of adversity are some of the most inspiring, for they are stories about the power of inspiration itself. Inspiration is the fuel that enables us to make meaning from our failures, to reframe them, and to learn and grow through them all.

My own studies into spiritually intelligent individuals revealed that nearly all of them spoke of finding meaning in their disappointment, pain, and suffering, and accepting agony as an inevitable part of every life. One person said, "Pain is my teacher. I allow myself to experience it as fully as I can and ask myself, what is it inviting me to practice or learn?"

Spiritually intelligent people practice staying open to the full range of life's experiences, making it a habit to embrace "yes." When facing difficulties, they begin by accepting what is (including all their emotions). Then asking themselves what those problems are calling forth in them, what might they be required to take on, release, or learn. They acknowledge the need to let go of any expectations they might have about how the future should unfold. This allows them to see new possibilities and find creative solutions. Reframing their problems as opportunities maximizes their potential to learn and reduces their suffering. Rather than becoming fixated on any end goal, they see life itself as their spiritual path of learning and growth and feel grateful for its gifts. As one person put it, "The universe is incredibly generous. When I don't get the lesson the first time, I invariably get another chance at it." Having this capacity is integral to spiritual intelligence and correlates significantly with effective leadership.

UNCOVERING OUR HIDDEN BLESSINGS

One of my favorite rituals when hosting Thanksgiving dinner is to invite my guests to recount a difficult experience they've had that, in hindsight, turned out for the good. My guests often speak about how being laid off from work, though financially challenging for a while, eventually led to a much more satisfying or lucrative position somewhere else. Some have spoken about the painful ending of a relationship that made it possible to find a deeper and more soulful love connection. Others have talked about how receiving a cancer diagnosis put them on a life-changing healing journey. I've already shared some about having been pushed out of the company I founded, Individual. Though devastating at the time, that experience put me on a path of spiritual growth and healing, which has made my life richer and more fulfilling.

Mei's story reflects how difficulties don't have to hinder our lives, but rather how they can actually help develop our gifts and motivate us to share them. The hardship her family endured as refugees in a new country struggling to make a living running a beauty salon energized her to support similar populations and businesses. It was this inspiration that gave her the commitment to recover from each setback and learn, grow, and keep moving forward. And when her work no longer stirred her, she tapped into other sources of inspiration to keep her energized, traveling, exploring, until she was ready for work again.

My client Charles, the founder and CEO of a rapidly growing start-up, attributes his ability at tuning in to people and reading the room to his childhood, a time when he needed to be attuned to his parents' volatile moods to stay safe. Another client, Hank, who built a multiplayer online video gaming business with hundreds of millions in revenue, was inspired to do so because computer games were the one arena in which he excelled and could connect with others as a child. Building his company was his way of helping others like him.

Such stories are not limited to entrepreneurs. I know a man whose teenage son was victimized in sudden, random violence by a gang member who was only trying to prove his toughness. His father went on to form a nonprofit with the mission of reducing gang violence through education and alternative routes for troubled young men to help them gain status, self-esteem, and community. Author Janet Attwood recounts how after she was raped at age seventeen, she became motivated to help other rape victims she encounters. Decades later, contemplating whether she wished her trauma never happened, she ultimately believed the positive impact and the rewards of helping others outweighed the pain and suffering she had experienced. Such stories demonstrate how part of our healing journey involves finding meaning in our wounds, making them sacred, and using them to motivate us in service of others. In the words of Victor Frankl, "What is to give light must endure burning."

YOUR TURN: DISCOVERING OPPORTUNITY IN A DIFFICULTY

Find a comfortable seated position and ground yourself, sensing the weight of your body and legs. Take a moment to simply pay attention to your breath. Sense and wiggle your toes. Sense and move your fingers. Now see if you can sense your hands, feet, arms, and legs at the same time. As you begin to settle, relax, and become present, recall a challenge you're currently facing. As you continue, notice any shifts in your body and breath through the sensations and emotions that may surface.

Consider what opportunities might be hiding in this challenge by asking yourself the following:

What is the situation calling forth in me? Perhaps it's resilience or patience, creativity, or dedication.

What qualities would support me in getting through this?

What would I need to believe about myself, others, or the world for me to handle it?

If this were happening to someone else, what gifts would I imagine it was offering them? How might they emerge as better equipped for the future?

Review your answers to the first two questions. Ask yourself whether you already possess those qualities, even to some small extent. Then call them forth and notice what they feel like.

Revisit the challenge you are facing now. Does it feel any different? What new resources do you feel you have access to now? Is your sense of confidence and capability stronger now?

There are no wrong answers. Stay open and see what arises without shame or blame. Take notes on what you feel, and what capabilities and insights have arisen.

When we're feeling challenged, it's easy to judge and berate ourselves for our shortcomings. We assume that we or someone else are at fault. Either we must have done something wrong, a cause for blame or shame, or we defend against that shame by blaming someone else. Neither way is helpful as it only disempowers us.

If nothing else, our difficulties are opportunities to practice open acceptance of the truth and cultivate compassion for ourselves. Self-compassion, though that alone can be a challenge for many of us, is often the first step toward finding the resources we need to deal with any situation.

The first step to self-compassion is to notice your pain, your difficulty, and your suffering, and be open to feeling it rather than denying, rejecting, or pretending it isn't there. Then, consider how you would feel if someone you love were in pain. Remind yourself that you're on your own side and you can do what soothes you most. I have found it helpful simply to put my right hand flat on my heart with my left on top while acknowledging and saying to myself, "Yosi, this is a really difficult situation for you. I'm sorry. Unfortunately, life involves pain. I'm here with you, and we'll get through all this together." I feel the flow of gentle energy between my hands and heart. I imagine what someone kind and compassionate who loves me deeply might say or do. This enables me to connect with a wise part inside that can offer some compassion to the part of me that is hurting; often that part is my younger self. To help my clients access this kind of self-compassion, I remind them of the Buddha's statement, "You can search the ten-fold universe and not find a single being more worthy of loving kindness than yourself."

If it's hard for you to find gifts in your difficult situation, you're not alone. Most of us only recognize those gifts in hindsight. In fact, it can take decades before they are revealed to us, especially from traumatic events. To this day, I am still unpacking the meaning of a stranger in a movie theater molesting me when I was nine years old. It was only at the age of forty, when I had been pushed out of my company and started therapy, that the memory, which I had tried to repress, resurfaced, and I dared to share it with someone. Every victim holds some shame and sense of responsibility for their experiences. For many years I believed I was damaged goods. But, in finding more understanding, I uncovered my hidden strengths. I can see now how the experience has also given me a depth of compassion for other children who have been sexually assaulted and has made me better able to protect my own children.

Working through my anger, I found it possible to discharge my remaining toxic resentment by practicing compassion and forgiveness. Over time, I began to feel the warm expansion of my heart's capacity for compassion, even for my perpetrator, the same ability that I have encountered in the spiritually intelligent people I admire most.

But what about the difficulties we create ourselves? Suffering we bring about to others and ourselves when we act out of alignment with our values? When we feel guilty or ashamed and down on ourselves? It is then that we can reframe our perspective from "I am bad" to "I made a mistake."

When we see our failures and shortcomings as mistakes, we can find a way out of wallowing in our guilt and suffering and see them as opportunities to learn better ways to live in alignment with our values. In fact, in the Jewish tradition I grew up in, when we make amends and resolve to do better in the future, even our sins can turn into merits.

Similarly, the Japanese kintsugi art involves piecing together broken pottery with melted gold. The result is resilient, unique, and more beautiful than the original. Kintsugi shows how healing our brokenness can highlight our gifts and beauty, letting the treasures shine in and through us.

Of course, some events are so horrible that the mere suggestion of hidden blessings may be offensive. I am not suggesting we look for the good side of atrocities. Indeed, I find it hard to reconcile my optimistic belief, my faith, and my trust that the universe is fundamentally friendly toward life when there is the reality of horrors. Certainly, Victor Frankl, living in the unmitigated hell of a Nazi extermination camp, had no reason to believe in a benevolent universe—yet he championed the ability of free will to choose to believe so. I choose to hold onto faith and trust and find this to be empowering as opposed to the alternatives of victimhood and despair from living in a hostile universe. Surmounting this paradox of a friendly benevolent universe that also gives rise to such horrors is beyond my rational mind's capacity to understand. But recognizing and holding this paradox nonetheless catapults me into a new level of humility, while my spirit remains high.

Whether we find meaning sooner or later, the mere act of looking for it and assuming it's there in our suffering transforms us. No longer are we victims of life's tragic horrors, nor is the universe reduced to just random quantum fluctuations and genetic mutations. Life is a sacred teaching journey packed with significance and purpose, and we are active agents able to respond, learn, and grow through it. To remain trusting and optimistic about the possibilities ahead.

CHAPTER 3

INTERACTING WITH GRACE

*The winds of grace are always
blowing; it is for us to raise our sails.*
—Ramakrishna

GRACE, AS EXPRESSED IN TERMS of Spiritually Intelligent Leadership, is the ability to lead with dignity, beauty, and joy in such a way as to awaken hope, trust, celebration, and gratitude in ourselves and others. This ability rests on four essential competencies: Trust, Beauty, Joy, and Gratitude.

- *Trust*: Inspiring confidence, optimism, and hope for the future in yourself and in others.

- *Beauty*: Recognizing the sparkle of life's creative intelligence that shines through, in, and around us.

- *Joy*: Radiating delight and bringing lighthearted playfulness, humor, and celebration to your engagements.

- *Gratitude*: Appreciating ourselves, the people, the learning, and all the gifts we receive along the way.

TRUST

TRUSTING OURSELVES AND OPENING UP TO LIFE: THE CASE OF LLOYD

After successfully selling his first company, Lloyd started his second business brimming with confidence. With investors eager to fund him, his self-assurance bordered on arrogance. Then his product launched and received a dismal response.

"How could I have been so wrong?" he laments in our session. Having attempted several changes to his product without any measurable success, he's nearly paralyzed by his fear of failure. I invite him to acknowledge and feel his anxiety and fear, which he first describes as a tight knot in his stomach before bringing his gentle awareness to it and starting to relax. With some relaxation he begins to sense a "fog" in the center of his head behind his eyes.

I draw his focus to this fog, inviting him to travel to its center using his imagination. He's scared to enter it at first, but eventually, after settling his attention on it, the fog begins to lift. "Not all the way but at least partially; it's like I can see a few steps ahead," he says.

With his sense of being paralyzed by fear subsiding and the fog partially clearing, he sits noticeably more upright with his energy more expansive. By naming and sensing his fear, as well as moving toward what seems like fog, Lloyd tells me he feels more hopeful and optimistic about his future. Over the coming weeks, he and his team are back at work creatively iterating, testing, and improving their product. Though the fog visits him periodically, he is now empowered and trusts himself to turn toward it and face it head on, after which he regains his clarity.

Trust is a state of being and living in open confidence and flow with life—an embodied inner knowing that things work out, that we are and will continue to be okay. We begin to restore this trust by increasingly opening to and bringing our full presence to our inner experiences. When we turn toward difficult emotions and allow ourselves to feel what we feel, we increase our tolerance for life and affirm our capacity to deal with the truth. We trust that whatever the storm, we can weather it.

Opening to our feelings means we can consciously feel our anger without reacting violently. That we can be aware of our fear without hiding under the covers. In fact, being mindful and present with our feelings makes it possible to choose how we want to respond instead of reacting impulsively when we're triggered. As Victor Frankl pointed out, "Between stimulus and response there is a space. In that space is our power to choose our response. In our response lies our growth and our freedom."

YOUR TURN: TRUSTING IN OUR EXPERIENCE OF LIFE

Without adjusting your breath or posture, notice what you are experiencing right now. What are you sensing in your body? What emotions are stirring in you? What is happening in your mind?

If you sense any tension, notice how it feels before you make any changes. How does your body and your breathing shift when you bring your awareness to discomfort?

Now, allow yourself to adjust to find more comfort in your body. What happens when you bring background tensions to the foreground of your awareness? Do they dissolve or get worse?

See if, just for a moment, you can open to your experience a little more. If there is fog, enter it; if there is anxiety, soften and breathe into it. Slow down to give it lots of space and permission to be there, just as it is, for the next three breaths.

Notice what changes as you breathe. If it began as an uncomfortable feeling, has it shifted? How? And if it was a pleasant one, what happened when you opened to it and allowed it in more deeply? Are you breathing more deeply?

What have you learned through this brief exercise?

If you just followed this guided exercise, you have had an experience of meditating! Practicing meditation can help you become more conscious of your state and stay present with your experience. As we learn to be more in touch with ourselves, we open to the depth, beauty, and richness of our inner life and our universe, and we develop deeper trust in ourselves.

From that depth of connection with ourselves, we can approach and respond to just about anything. Being able to respond, we are response-able, *responsible*, and empowered.

Every feeling communicates something important. By staying open to our feelings, we can discern what response is most appropriate. Anger often indicates that something we value is being threatened. It mobilizes the energy, motivation, and strength we need to fight. Fear alerts us to when a judgment must be made to either proceed with courage or take precautions. We can trust and learn from our feelings when we trust ourselves to feel them nonjudgmentally from a position of being open to the information they have for us. In the words of James Allen, "Self-trust is the essence of heroism." Noticing and labeling our difficult emotions gives us some space and distance from them. As we observe and name them, we are no longer simply reacting, lost in them like young children. And from that space of noticing and labeling, bringing our language center in the neocortical part of our brain online, we have greater freedom to skillfully choose our responses.[1]

WORKING WITH DIFFICULT FEELINGS: THE CASE OF PETER

Peter was reluctant to experience "negative emotions" and was trying to rid himself of them. Seeing that he was okay after acknowledging and feeling his sadness and fear, he agreed to conduct an experiment for a week. To the best of his ability, he would welcome any difficult feelings that arose. Instead of distracting himself or pushing the feelings away, he would pause and observe his sensations, thoughts, and action impulses with curiosity and interest.

In our following meeting, Peter reported that he felt much calmer than the week before, even though he had tolerated more unpleasant states than usual. "I wasn't fighting with myself trying to push away the negative feelings," he told me, and by welcoming them, he added, "The negative emotions moved through me faster."

Peter described how during the week he had become annoyed with his head of finance at his rapidly growing tech start-up. Instead of subtly chiding her as he would have normally done, he took a moment to notice his experience and then to communicate both the issue and its effect on him, even naming his "annoyance," honestly and with care. Although at first she was taken aback, it resulted in a constructive, honest conversation for both. Peter believed it turned out much better than if he had tried to suppress and ignore his feelings or had acted irritated without being transparent and direct.

During another meeting Peter felt "intensely sad" when his company's first product manager, a longtime stellar performer, said he was leaving the company. Rather than moving away from his feelings, Peter allowed his sadness to show on his face, and both he and the product manager shared a moment of sadness in silence together. It was a profound connection in which they both acknowledged their mutual appreciation and loss. In our session, Peter acknowledged that this moment of sadness was rooted in love.

THE RESEARCH: IN LIFE WE TRUST

In my interviews with spiritually intelligent individuals, the majority spoke about how trust is the foundation for their orientation to life—a faith that, even if things don't turn out the way they plan or wish for, events will still somehow work out for the best. They exhibit deep confidence in life, the universe, or the divine. And that confidence produces a hopeful, optimistic orientation to the future. "Love is stronger than hate, and life is stronger than death. And there is always renewal, always renewal," said one.

Others spoke of the confidence that naturally arises when they feel aligned with their higher purpose and trust that the universe would support their efforts. Some spoke of the importance of hope. One described, "We know that people recover from major illness when they have hope. . . . My parents were survivors of Auschwitz, and they didn't give up hope. That was what kept them alive, it was just having hope."

We confirmed that the capacity for trust is integral to spiritual intelligence and correlates significantly with effective leadership. Thus, if we trust that the world is fundamentally friendly, we can live fully, boldly, and passionately, because when feeling held and safe, we don't have to hold back. Such trust gives us the motivation and hope that our efforts are meaningfully worthwhile, even if things don't turn out exactly as we wish. As Václav Havel clarifies, "Hope is not the conviction that something will turn out well, but the certainty that something is worth doing no matter how it turns out."

Developing such basic trust starts with understanding.

According to eminent developmental psychologist Erik Erikson, the process of developing trust defines our lives from birth through the first eighteen months. Our sense of safety, and how our basic needs were attended to by our primary caregivers through feeding, nurturing, holding, and touching, determine whether we develop a trusting and hopeful attitude.

Erikson's next stage of early development weighs autonomy versus shame. When we don't get the love and mirroring—when others are well-attuned to our moods, wants, and needs and can reflect them back to us—we require as young children, we often unconsciously believe it is our fault, that we are broken, lacking, and deficient in some way. And since no caretakers can provide perfect attunement, most of us end up with some level of internalized shame. This effect can grow exponentially given that we often feel shame about our shame—further repressing it. Repression robs us of opportunities to work through feelings and inhibits our ability to experience our whole being. Feeling shame is both an internalized judgment ("I am bad") and a social feeling ("Others won't want to be with me"), and it has rather disastrous consequences on our capacity for trusting ourselves and others. Expecting rejection, we go into hiding from others, not trusting that they will accept us as we are, thus tragically bringing about the isolation and loneliness we most fear.

Spanning Erikson's first two developmental stages, more recent research has focused on the establishment of secure versus insecure, or anxious attachment, between babies and their primary caregivers, usually mothers. With secure attachment, children attain complementary capacities: autonomy and the capacity for self-regulation, as well as the capacity for bonding, intimacy, and connection.

Secure attachment naturally arises when the primary caregiver is reliably available and attuned so that the young child learns to trust that they have someone to turn to for comfort when needed. With greater autonomy, these children display the courage to take initiative and explore the world around them, knowing they have a trusted base to return to when needed. Whereas when the caregiver is not available, unresponsive, or mis-attuned, the child can develop what is called *anxious-avoidant attachment*, internalizing the message that others can't be trusted. They focus on being self-reliant, while still needing and longing for connection underneath it all. Similarly, those with *anxious-ambivalent* attachment have difficulty being vulnerable and trusting of others and of themselves. They tend to move toward and away from others in waves, wanting trusted relationships but unable to relax into them.

So, what if you weren't raised in an environment conducive for secure attachment? First, you're not alone. About half the population struggles with this insecurity. Fortunately, there's hope. Trust can be developed and attachment wounds repaired over time through a relationship with a reliable therapist or partner. If you haven't found a reliable therapist or partner, there are tools and practices available for developing secure attachment with the divine, a spiritual figure such as Jesus or Mother Mary, or an internalized parental figure.[2]

While our first years of life have the biggest impact on our ability to trust, the capacity for trust is also affected by our environment, traumas, and events throughout our entire lifespan. And since most of us grow up in environments with varying degrees of attunement or safety, our sense of trust is never perfect. Healing those wounds can be a long process, but it is crucial for trust in relationships.

For my own life, I think of my grandfather who often repeated the ancient Hebrew sages' phrase, "*Kol akuva le'tovah*," meaning, "Every mishap is for the good." His faith gave him the strength he needed to face difficult obstacles. And, as his name Sasson, Hebrew for "joy," denotes, he never ceased to radiate delight and happiness. He was able to radiate such joy despite facing much hardship and many traumas in his life, including escaping anti-Semitism around World War II and fleeing to Israel as a refugee with nothing but his bag of clothes. His memory continues to inspire me to trust that I'll find the blessings hidden in life's inevitable difficulties.

As interconnected, interdependent beings, we require trust in three realms: self, others, and the universe or life in general. And within each realm are multiple aspects: we can trust our thoughts but not our emotions. We can trust someone's intention, but not their skill. We can trust life's capacity to heal and return in general, but not from destructiveness.

With these interconnected dimensions of trust, SILeaders can risk aiming high, rallying support behind their cause, believing what they're doing is possible, and then bounce back, learn, and adjust if things don't turn out exactly according to plan. Albert Einstein eloquently put it this way: "It is better to believe than to disbelieve; in so doing, you bring everything to the realm of possibility."

In the *Harvard Business Review* article "The Neuroscience of Trust,"[3] Paul Zak cites research indicating that, "Compared with people at low-trust companies, people at high-trust companies report 74% less stress, 106% more energy at work, 50% higher productivity, 13% fewer sick days, 76% more engagement, 29% more satisfaction with their lives, 40% less burnout." A culture of trust yields positive results at any and every level of management.

Dr. Zak found that when we are trusted, and when we trust others, oxytocin levels in our body increase. Oxytocin is the neurotransmitter mothers and babies release during moments of attachment, such as breastfeeding or comforting touch. Oxytocin is also released during lovemaking between adults, or in more routine empathetic connections between friends and colleagues. Some call oxytocin the love hormone. Warming and opening our heart, it feels good.

And, while we can't directly change people's oxytocin levels as leaders, we can create a culture that fosters it by trusting others and being trustworthy ourselves. As we see and mirror others' positive qualities, and appropriately empower them, our coworkers feel validated and affirmed. Feeling trusted, they do their best to validate our positive expectations. And as they succeed and grow, they thrive and become more trustworthy.

Our sense of trust in ourselves, our belief in our teammates, as well as our confidence in life play a crucial role in our approach to every moment. Are we battling alone to survive in a dog-eat-dog world, or are there others we can lean on, and for what? Where can we find safety and support when danger and threat are real? Do we have people outside our work life upon whom we can rely? We need to discern and trust our judgment, confident that things will work out, even when we can't know the exact outcome. It's no surprise that the word *confidence* is derived from the Latin *confidential*, meaning "trust."

YOUR TURN: TRUST INVENTORY AND EXPERIMENT

Part 1: Take a few moments and reflect on your own relationship to the three domains of trust: self, others, and the universe. Reflect on a specific situation and rank your degree of trust from 1 to 10 (1 being the lowest, 10 the highest):

Trust in yourself to understand and respond optimally?

Trust in others to do their part or provide the right kind of support to you?

Attitude toward the factors ("life") you can't control in this situation?

Now reflect on what would be possible if you had a little more trust. Think of someone you know of who embodies a higher level of trust. Next recall someone—a friend, a loved one, or your favorite pet—who easily evokes love, gratitude, and appreciation in your heart. Imagine them in the center of your chest while taking a few deep breaths into your heart area. This will naturally release some oxytocin into your system. Notice whether your level of trust shifts in any of the realms in how you can go about dealing with your situation now.

Part 2: Reflect on the following and take notes:

Think of a time when your trust in others increased. What did they do that helped you trust them more?

What attitudes do others exhibit that enhance your capacity to trust them? What behaviors and attitudes limit it?

What events or circumstances in your life had the biggest impact on shaping your relationship to trust in each of the three domains?

Part 3: Reflect on the question:

How do I feel and behave when I trust more?

Make notes about specific bodily sensations, emotions, and energetic movements you experience when you're feeling trusting. How is your attention focused, what kinds of thoughts are engaged, and what kinds of behaviors do you exhibit when you are more trusting?

Part 4: Identify three people on your team and, one at a time, reflect on what ways you trust them and in what ways you don't. Do you trust their intention, loyalty and dedication, skill, or ability to solve problems and get results in certain domains?

> Now, review your list and consider what might be limiting your trust. Imagine what might be possible if you took a little risk and trusted them just a little more. Experiment with trusting them to partner with you in identifying their potential growth opportunities. That might mean giving them 5 or 10 percent more responsibility, or it might mean being more honest with them about your own challenge with their performance and your trust that they can receive your feedback in a constructive way.

You may be surprised at what trust makes possible. As Angeles Arrien says, "The opposite of trusting in the unexpected is trying to control the uncontrollable." Seeing the highest potential in others and acting accordingly by trusting them to manifest it helps activate their ability to actualize it. Doing so incrementally helps them build confidence and trust in themselves, as does yours in them.

But just as others become more trustworthy to us over time as they prove themselves to be reliable, so too do we develop greater trust in ourselves, and others develop greater trust in us by observing how we honor our commitments.

My client Randy, a general manager of a business unit within a larger company, often showed up to our meetings late, frequently walking in while still talking on the phone. At one point I chose to confront him, pointing out the impact it had on me—I felt less connected, with lower energy and motivation to help him. As you might expect, he was habitually late to most meetings with others as well. Taken aback by my disclosure at first, he acknowledged that he often began such meetings feeling scattered and needing to apologize. He felt defensive and undermined his own authority and power in those situations. And it was indeed part of a larger pattern of procrastination in which he was often late in delivering on his promises, something others found frustrating, as reflected in his 360-feedback. And not only did he undermine others' trust, but he also undermined his own self-confidence as he did not trust himself to deliver on his commitments to himself or others. Realizing the heavy price he was paying, Randy resolved to hang up the phone at least two minutes before walking into my office and set the intention of showing up on time. He lived up to his first commitment and started showing up to meetings on time more often. Within a year or so he would rarely show up more than a minute or two late to our meetings and would more consistently show up to work meetings on time.

As leaders we need to feel trustworthy in our own eyes by living in alignment with our own values and following up on our commitments to ourselves. And certainly, we need to earn the trust of those we lead by walking our talk, delivering on our commitments, showing others respect, empathy, and care, accurately recognizing their strengths and weaknesses, openly sharing information with them, and showing up authentically and vulnerably ourselves. When we trust others with our vulnerability—apologizing, owning our mistakes and limitations, they are more likely to reciprocate in kind. And through this greater mutual trust, deeper bonds develop, enabling more open and direct feedback to support collective growth and learning.

YOUR TURN: BECOMING TRUSTWORTHY

Take a few moments to reflect on your actions and behavior, considering which of your behaviors enhance your trustworthiness in your own and in others' eyes.

Next, pick one small, doable change you can implement to enhance your trustworthiness in your own eyes and in the eyes of others. It's very important that the goals you pick are doable, else you will be undermining your trust in yourself.

Faithfully practice making that change every time the situation arises. Once these new behaviors become a habit, you can pick another doable goal, thus building your trustworthiness consistently over time.

BEAUTY

BEING NATURALLY DRAWN TO BEAUTY: THE CASE OF PERLA

Over Zoom my client Perla sits with me while in her office having weathered a period of economic downturn for her company. With both relief and trepidation in her voice, she tells me, "I feel great to finally be clear on our direction. But I'm really nervous about our future financing." Before she can shift to discussing her anxiety, I interrupt. "Let's slow down," I suggest. "Tell me a little more about how 'feeling great' actually feels." Perla describes the clarity and excitement she's achieved—how her chest feels open and spacious while energy flows through her limbs.

I ask Perla what, if any, images arise as she focuses on these sensations. Closing her eyes, she's reminded of sitting on a rock in the middle of a forest stream. She can sense rushing water, birds, and the giant trees all around her. As she experiences it, her breath deepens, and she begins to smile.

I prompt her to open her eyes and look around, seeing what her eyes are drawn to now. She says, "Nothing, my office is really messy." After another moment, she says, "I'm drawn to the curved shape of the back rest on that chair. Its graceful, flowing shape is beautiful."

I ask if she still feels anxious. She says she still does but also feels more optimistic that she will find the right answers for her business.

We are all naturally drawn to, and moved by, beauty, be it a piece of music, a sunset, a work of art, a physics equation, or a skier gliding down the mountain. Taking in beauty, our racing minds slow down. "In difficult times carry something beautiful in your heart," reminds Blaise Pascal. It's as if time stops, pulling us out of our limited sense of a separate self. Absorbed in the beauty, we feel connected, expanded, and in a state of coherence. Our very nervous system calms. Once there, marveling at the beauty before us, we more readily feel inspired and hopeful. Beauty is medicine for the soul. It enlivens, rejuvenates, and uplifts us. Noticing and taking in beauty, we become more fully alive.

THE RESEARCH: TAKING TIME TO RECOGNIZE AND APPRECIATE BEAUTY

In my interviews with spiritually intelligent people, nearly every one of them spoke of how beauty fed their soul. They reported living in awe of the mystery of all the beauty in the world and in the small details around them. One said, "The little things, cleaning up after meals, helping my wife with grocery shopping, those things that I used to think of as being in the way of the important things, I now see as having their own beauty."

And while on the face of it creative self-expression may seem unrelated to the quality of beauty, it is in fact an embodiment of life's creative intelligence, the source of all beauty. "To love beauty is to see light," writes Victor Hugo. Indeed, beauty is integral to spiritual intelligence and to inspired leadership.

YOUR TURN: RECOGNIZING THE BEAUTY AROUND YOU

Find a comfortable seated position with your feet flat on the ground as you tune in and follow the INSPIRED protocol (see page 14).

Now, resting your attention at the center of your chest, recall an image of something beautiful. It can be a landscape, a face, a piece of art, a color, or a piece of music, anything. Marinate in its beauty, letting it seep into every cell of your body. Allow it to spread down your torso, arms, and legs, and just notice the effect. Enjoy.

Look around at your surroundings again and notice whether there's any difference in your perception from before. How do the colors, light, textures, and shapes look now? Does the space look softer? Do colors look more vibrant?

Take some notes or draw in your journal. Over the coming week, try taking a few minutes to ponder a beautiful image or memory. See how it shifts your state of mind, level of presence, and quality of interactions with others. And see if you can integrate a beauty break into your daily routine.

One of my favorite daily practices is walking on the Northern California beach near my house at dawn, enjoying the soft golden hue of the sky and the white foaming waves as they lap at the shore. Watching the immense power, depth, and vastness of the ocean, I occasionally spot seals and dolphins. Pelicans fly in formation high above, while others gracefully glide slightly above the water's surface before diving to catch a fish. Plovers skitter across the sand pecking at insects. As I take in this encompassing beauty, I am often inspired and receive my best creative ideas.

The easiest place for most of us to find beauty is in nature—where the creative intelligence of life shines through its infinite possibilities; in symbiotic relationships, where the fallen leaf composts to feed the next sprout. Whether we call life's creative intelligence God, spirit, or simply evolution, we can appreciate the magnificent diversity of its creations.

REACHING FOR THE SKY: THE CASE OF KAITO

Kaito is facing issues with his newest product launch—a mobile game that enables users to experience the beauty and magic of flying like a bird, exploring various landscapes. The product concept is inspired by his own passion for flying and the beautiful vistas he enjoys seeing while doing so.

Feeling discouraged over the past few weeks, he tells me how he has been drawn to and found solace in his backyard garden. Yet moving quickly past it, Kaito is eager to dig into his product's user adoption problems. I ask him to slow down and describe his experience in the garden first.

There is an understanding in positive psychology that if you can help a person find their resource, you can help them find their resilience. Kaito was instinctively drawn to his garden whenever he felt overwhelmed, and, knowing the power of nature to inspire, I suspected it was probably his resource.

Something in him changes as he describes his experience in the garden. He revels in the beauty of the flowers, roses and hydrangeas, and fresh fruit and vegetables—cucumbers, tomatoes, and strawberries. As he tells me of his time in the garden, he adds that his chest feels more open and lighter, like a weight is lifting. I prompt him to imagine the garden as if it were growing within his chest. He takes a deeper breath and says his entire body feels like it's brimming with energy. As he shifts his attention back to us, away from his garden, he brings that energy with him, ready to resume work on turning his company around.

For Kaito, just visualizing his resource in nature is enough to break him away from his discouraged state of mind. I don't think he'd ever wondered why he was so drawn to his garden in times of stress. But once he realized its impact, he is even more ready to harness its inspiring power.

There's an abundant amount of research demonstrating the benefits of spending time in nature. For example, the Japanese coined the term *forest bathing*, which refers to spending time in nature absorbing its beauty. And research also demonstrates its abundant health benefits.[1] As we connect with beauty and the effortless perfection of nature, we can connect with our own perfection as part of nature. Self-acceptance and self-compassion often spontaneously arise. Even watching an image or a video or imagining ourselves in nature can calm our nervous system and enhance our well-being. As we witness and feel gratitude for the beauty of life's creative intelligence, we can be inspired and more readily able to activate our own creative potential.

CREATIVELY HARMONIZING FORM AND FUNCTION: THE CASE OF ED

Ed calls in from a business trip in Switzerland for one of our sessions. He's marveling at the beauty of the architecture and cleanliness of Geneva. I ask if he can recall something in his work that touches him the same way. He responds, "Last month looking at our financial report, it was beautiful to see our numbers—all above plan."

"And this month?" I ask.

"The numbers are mixed," Ed replies.

"Was there anything beautiful about the report?"

After a moment, he acknowledges that his finance team did a great job providing clear graphs and charts highlighting useful insights. "I guess there's beauty in that."

I ask him how this beautiful presentation came into being, and he launches into an explanation of how one team member provides data while another makes a dashboard for it, and how the two collaborate smoothly to create the analysis and projections. I ask him where the beauty in this process lays, and he responds that it is in how his team members fit with each other. He values his colleagues saying that they not only "have their own unique talents," but that they also "work beautifully together."

When form, function, and purpose are imaginatively and intelligently aligned, it's a beautiful thing. Good science is characterized by beauty, the aesthetics of elegance and parsimony, like the qualities Ed values. Elegance is about grace, style, and refinement, whereas parsimony is about the simplest solution, no excess, no waste—just like nature. These qualities characterize good practice and theory in all kinds of work applications. In the words of Ralph Waldo Emerson, "Love of beauty is taste. The creation of beauty is art." Appreciating beauty as it is revealed in our work further enhances everyone's productivity and joy.

YOUR TURN PART 1: FINDING BEAUTY IN OUR WORK

Take a few moments to reflect on a recent work product or interaction, whether your own or someone else's (a presentation, a report, or even a well-crafted email) that delivered on its function and purpose.

What is the impact on you when you call it to mind?

What is beautiful about it?

How does it feel to appreciate that beauty? How can you express your appreciation?

Take a few moments to reflect on the people you work with who have contributed to a work product that delivered on its function and purpose.

Call each person to mind, one by one, and consider their talents, gifts, and strengths. Consider how they each contribute to your overall mission. It might be their creativity, intelligence, dedication, compassionate presence, or team spirit.

Consider the journey you've shared with them, the difficulties and challenges you've taken on together.

To the extent that you are able, reflect on their background and history. How did they end up working with you?

Now take a leap and sense into their essence, the deep qualities that make them the unique individuals they are. Imagine each of them standing right in front of you as you appreciate their intrinsic beauty.

As you might have been able to discern from this exercise, it's not just through nature that we can see the beauty of life. And if you find it difficult to see the beauty in the people you work with, especially in those who are difficult, stay open and curious and without harsh judgment toward yourself or them. Perhaps think of the beauty of your children or of other babies. Now try to imagine those difficult people as children, before their wounds and armor covered their radiance. Hurt and wounded, they have developed some scar tissue to protect themselves, just as in a forest where no perfect trees exist, each with broken branches, yet each with its own unique beauty expressing life's limitless creativity. So it is with every person we meet. Each person's soul print is a distinct expression of life's creative intelligence. It shimmers through them, manifesting into qualities. And though beauty may be hard to define, we are easily impacted by its radiant presence in others.

A well-matched team is just like an orchestra. Like the different instruments with their unique sounds, each individual brings their own distinct contribution to the whole. And when they play their own instrument or exercise, their unique gifts in harmony with others, the result—in a concert hall or in a workplace—is beauty. Recognizing beauty while in nature is easy. Finding the beauty while at work is harder.

YOUR TURN PART 2: FINDING BEAUTY IN OUR WORK

How do you feel now toward the coworkers you envisioned before? How do you feel about how they play together? What do you sense in your chest area? If you have some sense of their beauty, let it touch you. When you see each of these colleagues again, call to mind the beauty you experienced in them from this exercise and, without necessarily saying anything, notice the difference it makes in your interaction.

Seeing the beauty in ourselves can be the hardest mindset of all to develop. Close up with ourselves, we tend to focus so much on our flaws and limitations that we miss the appeal and grandeur of our essential nature.

Appreciating our own beauty doesn't make us arrogant or egotistical. Our beauty need not make us more special or better than others.

But just as every flower, tree, bird, and insect has its own beauty that is beyond comparison, so too does every person. And it doesn't have to revolve around physical appearance. As Kahlil Gibran so eloquently writes, "Beauty is not in the face; beauty is a light in the heart."

Each of us is a unique creation upon which the universe has bestowed distinct gifts. When we appreciate the intrinsic beauty of these gifts, the most natural response is to want to utilize them and apply them to their greatest potential—using them to contribute as broadly and generously as we can in service of as many as we can—not in service to our egos. This way we can value the beauty of each being, imperfections and all.

Furthermore, when we struggle to recognize our own beauty, it can be difficult to realize its presence, even when others appreciate and give us positive feedback.

FINDING BEAUTY IN OURSELVES: THE CASE OF TOM

Tom tells me about recently gathering his team to celebrate a successful year together following their IPO. How, as they go around the table, most everyone acknowledges his leadership, commitment, and relentless drive to see the process through. He's happy to report on this recognition but changes subjects quickly to discuss the challenges ahead.

I invite Tom to slow down and tell me how it feels to hear his team's feedback. "It was nice to hear, but four different people mentioned my creativity, and I don't have a creative bone in my body." He did not realize the creativity it takes to reinvent a business three times after it hits a dead end, as he has done. And I remind him how rare it is for people in Silicon Valley to exhibit the level of loyalty he has earned from his team.

I suggest Tom step outside his skin and look at himself the way a good friend would. I point out the devotion he has demonstrated in the past eighteen years to the business, his team, and his customers. I prompt him to consider the emotional and financial support he has consistently provided his mom and disabled brother since his father died ten years earlier. And also the support he provides his son and daughter through schoolwork, saving money to enable them to attend and graduate from their college of choice.

I ask if he could see any beauty in his journey, his background, his own growth, and his contributions. After a moment of silence, Tom nods. "It feels like a smile," and a soft, innocent sweetness appears on his face.

It can be easier to see the beauty of our journey, the gifts it has ripened in us, and the contributions we have been able to make by stepping back as if looking from outside ourselves. By savoring our gifts and the beauty they create, they can grow and offer us more to give. "Lord, help me to see myself the way my dog sees me," to quote a funny bumper sticker.

YOUR TURN: SEEING THE BEAUTY WITHIN

Find a comfortable position, take a few moments to close your eyes and turn inward, relaxing and following your breath. As you settle in, imagine yourself sitting around a circle in your home with the people who have loved you most.

Now go around and let each share their appreciation of your journey through life so far, both personally and professionally. Let them point out how you have overcome the difficulties you've encountered, how you have developed psychologically and spiritually, and how your qualities have helped to improve their own lives.

Listen to each person and acknowledge the truth of what they see in you. What are the plot lines? What experiences developed your resilience? How have you inspired others? What light in you has shined throughout your life?

Feel the beauty that you are.

As you move through the rest of your day, enjoy the beauty of the world, the products you create, and the people you work with. But, perhaps most importantly, let your own beauty shine brightly to illuminate the way for others.

JOY

CHOOSING JOY: THE CASE OF CHARLES

Charles's start-up is still struggling to raise funds after more than eighteen months of trying. To stay afloat, he's been forced to lay off employees and request last-minute emergency loans from his existing investors. He works seventy- to eighty-hour weeks, and with a two-year-old and a newborn, rarely gets enough sleep.

He has a low financing offer, but with his back against the wall he's thinking he'll have to acquiesce and take it. Especially since the new board is pressuring him to launch a revised product within three months.

Through all the trials he's facing, he consistently denies making his happiness a priority, under the constant belief that it will find him once he reaches a certain goal. I urge him to take time for himself and for his family, to relax and have some fun, and he assures me again and again that he'll do it "as soon as . . ." But "soon" never seems to arrive as there's always the next hill for him to climb. After years of relentless pressure, Charles is worn down and, on top of it, experiencing new, intense back pain.

In our session, I invite Charles to sense into the tension in his body and explore any wisdom it might have to offer him. He takes a few deep breaths and adjusts his posture as I ask, "What message do you have for Charles? What do you want or need?" He channels the pain's message out loud very quickly, "Charles needs to take better care of himself. He needs more sleep and regular exercise. Most importantly, he needs some fun."

I invite Charles to imagine what might be different if he listened to his back. His face brightens and he sits up. He tells me he would be happier. I jokingly ask, "Oh, who cares?" He looks taken aback at my response. Smiling I continue to ask, "Who cares?" He cracks a grin. He eventually responds, "I care." After I press him even more, repeating, "Who cares?" he adds, "My partner." I ask again, and he offers, "My kids." I persist with "Who cares?" and he pauses, then says, "My team and employees." He finally sees the connection between his own outlook and that of those around him. In this case, my joking around helps drive the message home.

Then, I prompt Charles to imagine leading his company, which creates and publishes apps, from this sense of well-being and joy. He visualizes himself interacting and collaborating with ease in an atmosphere that's lighthearted and playful. He sees a company where his employees would be free to joke around, one where he would be more creative and better able to make effective decisions. "In fact," he says, "I think we'd be much more likely to make a fun and engaging app for our users."

Charles acknowledges the effect his own frustrated, overburdened state can have on those around him, and he discovers how finding his own joy would inspire his employees to do the same. He resolves to bring a more joyful attitude to his company, starting with an in-person outdoor gathering for his employees and their families to celebrate their new financing.

As our coaching session ends, I ask Charles how his back feels. He pauses, checking in, and exclaims with surprise, "Wow—I can hardly believe it!? It's much better—the pain is almost gone!"

Overworking has not only affected his health, but it has also squeezed any time for relaxation, joy, and fun out of his life. Over the next few months we work on creating a schedule that enables Charles to rejuvenate himself by finding time for play and joy. He also shifts his company culture by establishing fun and joy as core values, and over time reaps the rewards of higher energy, morale, and initiative among his employees.

Charles learned firsthand that emotions are contagious. In fact, the modern discovery and understanding of mirror neurons has corroborated what we already intuitively know and feel—that encountering a colleague or a friend who is sad, or joyful, tuning into their body language and energy, immediately influences us. Our emotional state has more impact on the people around us than anything we say or do. The frequency we transmit gets picked up by everyone around us. So, when we cultivate joy, it's not only for ourselves, our well-being ripples into happier teams. And research shows that happier teams are more creative, productive, and better at solving problems.[1, 2, 3]

The good news is that joy is our natural state and integral to our true nature. Unlike pleasure or momentary happiness, which can vary from mild contentment to ecstasy and is usually a transient state caused by external factors, joy is a constant sense of optimism, vitality, and "okayness" that comes from within. As babies, we are born with boundless curiosity, wonderment, and playfulness, exploring the world around us with enthusiasm, excitement, and joy. Even when we fall or get hurt, we might cry for only five minutes or so. And before we know it, we are back to laughing and playing. That is why watching and playing with babies and young children is so relaxing, fun, and inspiring. We can directly experience their radiance, the incredible lightness of their being. Our true nature never leaves us. We just need to tune into it. The spark of the divine, the spark of life, shines brightly within us.

THE RESEARCH: A JOYFUL CELEBRATION OF SERVICE, LAUGHTER, AND PLAY

Joy enlivens, energizes, and motivates us. It opens us internally and externally. It makes our creative juices flow and provides an intrinsic reward for the journey.

In my interviews with spiritually intelligent people, nearly every one of them spoke of how joy fueled their love of life and the many ways joy shows up in their lives. Here are a few examples:

"One of the things that's happened for me as I've been doing this work is I've discovered the true joy of service, of doing meaningful work—it brings abiding happiness and I just laugh more often."

"There is an absolute joy of having the opportunity to be a part of the celebration of life. And that doesn't mean that I don't experience pain or grief. But even amidst pain or grief, there's a deep sense of meaning in life and purpose and the joy and celebration of being alive."

"With the profound wisdom of play and the sense of freedom it entails comes joy in the present moment, and the ability to appreciate the lighter side of life."

The sense of inner freedom naturally results in greater joy. And indeed, my research found joy to be integral to spiritual intelligence and SILeadership, contributing positively to effective management.

In fact, everything we do, however misguided, is motivated by the desire to feel good. Joy is the holy grail for almost every personal growth path, and therefore it has garnered much interest from the business community. That's because not only are there obvious intrinsic benefits to feeling good, but the research also shows that joy makes us more productive, creative, loyal, and effective. It brings us into an open state, which is the foundation for effectiveness, mastery, and ultimately success.

Yet, do you consider joy, as I used to, a luxury that we can only afford once we attain "enough," be it wealth, power, or recognition? Or when we've found the right "one"—be it a job, a house, or a mate? When we defer joy, our spirit dims, and we lose our inspiration. Eventually we burn out, or even get depressed as life passes us by.

Hardly anyone on their deathbed wishes they had been more successful, made more money, or attained greater fame. Most wish they had led a life of greater meaning, love, and joy. Research with those who counsel the dying in their last days reveals the most common regrets we have at the end of our lives:

1. I wish I had the courage to live a life true to myself, not to others' expectations.

2. I wish I hadn't worked so hard.

3. I wish I'd had the courage to express my feelings.

4. I wish I had stayed in touch with my friends.

5. I wish I had let myself be happier.

We can find joy just by looking for it, and we can also cultivate joy by doing certain activities. But the deepest, most satisfying joy is only found when we are abiding in and living rooted in our essential nature. How and where do you experience it in your daily life?

YOUR TURN: FINDING YOUR JOY

Recall a small problem you have been wrestling with recently. Notice what happens to your experience, facial expression, body posture, tension level, breathing, and physiology.

Now recall some moments of joy in your recent or distant past. It could be the time you laughed so hard you couldn't breathe and your sides hurt. Or the time you felt music coursing through you. Or entering a state of flow while engaging in some activity, be it painting or writing, or anything else that has uplifted you. Or maybe some smaller, more passive moments like the smell of opening a new box of crayons, or getting into a hot shower after a long day, or enjoying the satisfied tired but energized feeling of your body after a good workout. Joy, like beauty, is everywhere.

With your eyes closed, see the image of yourself as you were in those moments as if it were a hologram at the center of your chest. Take a few full deep breaths, bringing this memory to life as vividly as possible, as if it were happening right now.

Notice what happens to your experience and to your body.

Now reconsider the problem above. How do you feel and relate to it now? What difference does a drop of joy make in your perspective on it? What options and creative solutions are available now?

> If you don't notice a difference, keep tapping into a state of joy as you face the challenges in your life. You'll likely find that the more open, playful, and joyful you feel, the more creative possibilities will begin to emerge.

Many of us think of play as a frivolous pastime, but a consistent diet of play is essential not just to a balanced adult life, but to our own and others' well-being, development, and creativity.[4, 5, 6, 7] As George Bernard Shaw writes, "We don't stop playing because we grow old; we grow old because we stop playing."

CREATING LEVITY: THE CASE OF DAVE

When Dave complained about feeling burned out, I asked him where he finds joy and play in his life. He told me how he loves rolling around and wrestling with his four-year-old son and making silly faces at his three-month-old daughter. He also enjoys boating with his wife, his monthly fantasy football game with his friends, and mentoring younger entrepreneurs.

I invite Dave to experiment over the next two weeks by intentionally making time for a weekly boating date with his wife and daily play sessions with his kids. Now, on the days he works from home, he squeezes in a few minutes between meetings to play with his daughter. "Even thirty seconds of holding and smiling with her completely uplifts my mood. I'm more present and relaxed in the meetings right after, and everyone else's mood seems to be affected as well. Our discussions tend to be more creative and productive on the whole," he tells me, beaming with joy.

Another one of my clients, Osher, incorporates play into his business culture through a game in which his team places bets on their quarterly results. The person with the most accurate prediction has the honor of bringing everyone else a treat. This game has consistently resulted in greater engagement among his team members, as well as more diligent thinking through their forecasting.

LAUGHING ALL THE WAY TO THE BANK:
THE CASE OF FAROOQ

Farooq is a second-time entrepreneur and CEO who understands his tendency to get carried away with optimism, as so many entrepreneurs do. He'll often give talks to other entrepreneurs during which he warns them against this instinct, urging them to make realistic plans for their organizations.

One day, Farooq tells me that a product vital to his company's revenue projections will now be delayed. His brow furrows as he tells me he's worried about his company's future. He's also frustrated because he is confident that he found a workaround, but his head of engineering doesn't agree, pushing back on the idea in a way that they end up in a heated and unproductive argument. As Farooq recounts this to me, his brow once again furrows. He isn't sure what strategy to pursue next and is even less certain of how to approach an upcoming meeting with his head of engineering, which is sure to be awkward.

I can't help but smile at this as yet again Farooq has run into trouble practicing what he preaches to entrepreneurs. Farooq notices me smiling and begins to laugh as well, his brow softening. He and I joke around for a bit about how often it is we need to learn what we teach, and he tells me afterward that it has helped him clear his head.

I urge him to reflect on what brought clarity to him just now: humor. "Perhaps you need to joke around with your head of engineering, and that's no joke."

When I see him one week later, Farooq tells me that he began his meeting with the head of engineering by suggesting silly, obviously fantastical solutions. There was a moment of confusion, but soon the two joined in the game together, adding more ridiculous options. The tension evaporated. After Farooq had reset the tone of their meeting, they were able to have a collaborative discussion and come up with a creative solution they both liked.

Consider some of the most impactful speeches you've witnessed. Invariably, humor, whether confined to an opening joke or laced throughout, played a big part. Humor gets our attention, draws us in, and opens us up, cognitively and emotionally.[8] Though not all problems are laughing matters, appropriately timed humor can boost productivity and generate creativity. Like play, humor evokes joy, generates an open state of mind, supports emotional regulation,[9] boosts immune system responses, and expands creativity.[10, 11]

For example, hearing the punch line of a funny joke shatters our cognitive schemas, expectations, and models of reality. With our minds blown open, our familiar sense of egoic self momentarily dissolves. In that momentary experience of "no-self," even if we are not aware of it as such, we are much more creative. Freed of our ego's habitual mental constraints, we can bring new perspective to problems and challenges.

Fortunately, you don't have to be a comedian to bring humor to the workplace. I'm not particularly smooth or comfortable telling jokes, but I do still like to fool around. From time to time, I might even use cartoon strips or funny YouTube videos in my talks. When the humor is coming from the voice of authority in the room, it helps all present give themselves permission to loosen up and relax.

YOUR TURN: FINDING LAUGHTER AND PLAY

Take a moment to reflect on your own relationship with laughter and play. Review the following questions and note your responses in a journal:

How do you like to play?

What makes you laugh?

How does it feel to reflect on the previous two questions?

How and when have you found humor and play to be beneficial or productive?

How might you bring more humor and play into your life and your work?

How might it benefit you to be able to laugh at yourself with your colleagues?

What is a topic at work whose discussion could use a healthy dose of levity?

Over the coming week, experiment by implementing one of your ideas above. How does it feel to simply contemplate this possibility?

GRATITUDE

Research overwhelmingly points to a vast range of physical, social, and psychological benefits that come from the attitude of gratitude.[1,2] Gratitude increases physical alertness, vitality, determination, and energy, while also improving the quality of sleep and reducing inflammation.[3] Increasing our gratitude reduces loneliness by strengthening social bonds[3,4] and the overall feeling of being loved. It touches every aspect of our lives, boosting our happiness, optimism, and overall life satisfaction. In the words of David Steindl-Rast, "It's not happiness that makes you grateful, it's gratefulness that makes you happy."

FEELING GRATEFUL: THE CASE OF FRANK

For my session with Frank, the CEO of a rapidly growing Silicon Valley start-up, I have prepared a 360-degree feedback report. Based on my interviews with six of his direct reports and four board members, I've learned how he's admired for his vision, strategic thinking, passion for product execution, and attention to detail. They also commend, among other things, his energy, drive, and focus on results.

I begin to share this positive feedback with Frank, but he interrupts me, "I know, I know, just tell me where I need to improve." "We'll get there," I assure him. I summarize what his colleagues shared with me, then hand him seven pages of anonymous quotes appreciating him and all he contributes. As he reads, his expression changes. I can tell this is a new kind of experience for him, and I don't want him to miss a moment of it.

After about ten minutes, I ask him how he feels. He simply responds, "Great." I urge him to elaborate while sensing himself. He shares with me that he feels expanded and stronger. His presence fills the entire room. We spend a few more moments experiencing this state together and acknowledging his goodness.

With Frank feeling grounded, empowered, and appreciated, he is now more ready to hear the negative feedback his colleagues offered. For Frank, this part of the process is vital, as it was reported that he has a serious issue with how he behaves toward his employees. His board members and direct reports are frustrated by his harsh tone and lack of positive feedback, calling him "extremely difficult" to work with. It's clear that he is just as critical of his employees as he is of himself.

I share with Frank an account of how a junior employee felt crushed when, after completing a long and arduous project, the only acknowledgement he got from Frank was, "This is shit." Without fail, Frank's instinct has been to quickly, and often harshly, identify what's wrong with a product, never to first appreciate the work someone put into it. While Frank's relentless drive toward excellence can contribute to his company's success, it can also sink morale, both for himself and others. Frank takes these thoughts in.

I share with him how research shows that in healthy romantic relationships, partners will give five times more positive feedback than critical feedback. In healthy work situations, this ratio is at least three to one. Harsh criticism is demotivating, and if it is frequent enough, eventually we just tune it out. Or even worse, the person gets demotivated and their performance only spirals down further. But if, on the other hand, we are used to receiving lots of expressions of gratitude which further motivate us, the negative criticism resounds with us, and we have the energy and motivation we need to address it and improve ourselves.

By trying to focus so narrowly on what needs improvement, Frank consistently misses the benefits that come from recognizing and appreciating what he's doing well. He admits in our session that had he focused only on the negative comments provided, he would have been less motivated to work on his shortcomings.

For Frank, this lesson is twofold: first, receiving appreciation uplifts him and inspires him to grow; and second, the very growth Frank needs most is learning to express gratitude, both toward himself and others.

So, for Frank's well-being, I recommend that every night he recount at least three things from the day for which he feels grateful. And to help with his issues at work, I suggest he share with at least one person each day what he appreciates about them. Last, I tell him whenever he feels frustrated and unmotivated to remember how those seven pages of appreciation from his colleagues make him feel, how they move and energize him.

At the end of our session, Frank shares his gratitude for the effort I took to create such a detailed feedback report. I'm touched since it took over two years to convince him of the process's power. I offer my own deep appreciation for the vulnerability and courage it took for him to agree to such an extensive review. Our exchange of mutual gratitude and appreciation creates a palpable connection, strengthening the bond between us.

Soon Frank decides to implement the same feedback process with his staff and to use it to both celebrate their positive qualities and highlight their developmental opportunities. Now, on a regular basis, he looks for chances to express gratitude for work well done, which increases his employees' morale, motivation, and appreciation of him in turn.

THE RESEARCH: COUNTING OUR BLESSINGS

As with beauty, nearly all the spiritually intelligent people I interviewed in my research also spoke about gratitude, especially for the things many of us tend to take for granted, like the gift of life, our bodies, running water, and electricity. They mentioned how much they enjoy expressing their appreciation for others and how it deepens their relationships. And, as a more proactive act, they spoke about looking for the hidden blessings in difficult circumstances. Here are some of their comments:

"When my first grandniece was born, I sat there and held her for two hours while she was sleeping, and I felt the grace and the love of our reality and the miracle of life and existence—the miracle that there is anything here at all. We take it for granted, but I often remind myself of the grace through which we receive the gift of life."

"When a server brings me tea, I try to be conscious of how I receive it from them, to make it a conscious interaction where the server feels gratitude for the opportunity to provide and I feel gratitude for the opportunity to receive. It creates a moment of connection between us."

"When I help less fortunate people, I try to see it as an act of gratitude for what God has given us—the extraordinary power of nature to sustain humans and other living beings in this world. The earth gives us so much abundance, and we express our gratitude by sharing it with all."

Based on the study results, we found Gratitude to contribute significantly to spiritual intelligence and to inspired leadership. As Brené Brown writes, "What separates privilege from entitlement is gratitude."

YOUR TURN: COUNT YOUR BLESSINGS

Think of a relatively minor challenge you are currently facing. Notice what happens to your breath, posture, tension level, clarity of mind, and overall state.

Now contemplate a recent experience that generates a sense of gratitude. It could be anything, from a productive discussion to enjoying your morning coffee. Where are you? Who are you with? What's happening? How does it feel? As you vividly recall the details of the experience, take a few deep breaths, soaking in this goodness.

Now notice what happens to your breath, posture, tension level, clarity of mind, and overall state.

Reconsider the challenge you are currently facing. How do you feel about it? Has anything shifted?

It's true that gratitude doesn't come easily for many of us. We're wired with what neuroscientists call a negativity bias, the orientation to look for potential threats—no doubt derived from prehistoric threats like tigers hiding in the bushes. This bias and its associated vigilance in our nervous system help us survive—survive but not necessarily thrive, especially since we so rarely face such existential or physical threats as tigers in the modern world. Yet, in our evolution gratitude is highly valuable and practical. It balances out our negativity bias, helping us take in the good and enhance our health and longevity.

Practicing gratitude creates a positive feedback loop in our lives. Even animals, from mammals to fish to birds, repay good deeds with generous acts of their own in what evolutionary biologists call reciprocal altruism—responding to kindness with kindness. Chimpanzees, for example, are more likely to share food with other chimps that have groomed or helped them in some way.

As all the world's contemplative traditions teach, and modern research shows, the attitude of gratitude contributes to our well-being, energy, and motivation, rendering problems more manageable, all of which endows us with even more to be grateful for. The process includes our realization that we are doubly blessed—first by all the gifts life has given us, and second by having the capacity to appreciate those gifts. Without recognizing our blessings, we could have all the wealth in the world but still feel poor. It is our gratitude that endows us with a sense of richness.

THE PERSONAL BENEFITS OF
GRATITUDE: THE CASE OF KRTAJNA

Top-tier venture capital firms had recently invested tens of millions of dollars in Krtajna's company, and their expectations were high. When the company failed to meet those expectations, he, as the founder and CEO, had to cut expenses significantly, including implementing several layoffs. He was feeling somewhat depressed when we met.

I suggested that Krtajna begin a gratitude journal—spending a few minutes before going to bed logging at least three positive things that happened to him at the company during the day. It might be a high-quality report he got from an employee, a new sales order, or a milestone in the engineering development schedule.

There's no way to know precisely what role this gratitude practice played, but over the coming year Krtajna's mood began to improve simultaneously with the company's growth. And with the expansion came new challenges. The demand stretched the company's systems with more users and a heavier load, grinding operations to a halt. This, naturally, frustrated their customer support and sales teams and forced the engineering team to scramble to redesign and rewrite the software. The tensions this created began to erode trust and made it impossible to plan future growth.

Having experienced the benefits of his own gratitude practice, Krtajna decided to reorient the team. At one planning meeting, when people started to unproductively blame others, he interrupted and invited everyone to go around the table, reflect on the past year, and name something they were grateful for. Their comments included appreciation for "what we've learned," "how we recovered from our slump," "the personal and business growth we've experienced," "our creative freedom," "how we solve the gnarly big problems," "that we get to be a part of a winning team," and "everyone's passionate engagement and care."

After his colleagues recognized their many blessings together, their challenges looked much more manageable, and they ended up having a fruitful planning discussion. At the end of the meeting, everyone felt more energized and hopeful about their future. Reflecting on how the same people they were having conflicts with now had helped get the company through difficult challenges in the past helped renew their appreciation and trust in themselves and their teammates. This boosted their confidence in their ability to meet the challenges ahead.

Gratitude and appreciation are not only good for teams, but also for communities and societies at large. People who have been appreciated by others are more likely to get along with each other and contribute to the collective. Voters who received a thank-you postcard for voting in an election have been shown to be significantly more likely to vote in the next one compared to those who only receive a postcard encouraging them to vote.[5] Acknowledging coworkers and giving them positive feedback motivates them to do a better job more than merely pressuring them to improve.

YOUR TURN: GIVING THANKS

For the coming week, as you go about each day, find three moments when you can acknowledge someone and thank them directly and personally. Make your appreciation as specific as possible, and let them know what their actions mean to you.

For example, instead of a simple "Thank you for your feedback," you might say, "Thank you for working late under a tight deadline to give me feedback about XYZ. I really liked and was motivated by your encouragement and suggestions. Not only did it improve the end product, but it also helped me feel supported as part of a team working on this important initiative." Can you sense the different impact the more specific feedback can have on the recipient?

If you can express your appreciation in real time, great. If not, reflect on it, then reach out to those people by the next day.

Pay attention to how it feels each step of the way, from finding something to appreciate to expressing your appreciation. Notice the impact on the people you appreciate and on your relationship with them.

And don't forget to appreciate your increasing capacity to appreciate as the virtuous cycle continues! Now, contemplate what you appreciate about yourself. How hard do you work? Your commitment to personal and spiritual growth?

In your mind's eye imagine the whole of your life and complete the following sentence in your journal:

I appreciate and am grateful to my historical self for _____.

CHAPTER 4

BECOMING INNER-DIRECTED

There was a new voice,
Which you slowly recognized as your own,
That kept you company
as you strode deeper and deeper
into the world.
—Mary Oliver

THE INNER-DIRECTED DIMENSION OF spiritually intelligent inspired leadership is the ability to align with your inner compass. This ability rests on four essential qualities: Centeredness, Integrity, Confidence, and Freedom:

- *Centeredness*: Staying grounded and openhearted amid chaos.

- *Integrity*: Standing firmly in alignment with your values.

- *Confidence*: Expressing your unique whole self with ease.

- *Freedom*: Playing in the realm of limitless possibilities.

CENTEREDNESS

RETURNING HOME TO CENTER: THE CASE OF CARTER

Carter is the CEO and general manager of a security software division with about $150 million in annual revenues. A few years ago, he chose to sell his company based on the understanding that his team would maintain autonomy. Recently, Carter and his team have been facing increasing pressure to integrate their sales team into the parent company. After much deliberation, he concludes that this move would in fact better serve their customers. But he's torn: on the one hand, he is worried that if he moves forward with the integration, he will be breaking the promises he made to his team. On the other hand, if he pushes to keep the sales force independent, he could be failing the parent company and their customers.

He has just received a flurry of emails from the parent company's executive team insisting he proceed with the integration, all while his own team speaks loudly in opposition. As he describes the situation, his speech accelerates and his eyes dart around the room.

Before getting into the content of the dilemma, I ask him what he is feeling in his body. He ignores the question and continues with his stream of thought, so I try instead asking him what he is feeling emotionally. He pauses for a moment, then reports that he's anxious and overwhelmed. I ask him how he sees himself when he's feeling this overwhelming anxiety. He responds, "I'm going to fail, I can't handle this—it's too much . . . I'm defective." I ask him how the world looks from this place. He answers, "The world is narrow and threatening. Other people are alien."

Carter, now sitting hunched over, describes to me nervous energy streaming throughout his limbs and a ball of tension in his lower belly. I suggest he continue to allow his thoughts and physical/emotional states to simply be, just as they are, without judging or trying to change them. While I invite him to give space to any anxious feelings, I also guide him to sense the weight of his legs and tor-so as they are pulled down toward the ground by gravity. Once he connects to this gravitational pull, I direct him to include in his experience the support of the floor under his feet and the seat on his bottom—as they hold him in place while his feelings continue to arise.

Carter allows himself to experience his anxiety and other emotions, giving them space, and then opens the aperture of his awareness to include the support of the ground. His breath starts to deepen, his posture straightens, and his eyes settle. As he welcomes the fullness of the experience without resistance, he tells me that the ball of tension in his belly is beginning to soften.

I invite him to next become aware of his spine, and then to explore the way his breath can draw energy from the earth and sky through his spine and circulate in his heart. Seated upright with an erect spine and open chest, he describes how his sense of self, the world, and other people has shifted: "I am capable . . . The world is diverse, rich, and full of opportunities . . . and other people are interest-ing." Carter's posture and presence carry an air of dignity that fills the room.

Feeling empowered and enlivened, he reports that he feels vibrating energy throughout his body. It seems to emanate from a sun-like ball in his lower belly where the tension used to be. He says his chest feels open and spacious. He gives himself a moment to ex-plore and sense that spaciousness and notices a tender, yet bright yellow star around his heart.

From this open and relaxed state, Carter can think more clearly. He decides to call a meeting among the key parties affected by this potential change. Eventually, most of his team embrace the decision to integrate the sales organizations and work together to develop a strategy for a gradual transition. And while one or two employees never come around to supporting the integration and even leave the company, many others thrive, finding important and rewarding roles for themselves in the combined organization.

Carter was able to navigate a challenging, complex organizational situation in a principled and centered way. And when he had lost his center, he was able to find it again simply by accepting himself as he was and allowing his experience to be as it was. This meant not holding onto it nor pushing it away, all the while also expanding the aperture of his awareness to include more, particularly his relationship to his spine and to the ground underneath him. He helped himself become grounded by connecting to his own powerful life force of energy and connecting to others as well.

I call this approach "Allow and Include," or "AI," and developed it building on various somatic and meditative modalities as I referenced in Chapter 1. I've found it to be particularly effective in working with difficult emotions of any kind. With nothing rejected, allowing and including all, and with the support of Mother Earth below, we enter a state of co-regulation whereby we can return to our center, the core of our being, where we rediscover and reconnect to our essence—our consciousness that is always there simply aware, like a mirror reflecting all in its loving embrace, yet never itself affected by the particulars of our experience.

Connected to our center, our sacred life force, we are grounded, empowered, and openhearted. There, rooted in our spirit, we are resourced. Our thoughts stop racing and our mind quiets down. We have access to greater clarity and creativity to deal with whatever challenges we face. And in contrast to AI as usually referencing artificial intelligence, with Allow and Include we tap into the natural intelligence of our being—a grounded and expanded state of open awareness and presence.

THE RESEARCH: FINDING PEACE AT THE EYE OF THE STORM

All my spiritual intelligence research participants highlighted the importance of returning to their centers amid life's inevitable challenges.

And while each person's center may be found and experienced different-ly, they all expressed how only when they were centered could they find the peace, equanimity, clarity, openheartedness, and creativity it takes to face adversity with skill. In the words of Alan Watts, "Stay in the center, and you will be ready to move in any direction." It is worth noting that equanimity does not mean we never get angry or frightened. It simply means that we don't get overly disturbed by those emotions and don't add more levels of agitation or inner conflict in relating to them.

The participants' comments below reflect the importance of returning to center:

"My first step to regaining center is noticing where I start to get hooked, noticing where my ego becomes engaged, and I'm getting either offen-sive or defensive. There's a wonderful term in Buddhism called 'equa-nimity.' I know that when I'm in that place and I don't have a big ego that I'm defending, my response is more holistically skillful."

"When the attorneys were going at it and trying to fire my colleagues and all this stuff, I just thought, 'This is what I choose to do,' and there was no fear. There was just this sense of peace and rootedness in what I truly believed."

"It's right beneath the surface. In water, there might be all these waves and turbulence on the surface, but underneath that there is this power and this depth of silence and peace. And from that place I can intelli-gently respond rather than mindlessly react."

As might be expected, Centeredness is found to contribute significantly to spiritual intelligence and to effectiveness as inspired leaders.

YOUR TURN: RETURNING TO CENTER

Think of a worrisome situation. Notice what's happening in your body as you consider this situation. What happens to your breath? Posture? Tension level in your belly? Chest? Jaw? Eyes? Toes?

Now, shift focus and look around. How does the world look? How bright are the colors? How sharply defined are the shapes? Are they clear or fuzzy? Do they feel friendly? Or threatening? Then check inside again. Is your mind calm or racing?

Now notice your emotional state. What are you feeling? Anxiety? Fear? Anger? Sadness? Overwhelm? Allow your state to be as it is as you complete these sentences:

I am _____

The world is _____.

Other people are _____.

Rather than rushing to change the situation, give yourself full permission to be as you are. Simply notice, shining the light of your awareness on your experience.

After a moment, begin to open your awareness and sense your feet. Feel their weight. Their temperature. Sense each toe. Now feel the pressure of the ground underneath you. Let your feet, legs, and the floor support you as you feel whatever arises.

Keep noticing your experience without judging or trying to change it.

Now open your awareness to include the ground under you. Imagine your breath is drawing in air and energy from the earth. Let it travel up your legs and spine to the top of your head. Once you feel the energy reaching the top of your head, release your breath and exhale the energy back down into the earth. It can help to make a sound as you exhale. Do this for several breaths.

Now take a few more breaths, inhaling the energy up your spine to the center of your chest and exhaling out through your arms and shoulders, making an audible nonverbal sound. Breathe like this for three or four cycles. Then let your breath return to normal.

Notice your state of being now. Has it shifted or stayed the same? Again, complete these same sentences:

I am _____

The world is _____.

Other people are _____.

How has your experience of yourself, the world, and other people shifted, if at all? Do you feel more energized? More relaxed? More open? Or can you imagine more possibilities? Can you more readily tap into your life force? Can you locate its center? What happens if you take a few more breaths, sensing into it all, and letting yourself be as you are?

Now, bring your worrisome situation to mind again. How do you feel about it now? What actions, if any, seem wisest now?

In a survey of two thousand employees, Bain & Company found that among thirty-three traits, the ability to be present and centered were considered among the top hallmarks of leadership.[1] Their report says, "Centeredness consists of being fully present and aware of the situation so that you can bring your best traits to bear on the problem. This is not easy, and a completely cognitive approach—which business leaders often rely on—cannot work. Instead, leaders must apply both physical and mental exercises, such as controlled breathing, to create a state of greater mindfulness. If that sounds like a bit of spiritual advice coming from management consultants, it is."

There are many ways to get centered. You can exercise, spend time in nature, listen to music, pray, take a shower, talk to an attentive witness, write in your journal, or meditate. Or clean, cook, dance. Or anything else—each method possesses its own unique advantages. Sometimes you may need to try several or all of them before you find your way home.

I've found that establishing a regular spiritual practice, such as meditation, prayer, or time in nature, helps me become more deeply rooted in my center so that when disruptions do arise, I can more quickly remember myself, connect, and ground in my essence. Thus, the more readily you or I return to our center, the more we increase the tools available to us.

Though I use a variety of tools in this process, I find the Allow and Include approach to be particularly effective and relatively quick, especially by feeling the earth pulling me into her center with the loving embrace of gravity, while also supporting and keeping me in place where I am.

FEELING MOTHER EARTH: THE CASE OF VICTORIA

Victoria, the CEO of a rapidly growing personal health and wellness app, is facing a difficult situation with a board member. Speaking breathlessly in a high-pitched voice, she describes the board member as being extremely helpful and supportive much of the time, but who out of the blue can become domineering, bullying, and demeaning. Several of her outside advisers have recommended that she ask him to leave the board, something that she has already broached with him. Yet, she is reluctant to lose his immense contributions.

Tuning into her body, Victoria finds a ball of tension in her lower belly and a stabbing pain in her heart area. I invite her to simply notice those sensations and allow them to be as they are. I then suggest she include the sensation of her feet in contact with the ground, feeling the pressure that the floor creates to keep her feet and legs steady. After a moment, her breath begins to deepen, and she says the tension in her belly is softening.

I guide Victoria to imagine a pyramid between the ball of tension in her lower belly and her legs and feet, then to use this pyramid structure to support her in welcoming her feelings as they are. After a few more deep breaths, she reports that the tension has nearly disappeared, and her chest is beginning to feel more open. She adds, "I feel grounded and powerful," then states an affirmation: "I and others are capable of change, and the world can be a welcoming place."

Victoria then closes her eyes and imagines how she would like to speak to this challenging board member. Speaking from her heart, her voice is tender yet clear and powerful as she describes both how much she values his contributions and the pain she feels when he creates a counterproductive environment. Opening her eyes, she says, "It feels good to openly speak the truth."

A few days later, Victoria texted me that she had invited the board member for a hike and to talk. She told me she was excited because he had opened up and let down his defenses. He told her that he had PTSD, which could cause him to behave in ways he later regretted. The two established some ground rules on how to keep him on track. Though there were still occasional difficulties to overcome, through the next few months they both found their interactions more productive at the business level and more rewarding personally.

YOUR TURN: FINDING YOUR WAY HOME

Take inventory of the tools at your disposal for returning to your center when you are upset. Underline your favorites.

Now recall a time when by using them, you felt strong, grounded, open, and clearheaded, thus able to discern the right course of action in a difficulty.

Consider a dilemma you're facing now that might benefit from you being more centered. Make a commitment to use that tool in this situation.

Also practice using these tools for smaller challenges as they arise.

The more you practice navigating your way back to center, the more receptive you will be, and the faster you will be at accomplishing groundedness again. In fact, your center is always there. Where else could it be? It is only waiting for you to return.

INTEGRITY

INTEGRITY VERSUS EXPEDIENCY: THE CASE OF DAVE

Dave is the founder and CEO of a security software start-up. After extensive user research, design, and development, the company has launched its product and is beginning to gain momentum with new installations. But Dave knows his company lacks diversity. He has openings for three more software engineers and is considering making recruiting women a priority. He has in the past successfully hired women into key leadership positions and wants to do more of the same. The only issue is that the pool of qualified applicants is already quite small because of the unique skills needed, plus the tech industry's fierce competition for top software talent. He's worried that adding another constraint to the necessary qualifications will make an already difficult problem even more challenging.

I invite Dave to move to one end of the couch where he's seated and tell me all the reasons he wants to make hiring women engineers a high priority. He answers, "If the next three hires are all 'white dudes,' it'll be much harder to hire quality women and increase our engineering diversity in the future." I help him turn his attention to his internal experience, where he notices a lot of fear about handling this situation correctly.

I then invite Dave to move to the other end of the couch and tell me all the reasons *not* to make hiring women engineers a high priority. He describes an interview he'd seen with a very impressive founder and CEO who'd explained that the key to their success was moving fast and responding to customer needs swiftly. Dave feels intense pressure to move quickly, especially since some of his investors have echoed sentiments about speed to him as well. But given the scale of the launch, he might not have time to find the perfect candidates. As he describes this pressure, I notice that his energy drops. When

I ask him how it feels to articulate this perspective, he tells me that it seems practical, but he's still more concerned that if he doesn't commit to diversity now, it will be much harder later. He notices that his body feels tighter than it had on the other side of the couch.

I suggest Dave move to the center of the couch where he can synthesize the two perspectives: "Hiring a woman is important because building diversity into our culture's foundation is a high priority" versus "Hiring a woman and building our culture's foundation is not as high a priority as moving fast." After centering himself, taking a few deep breaths, and feeling his feet on the ground, he repeats each position out loud. When he declares the first statement about diversity and company culture, Dave notices his body feels more relaxed, and he breathes with ease. In contrast, when he asserts the second statement, he notices his breath becomes more labored, momentarily pausing at the bottom of each exhale, and his body is more tense.

His body is feeding him signals about which statement resonates more strongly with his deepest values. With renewed clarity, Dave reaffirms his determination to build a high-caliber, diverse team, and in doing so, a solid cultural foundation for his company's future.

Although it might take longer to reach certain business milestones and land the next round of funding, companies with solid reputations eventually attract more high-profile investors, accelerate product adoptions, and build loyalty with their customers.

By following your inner compass, you can build the culture and the products that reflect your values while retaining your integrity. As Janice Joplin said, "Don't compromise yourself, you're all you've got."

Often, we feel a conflict when our personal values appear to clash with external, societal, or cultural norms. These are true tests of our integrity, our ability to walk the talk and live in alignment with our core values. We must learn to do this despite our own and others' desires, foregoing what we want and risking rejection based on others' standards. When we are willing to give up that external validation to follow our inner compass, we gain not just self-respect, integrity, and freedom, but we also become powerful, authentic leaders.

THE RESEARCH: DISCERNING AND LIVING IN INTEGRITY

The people I interviewed for my research on spiritual intelligence were all nominated by their peers as ones who walk the talk and embody spiritual intelligence in their daily lives. This means integrity is implicit in understanding the nature of spiritual intelligence. The word integrity comes from the Latin *integer*, meaning "complete and whole." When our words and actions are congruent with our values and nature, we experience a sense of integration and wholeness. Thus, it's not surprising that nearly all the participants spoke of how essential it is to tune into their inner voice, and how discerning its message is what makes it possible to live wholeheartedly aligned with their values and to follow their soul's purpose, even in the face of enormous pressures to conform. Below are a few of their comments:

"Listening to what I call your inner guidance system, your inner GPS, or your inner BS meter, which is your God within . . . if you listen to your inner self, the truth is always there, and everybody has it. We just get into these habits of listening to the noise in the room. And when we wander off the path, we feel kind of 'yucky.'"

"If you read autobiographies of people who have done amazing things, they all feel called to do something, and whether it's Dorothy Day or Jane Goodall or Nelson Mandela, there is some light within them that they tune into, that they nurture, and that they uphold to the world."

"To say what you mean, do what you say, and say what's so when it's so."

Not surprisingly, we found Integrity contributes significantly to spiritual intelligence and to effectiveness as inspired leaders.

YOUR TURN: LIVING IN TRUTH

Take a moment to get centered, grounded, and INSPIRED following the protocol on page 14.

Now look around the room and say out loud the color the walls are painted. As an example, "The walls are off-white." As you do, simply notice the quality of your breath. Is it smooth and easy, or is there something holding you back? Where does your chest feel open and where does it feel tight?

Next, try saying out loud a color that the walls obviously are not. For instance, "The walls are red," when really they're off-white. Again, notice what happens to your breath as you make the false statement. Is it smooth, easy, and flowing, or is there tension? Where does your chest feel open and where does it feel tight?

What difference, if any, do you notice in your breath, energy, and overall physical tension as you make a true versus a false statement? You will probably notice a difference, but if you don't, it's possible that you'll need to take some more time to settle before trying the exercise again. Our bodies naturally relax and open when our words, thoughts, and actions align with our truth. With practice and close attention, we can learn to receive the wisdom of our bodies' messages.

Once you have tuned into this inner truth meter, try applying it to more complex situations. If you're facing a difficult choice, try sitting in one seat and naming all the reasons for choosing option A. As you do, notice your experience: your breathing, the opening or closing of your chest, your tension level, posture, and overall sense of aliveness.

Then move to another seat. Now, say out loud all the advantages of doing option B. Again, notice your breathing, tension level, posture, and overall sense of aliveness.

Finally, find a seat in between those two positions. Try saying "I am ready to choose A." Notice how it feels in your body. Is your breathing relaxed and flowing smoothly? Next try, "I am ready to choose B." Again, notice the effect on your body.

Does one feel truer? How does your body respond to each? Many people have difficulty sensing their body at all, much less discerning the differences between their somatic responses to various statements. If you find it difficult, take more time to settle into your breathing. With patience and practice, you can learn to discern these subtle differences, just as an experienced wine taster can discern subtle nuances in vintages that others would never perceive.

As choices become more complex, it may take longer to identify a decision that feels right. Have patience and try again, perhaps much later. When you return to the question, when you immerse yourself in it with enough careful attention, the truth will emerge even if it is only the best choice under the constraints and circumstances.

When we are in harmony with our deeply held values and living from our truth, we experience an inner alignment, a grounded strength, an expanded open spaciousness, relaxation, and ease. Devoted to truth, we can live undefended from our deepest nature.

In fact, research by the Center for Creative Leadership puts integrity at the top of their list of important leadership qualities, as does Bain & Company.[1, 2, 3] But what does integrity mean in action and on the ground? Most of us recognize that high-integrity leaders walk their talk. Their actions are consistent with their words. At a deeper level, integrity is an alignment with our truest nature, our spirit. Since our spirit is connected to all of life, when we are in integrity with our nature, our actions will naturally be kind, caring, and compassionate, as well as ethical and moral.

Most of us were given our sense of morality by external sources such as religion, society, and/or family. But it is our self-directed connection to our spirit that brings about a rise in our moral conscience that leads to integrity.

KEEPING HONEST: THE CASE OF STEVE

Steve, a first-time entrepreneur in his late twenties building a cloud-based software company, is having smashing success with his follow-on round of financing. It is so oversubscribed that he's even turning away some potential investors. That is until one of the committed investors suddenly backs out. Steve is upset, wondering why they would change their mind. He says they told him that in their final review they realized that the total annualized recurring revenue (ARR) base for the business was still smaller than they were comfortable with, even though they'd already known those numbers from his presentation meeting weeks before, and at which time they'd said yes, they would go in on the deal.

I ask Steve more about this presentation, which typically marks the final approval stage from a venture capital firm. After some questioning, he admits that he focused his investors' attention mostly on the number of new customer sign-ups. But due to limited product functionality and low price points, the number of customers wasn't drawing in the revenue one might think. And while his ARR was in the presentation, it was in a smaller font on the bottom of one of the slides and never explicitly discussed.

I know Steve to be an enthusiastic person who usually paints an optimistic view of his business. Having worked with him over three years, I know him to be a person of high integrity. Yet, I also know that his enthusiasm can sometimes get the better of him.

I ask him about his primary motivation. "Is it to get what you want? Or is it to do the right thing?" With an embarrassed chuckle, he admits, "I want to get what I want. I'm trying to get to a certain net worth, and the company is a vehicle for that."

I suggest we try an experiment. First, I help Steve center himself. After he settles down, I invite him to say out loud, "My primary motivation is to get what I want." As he completes the sentence, I notice a slight pause in Steve's breathing, which now sounds constricted and shallow. He notices it too and mentions it without my prompting.

After Steve re-centers himself and returns to breathing more calmly, I invite him to repeat the sentence, "My primary motivation is to do the right thing." This time Steve and I both notice that his breath appears to flow more smoothly. While part of him just wants what he wants, the wisdom of his higher self coming through his body is sounding a warning alert: focusing on simply getting what he (or likely his ego) wants is not aligned with his values and deeper truth. He does not need me to lecture him on conducting business with integrity. His body is already helping him discern that truth.

Our bodies contain a wealth of wisdom. To receive this guidance, we need only to tune in and listen. Our bodies don't lie.

Our egos do. Our egos are invariably resistant to reality and to the deepest truth of our nature. Such resistance shows up as consistent tension patterns in our bodies. For when we resist what is, and what some part of us knows to be true, our bodies contract and tighten up. These egoic tension patterns squeeze our life force and stifle our aliveness. It may take us a long time, but by noticing how and when we contract versus relax, we can soften that tight grip and return to our natural expanded state from which our deepest nature shines brightly and our life force flows with power and ease, leading the way for us and others.

YOUR TURN: LISTENING TO YOUR BODY

Take a moment to center yourself by sitting in a comfortable chair with your spine straight yet feeling relaxed and alert. Place your feet flat on the floor. Feel the weight of your legs and body as they are pulled by gravity toward the center of the earth. Notice the pressure of the floor under your feet and the cushion under your seat. Take a few belly-deep breaths and let go of any tension.

Recall an incident in which you stayed true to your values despite pressure from others. You might have spoken up, taking a contrarian view in a meeting, or gone out of your way to help someone. As you bring this incident to mind, notice how it feels. Does your chest feel open and spacious or tight and contracted? What is your posture? What's the quality of your breath?

Next, recall an incident in which you compromised your values. Perhaps the cashier at the checkout miscounted the change and gave you an extra dollar, but you didn't say anything. Or perhaps you held back your views in a meeting and went along with a direction you didn't really believe in for fear of reproach. How does your body feel? How open or closed is your chest? Your posture? Your breathing?

Can you notice a difference in your body's response to these two incidents? Your body is refereeing and keeping score. What's your scoreboard of late?

What feels best at the deepest level is what's best for you, for those you lead, and for the world.

CONFIDENCE

EMBRACING FEAR: THE CASE OF IMAAD

Imaad, a first-time entrepreneur in his late twenties who just completed his first round of professional VC funding from a top-tier firm, describes feeling profound anxiety as he prepares for the first meeting with his new board.

I prompt him to explore the roots of this fear, to explore the earliest examples he can come up with. He shares a memory of not getting an "A" on an exam in school, and how painful it was to disappoint his parents. Somehow this memory becomes linked with another from his past: being overweight and feeling unattractive when he was in his teens—I watch his chest collapse and his shoulders slump forward as he relives it all. As is typical for most of us, Imaad's first impulse is to push away those painful emotions and memories that cause him to feel shame, but I encourage him to stay present with these young parts of himself.

Imaad reports feeling sadness in his heart. I urge him to stay with the emotion. After another moment, he says a pleasant feeling of warmth and compassion is arising in him. He visualizes his younger self and tells him, "You'll be okay. You're a smart kid. You'll do just great!"

While this seems to help Imaad relax his face, I still notice tension in his shoulders and arms. I suggest he try telling his younger self, "You're okay, and you're valuable no matter what grade you get. I love you, I'm here, and I'll always be with you whenever you need me." Hearing my suggested words out loud, Imaad takes a deep breath. Something clicks. His arms and shoulders finally relax, and his queasiness subsides.

I ask him how he now would relate to his younger self. He says he can picture himself with his arm around little Imaad, which makes him feel relaxed, optimistic, and connected. Imaad smiles quietly as he tells me that his anxiety has been completely replaced with feelings of calm, strength, and confidence. He says he's comfortable contemplating the board meeting, being vulnerable, and letting his board know that he is new to this game and that he welcomes their feedback and guidance.

Imaad later told me his lead investor let him know that his openness to feedback and coaching inspired the board's confidence in his ability to lead the company. Most of us believe we have to suppress these younger parts of ourselves or they'll overwhelm us psychologically. In fact, the opposite is true. As Eleanor Roosevelt put it, "You gain strength, courage, and confidence by every experience in which you really stop to look fear in the face. You are able to say to yourself, 'I lived through this horror. I can take the next thing that comes along.'"

It takes immense courage to face our childhood demons hiding in the shadows. But when we look at them through the eyes of our adult self, we can recognize that they are not who we really are. They are parts of us that were hurt and now need our love. We can turn toward our trauma with our full-grown empathy, confident that it won't overwhelm us. These wounded parts and painful emotions want nothing more than our own unconditional acceptance and care. And, through recognizing that our true nature has that capacity and can offer us this gift of compassionate presence, our younger parts are healed, and we become more integrated.

If we can't find the fortitude to face these vulnerable younger parts inside ourselves, how can we expect to face present-day challenges? It all begins with trusting our capacity to face, feel, and welcome all parts of ourselves, making us whole.

THE RESEARCH: INNER-WHOLENESS IS OUR FOUNDATION FOR CONFIDENCE

Nearly all my spiritually intelligent research subjects spoke of radical self-acceptance[1] as a way to attain inner wholeness, resulting in ease, courage, and confidence to be all of who they are. Their comments included the following:

"Over time, I develop more self-acceptance and confidence and I am able to own that 'difficult' part that I used to try to deny. There's now more willingness and ease with more and more of myself. With this developing radical self-acceptance comes confidence to be *all* of who I am."

"In this state of inner-wholeness, recognizing that harmonious interplay of opposites, like self-esteem and humility, and being comfortable in expressing all of these energies, gives me the courage to be all of me and actualize all my potential."

"As I mature in my development, I find that my self-esteem doesn't have to be on the line. I can be grounded in who I am, where my esteem or my worth isn't precarious, it's not even questioned. It gives me a sense of ease to just be who and what I am without the worry if it is acceptable to myself or others."

As expected, confidence is a significant component of spiritual intelligence and strongly contributes to an inspired leader's effectiveness.

YOUR TURN: ACCEPTING YOUR WHOLE AUTHENTIC SELF

Note: The following exercise draws on several sophisticated psychospiritual modalities.[2, 3, 4, 5] If you find it challenging to follow and experience the resulting state of greater wholeness and confidence it can create, please go slow and be gentle with yourself. You might benefit from reading some of the references in the back of this book or utilizing the support of an experienced guide.

Find a comfortable seated position. Take a few deep breaths while sensing your body and the flow of air in and out of your lungs. Continue for a moment or two as you return home to center, becoming settled and grounded.

Once centered, recall a challenging situation that is causing you some concern. Do you notice any changes in your body? Your breathing? Simply notice and allow whatever bodily sensations, feelings, and thoughts arise. As you allow your experience to be as it is, notice whether it is familiar. Have you felt this way before? What is the earliest memory you have of feeling this way? It might be of a specific incident or of a general setting from the past. As you bring this memory to mind, picture yourself at that age, having that experience. What do you look like? What is your posture and expression?

Notice any thoughts that run through your mind about that part of you that felt challenged at the time. Do you judge it as weak? Do you try to push it aside, or are you feeling open, tender, and compassionate toward it? If you notice judgment arising, ask this inner critic what it wants for you. Simply hold the inner critic in your presence, thanking it and telling it to take a break for a moment or two while you contact these younger, vulnerable parts. (Dealing more fully with our inner critic requires much more involvement and work than can be discussed in this chapter.)

As you contact that younger you—that part of you that may have been overwhelmed—ask them what they want and need. Perhaps that part just needs to know you're there, since they have felt alone, desperate, and ignored for too long. Or perhaps they need a hug, or reassurance that they're lovable just the way they are.

Now imagine your current adult self giving your younger self exactly what they need, speaking the words they want to hear, and making the contact they find most comforting. Perhaps you're telling them that they are okay, as Imaad did. Or that you are willing to be with and support them whenever they call on you. Now, notice what happens when you give this part what it needs. It may be difficult for your younger self, who has been deprived for so long, to receive and absorb the love and support they long for most. Try to be patient and steadfast in caring for them. See if they can take it in small sips.

Notice what happens to both your current adult self, and the younger part, as you send this compassionate loving energy to them. What effect is it having on your younger self? Does it create a feeling of openness and relaxation? Greater ease and confidence?

Take some time to integrate any realizations or openings that have occurred through this process. When you feel ready, consider once again the challenge you are facing. How daunting or doable does it seem to you now? Do you feel more capable or confident in addressing it?

DEALING WITH DOUBTS: THE CASE OF MARY

Mary, the CEO of a cloud software company, is struggling through a business downturn from the pandemic and is just now closing on a new round of funding. Her other challenge is recruiting top talent for key product, engineering, and sales positions in one of the tightest labor markets out there.

She tells me how excited she is by some of her new hires in the product department. "They're the caliber of people who can take us all the way to an IPO!" Without pausing for a second, she rushes to add, "But I just don't know how to handle all our problems in engineering and sales." In that moment there's a palpable sense of her energy level dropping off, as the intonation in her voice confirms as well.

I ask Mary to take a breath and tell me again what invigorates her about the new hires. She simply repeats her original statement. I ask her what she notices now. She says she feels lighter, with streaming, bubbling energy throughout her body. I guide her to slow down and allow herself to dwell in the positive state, inviting her to feel her feet sturdily on the floor as well as to sense the verticality of her spine. Mary sits more upright. She tells me that now, in addition to the excitement, she also feels grounded, strong, present, and confident.

Taking more time to tune into her body, she senses a warm ball of energy, radiating like the sun, around her lower belly. When she focuses her attention on that area, she tells me that her sense of confidence increases. At the same time, she mentions that her chest feels open and spacious. I invite her to see what's in that space. Peering into it, she describes a small, shining yellow star. She shares with me that her mind feels calm, quiet, and clear, as if she were looking at the blue sky on a bright day.

From this state of clarity, Mary comes up with a plan to begin tackling her challenges in engineering and sales. She realizes she can do so better when feeling her three main energetic centers—belly, heart, and head—are in alignment and integrated.

While it's true authentic confidence requires that we deal with our fears, it also requires that we build on strengths we derive from our three main energetic centers:

1. Belly: the center of embodiment and action, giving a sense of capacity, grounding, and power

2. Heart: the center of courage and emotions, giving a sense of connection, peace, and joy

3. Head: the center of intelligence, knowing, and wisdom, giving a sense of clarity, vision, and purpose

YOUR TURN: LETTING YOUR STRENGTHS CARRY YOU

Take a moment to center yourself. Rest, being just as you are in this moment. Follow your breath, feeling your lower belly as it expands and contracts with each breath. Notice how relaxed or tight it feels and allow it to be just as it is. Then take a moment to explore the space in the center of your chest around your heart area. How open or closed does your chest feel? Again, simply notice and allow.

Now, think of a time when you *succeeded* in meeting a serious challenge. Review the situation and how you addressed it with as much vivid detail as possible. What qualities and capacities did you draw on to meet the challenge? Reflect on these strengths and others that you appreciate about yourself. Notice how your body feels now. Notice the effect on your energy level and overall sense of well-being. Are you more or less energized? Contracted or expanded? Hunched or upright? Include in your awareness your relationship to the ground underneath you, feeling your feet on the floor, and the weight of your body as it is pulled by gravity. Notice what happens to your energy and overall state as you do. What, if anything, shifts when you include the ground in your awareness?

Now, think of a challenging situation you are currently facing. How manageable does it feel? How confident do you now feel in your ability to handle it? How tamable does any anxiety feel now?

When you're facing a challenge that feels overwhelming, you can find hidden resources by tapping into your strengths first and then including the support of the ground underneath you. And as we've seen through this chapter, you can process simultaneously both your deficiencies and your strengths to find your confidence. Like the two wings of a bird, both help you fly.

Yet, there is an important distinction to be made here about confidence versus arrogance. Grounded in the wholeness of our being, our sense of self is anything but fragile. Our self-worth does not depend on other people's opinions or on our external successes or failures. We don't constantly compare ourselves to others and feel threatened by them. We can be open to feedback, be influenced by others, and stand corrected. We can recognize other people's value, and thus properly appreciate our connection to them.

With *true* confidence comes humility. Those who are humble, who can see and accept their limitations, are also the most likely to be able to work on them.

While it can look a lot like confidence, arrogance is entirely different. Arrogance puffs us up, inflating our sense of self-importance. Usually, we indulge our arrogance to compensate for deep-seated insecurities so that when we don't feel our own intrinsic value, we superficially elevate ourselves over others to land at a poor imitation of our true worth. With arrogance, we're closed off, threatened by other people's gifts, and driven by a need to be right.

YOUR TURN: UNDERSTANDING THE DIFFERENCE BETWEEN CONFIDENCE AND ARROGANCE

Recall a time when you felt true confidence. Maybe you were just walking down the street on a sunny day. Or maybe you were in the flow playing a sport you are good at. How does it feel in your body to recall that experience?

Now think of a time when you were overly confident to the point of arrogance. Perhaps you were closed off to considering others' input or acknowledging the possibility that you may be mistaken. How does it feel in your body to recall that state?

Or, think of someone you have found to be arrogant. How does it feel to be around them? What about their energy, demeanor, or behavior conveys arrogance? How connected do you feel? How is being with them different from being with someone who is confident? How can you tell they are overcompensating for their insecurity?

You can find strength, wholeness, and confidence by facing instead of avoiding fears and self-doubt, and by tapping into your strengths with enthusiasm. Both approaches take courage—the courage to be.[6] Both require trust—trust that you can allow yourself to be as you are, and still be okay.

FREEDOM

DREAMING OF A SOLUTION: THE CASE OF JOSEPH

Joseph, the cofounder and CEO of a mobile consumer app start-up, is seeing the strong start for his company now settling into a plateau. With funds dwindling, the board is pressuring him to sell the company, especially since a larger corporation is showing interest in a buyout.

He and his three cofounders have been trying relentlessly on their own to find new ways to pivot the company, none of which have become viable. But recently one of his cofounders came up with a new product idea that Joseph feels could help them turn the corner, except implementing it will take time—time they don't have.

Joseph feels conflicted. If he pushes back and convinces the board to turn down an offer, they risk losing everything. He feels burdened by the weight of his responsibility, though he is still intrigued by the new idea's potential and doesn't feel ready to give up on it just yet. Furthermore, Joseph and his cofounders are not interested in working for a larger corporation. He feels boxed in, unable to come up with any resolution.

I invite Joseph to explore the responsibility he feels toward his investors and employees—that is the pressure to sell rather than keep holding on. He tells me that his body feels both infused by strength and weighted by heaviness, while his mind plays the repeating message: "It's your duty." I tell him to place this state of being in his right hand.

I then suggest he explore the state of being associated with remaining independent. He reports feeling both excitement and anxiety at the prospect. Now I invite him to isolate this energy in his other hand.

I prompt him to alternate back and forth between the states represented in each of his hands, becoming familiar with them, and then to zoom out, opening the lens of his awareness to include both. Joseph takes a deep breath and sits up straighter. He tells me that the tension has softened, his mind has quieted down, and he feels more present and spatially aware. Although no clear resolution has emerged, he finds a new sense of inner freedom.

I suggest he repeat this exercise before bed, reconnecting to this opened state and inviting his subconscious to grant him some insight through his dreams. I also advise him to take walks in nature and do anything else he can to help him clear his mind from his obsessive efforts to solve the problem.

A few weeks later, Joseph told me that he had woken up in the middle of the night with a new approach to solving his dilemma. His workaround was this: because the promising new product concept has no relevance to the interested buyer, they might be willing to exclude it from the sale. He felt confident he could even negotiate spinning this initiative out into an entirely new company. The investors would get most of the proceeds from the sale of the existing company while retaining a smaller ownership stake in the new spinout, while Joseph and his cofounders, giving up some of the potential immediate return on the sale, would get to stay independent and explore their new product idea.

As good fortune would have it, four years later, Joseph's new entity became a smashing success. By relaxing his mind and moving beyond either-or thinking, he accessed a creative solution that provided a win for everyone.

Creative solutions often seem to arise out of the blue when our minds are most relaxed and open, be it while we are walking in nature, daydreaming, or sleeping. Rest, naps, and good sleep are not only beneficial for our physical health, but also for solving tough issues.

In fact, many of the most famous discoveries ever made arrived through dreams. Biologist August Kekulé discovered the structure of the benzene molecule one night in a dream. And Thomas Edison, when stuck, would take naps, often awakening to new insights. This napping method has been validated scientifically.[1] Indeed, repeated studies have confirmed that relaxing and quieting our habitual egoic mind,[2] allowing it to wander and free-associate while dreaming (REM sleep), stimulates insights[3] and creative problem-solving.[4] In the words of creative genius Wolfgang Amadeus Mozart, "When I am, as it were, completely myself, entirely alone, and of good cheer—say traveling in a carriage, or walking after a good meal, or during the night when I cannot sleep—it is on such occasions that my ideas flow best, and most abundantly. Whence and how they come, I know not, nor can I force them."

THE RESEARCH: COMMITMENT
AND NONATTACHMENT

Nearly all the people I interviewed for my spiritual intelligence research mentioned "inner freedom." For them, freedom means being whole-hearted in their commitment to their purpose while remaining unat-tached to the outcome. Doing so enabled them to stand their ground with strength while remaining receptive to others' influence. Such inner freedom keeps them open to possibilities as they engage the dynamic nature of reality with creativity and play. Some of their comments in-cluded the following:

"If I am on a trip and it's pouring rain on the day I want to go on the ferry, then of course I will experience disappointment. But I will also find the practice of 'Okay, this is what is,' and a deep curiosity about what else is possible now."

"One of my continuous practices is nonattachment. I distinguish very carefully between nonattachment and the risk of *being* detached and not caring. It doesn't mean disengaging. It means I am fully and whole-heartedly committed to an outcome but that I understand that there are larger forces involved that might not provide that particular outcome but provide another one. And I would be okay with that."

"When I experience inner freedom, I can see the playground before me. My play is really an expression of freedom. When there is little at stake, when I am not trying to protect myself, possibilities and play are avail-able for what wants to happen. Play is the enjoyment and generation of possibility, and that's life's force."

As might be expected, we found that a sense of Freedom contributes sig-nificantly to spiritual intelligence and effectiveness as an inspired leader.

MAKING MAGIC: THE CASE OF MOKSHA

After raising tens of millions of dollars, employing several hundred people, and pouring her heart and soul into her first start-up, Mok-sha was reeling from having shut down her company. Her investors had lost their money, and her employees had lost their jobs. She was heartbroken, deeply depressed, and saw her company's failure as her personal failure.

Now, three years past, after having taken some time off to recuperate and working at a larger company, she thinks she might be ready to try her hand at another start-up.

On the one hand, she knows that undertaking a new venture requires her to be a hundred and twenty percent committed to her vision—as she puts it, "Seeing and believing it in my bones." On the other hand, she is afraid of failing again. She's seen for herself the effect failure has on her and everyone else involved.

I invite Moksha to immerse herself in the passion and commitment she feels for her vision. This generates excitement, passion, and power for her, which she describes as "a fire in my belly." She also reports some tightening in her arms and legs, as if she's bracing for a fight. After exploring this energic and somatic state for a short time, I suggest she shake it off.

Next, I invite her to feel into the side of her that wants to and is willing to remain unattached to the outcome of her vision. As she does, she says her drive moves to the back seat and her body relaxes, as if she's being held by a great compassionate energy. She tells me that she can best associate what she's feeling with "the archetype of Divine Mother." As she describes feeling bathed in soft, golden light, I notice her breath beginning to slow and deepen, and her face visibly softening into a wide smile.

I suggest she put her passionate devotion into her right hand and her feelings of nonattachment into her left hand. Then to alternate and become comfortable with experiencing each of these states one at a time. Finally, I suggest she zoom out and allow herself to experience both simultaneously.

After a moment of blending the energetic states together, Moksha sits up straight. A sense of powerful yet gentle presence fills the room. She says, "In this place I can be both passionately devoted to what we do but also not take the outcome personally. I feel free— free to wholeheartedly pursue it without getting overly attached—I will be okay, regardless of the outcome."

While Moksha was able to integrate these two energies in that session, in subsequent ones she would periodically vacillate between them. This is to be expected. Integrating and stabilizing such seeming opposites can be the work of a lifetime. However, as William James writes, "The first act of freedom is to choose it." With practice, Moksha became increasingly able to find the center of her being rooted beyond polarities and move in new directions with greater ease.

Indeed, life calls on us to embody, integrate, and flow between polarities. We may desire autonomy and freedom in our relationships, yet we also require a sense of stability, safety, and connection. Or we may want to establish the structure and discipline to be productive while also wishing for joy and spontaneity. Or we may long to develop both our feminine and masculine energies, the Taoist principles of yin and yang.

The universe is made possible through polarities: up/down, left/right, positive/negative, and so on. By developing and harmonizing the energy of polarities, we can liberate ourselves from our confines, drawing from those energies, mixing and matching them to fit the needs of a situation, to give us more range, more freedom.

YOUR TURN: TRANSCENDING POLARITIES

Find a comfortable position and take a few deep breaths. Feel yourself settling into the here and now. Sense your presence deepening.

Once you feel centered in the present moment, think of a dilemma you're currently facing. Whatever the struggle might be, it likely involves two or more values that are important. Otherwise, the choice would be easy.

Next, focus on option A and the value it represents. It could be "living my mission." Let yourself feel this need. Notice what it is like to give yourself permission to feel it fully. Let yourself imagine what it would feel like to have this need met. How do your body, energy, posture, muscles, and breathing feel? What images come to mind that are associated with this state? How strong, spacious, grounded, and aligned do you feel? Simply notice this all without judgment.

Now focus on option B and the value it represents. It might be "needing some security." What is the essential need that this option might fulfill? What do you value about it? Whatever it is, let yourself feel how important it is to you. Notice what it feels like when you imagine having this need met. How do your body, energy, posture, muscles, and breathing feel now? Again, this is all without judgment.

Now, recall option A and let the feeling of having that need met permeate your being. Make friends with it. Get to know it intimately from the inside. Imagine holding it in one of your hands, palm facing up resting on your knee.

Now recall the experience associated with option B. Let it permeate your being, making friends with this state. Get to know it intimately from the inside. Then put its associated energy in your other hand, letting it rest palm facing up on your other knee.

Once you feel the energies of both options in your hands, try switching your focus back and forth between them slowly several times, letting each state take hold of you before shifting. As you get more familiar with both, you can switch back and forth more rapidly, spending less time in each.

As it becomes easier to transition between them, zoom out your awareness to give a broader view. Sense the energy present in both hands, holding and blending them together. Continuing for another moment, notice what happens to your mind and thoughts. Notice what happens to your body and emotions.

Now, check what your dilemma feels like from this new, integrated place. What, if anything, looks different from this perspective? What possibilities are now available?

Play with this exercise a few times, and perhaps right before you fall asleep at night, invite your dreams to provide guidance as well.[5]

CHAPTER 5

CULTIVATING COMMUNITY

*As people see their predicament
clearly—that our fates are
inextricably tied together, that
life is a mutually interdependent
web of relations—then universal
responsibility becomes the only
sane choice for thinking people.*
—Dalai Lama

A SENSE OF COMMUNITY IS built on three pillars: connectedness, synthesis, and holism.

■ *Connectedness*: Fostering a web of relationships based on mutual empathy, compassion, and shared values and purpose.

■ *Synthesis*: Finding common ground and integration among conflicting viewpoints by adopting a wider, more inclusive view.

■ *Holism*: Viewing situations through a holistic "systems perspective."

CONNECTEDNESS

RECEIVING SUPPORT, OVERCOMING LONELINESS: THE CASE OF BLAKE

As an only child having grown up in rural farmlands, Blake is used to spending a lot of time alone, and thus misses out on opportunities to develop his social skills. Those challenges imbue him with the passion to start up and become CEO of an artificial intelligence software company that will help people recognize and respond to social and emotional cues.

His company is struggling to raise its third round of financing, but at the eleventh hour, it manages to secure some funds. He begins our session telling me how grateful he is, first for my support, then for the incredible support of the people on his team, each of whom has contributed enormously to the funding efforts and are doing excellent work.

I invite Blake to reflect on how it feels to receive so much support. He says, "I've realized I'm not alone anymore, and that it's okay to ask for help and trust that others will be happy to do so when they can." He adds thoughtfully, "This support really has aided me in avoiding feeling despair when I face rejection. Plus, it makes everything a lot less lonely. . . . The other people help me get out of my stuck ideas. After all, problems are bigger than one mind. Not only is it more effective this way, but it's more enjoyable." Suddenly, his face lights up as he makes a connection: "Now I understand why pair programming has been such a success for us."

Pair programming is a development methodology in which two programmers work together at one station. One writes code while the other observes and reviews it, switching roles frequently. Blake describes how initially everyone had resisted it: "They didn't want others to scrutinize their code." But now, after nearly a year, his team recognizes how they are much more productive, turn out higher-quality projects, and feel more connected when working together.

These positive team experiences have been very healing for Blake, teaching him that he isn't so alone. As he starts to realize that he can trust others, he is becoming more vulnerable with them as well. This in turn is helping his team members be more vulnerable too in an environment in which they can each own and learn from their mistakes and feel more supportive of one another.

The ways in which teamwork, from study partners in school, to therapy support groups, to spiritual communities, to collaborative work teams, all promote individual growth and collective evolution is well documented.[1] As spiritual teacher Thich Nhat Hanh writes, "The next Buddha will be a *Sangha*." (*Sangha* means a spiritual community supporting our enlightenment.)

From the moment we're born, we depend on connection for survival and well-being.[2] In the critical first years of life, we need secure emotional bonds with our caregivers for healthy development and consistency in our relationships. As Brené Brown writes, "Connection is why we're here. We are hardwired to connect with others, it's what gives purpose and meaning to our lives, and without it there is suffering." The entire field of interpersonal neurobiology highlights how our brains are wired to seek and depend on relationships.[3] A seventy-five-year-long study tracking Harvard graduates and disadvantaged youths found that the quality of human connections and friendships in one's life is a more significant determinant of long-term health and longevity than class, education, or financial privilege, and that the absence of high-quality connections can be as deadly as a lack of exercise or smoking.[4]

Surveys show that nearly eight in ten Gen Zers, seven in ten millennials, and half of all baby boomers are lonely.[5] Loneliness, an epidemic in the US, is a leading cause of depression, anxiety, and schizophrenia. In addition to our mental health, loneliness affects our physical health, causing chronic inflammation, which increases the risk of heart disease, stroke, cancer, and Alzheimer's disease.[6]

Fortunately, positive connections with coworkers are especially effective in reducing loneliness. A survey of over ten thousand adults found that those who don't have good relations with their coworkers are significantly lonelier than those who do, taking not just an emotional and physical toll, but also resulting in more missed workdays, lower productivity, lower quality of work, and higher turnover rates.[7] These findings were also true for the younger Gen Zers and millennials, even though one might assume they experience more connection with each other through social media than boomers do. The results also suggest that many of us need shared physical presence, shared purpose, and positive emotional bonds, not just shallow, ephemeral online connections that can often turn toxic. Indeed, many of my clients report improved employee mood and morale as people begin at least partially returning to their offices as the pandemic came to an end.

Positive connections are important in every domain of life, but especially at work since the workplace is for many the primary community. This is increasingly true, with the percentage of single-adult households growing to 28 percent—more than one in five—in 2021 compared to 13 percent in 1960.[8] For leaders, this represents a great opportunity and an imperative to fulfill a universal need for belonging by cultivating a culture of committed and connected team members, benefiting individuals and the whole organization.

THE SI RESEARCH: WE ARE ALL
INTERCONNECTED AND INTERDEPENDENT

Every one of my spiritually intelligent research participants spoke of their sense of interconnectedness and interdependence with their intimate relationships, families, communities, and, for many, with all of life. They mentioned the importance of listening deeply, and of expressing empathy and compassion as foundational qualities for experiencing the connection of our shared humanity, whether in joy or in suffering. And they spoke of cultivating what philosopher Martin Buber referred to as I-Thou relationships—relationships based on a mutual recognition of each other's inherent value, dignity, and humanity, rather than I-It relationships, which are instrumental or transactional.[8] Their comments included the following:

"I ended up leading the integration of two IT departments where there was much potential for conflict and strife. I made it a point to create a space of openness and generosity—valuing and respecting everyone. From there, the two teams could cooperate and deal with conflict productively. And what emerged were projects that none of us could have come up with on our own."

"Each team member is a beautiful bead on a necklace. We thread ourselves together when we have conversations that are heart-centered, letting everyone express themselves and be heard."

"When I am interacting with someone at work or even in a mundane setting like the supermarket, my intention is always to see a sacred, precious human soul behind their eyes—and kindness and care naturally and effortlessly arise in me. It helps me connect with them, and our interactions tend to go much better."

As might be expected, we found Connectedness to contribute significantly to spiritual intelligence and to effectiveness as SILeaders.

HIVE INTELLIGENCE: THE CASE OF LLOYD

Lloyd, a designer, founder, and CEO of an extremely successful company that makes smart phone-connected medical devices, is struggling to build a team that can scale with the business. For a variety of reasons, including his parents' divorce, he is in deeply entrenched patterns of avoiding confrontation, of needing to please, and of controlling the flow of information between people. Exploring this tendency, he realizes it emerged as a survival strategy from his early childhood in always striving to be liked. Not surprisingly, this focus on being liked when reflected in a management style is disempowering to him and frustrating and inefficient for his team, making it difficult to recruit senior leadership talent.

At my suggestion, Lloyd hires a consultant to facilitate a two-day team-building off-site. With the facilitator's help, the team learns how to reveal and deal with difficult issues, balancing radical honesty with kindness and respect. And, over time, Lloyd works on processing the childhood traumas and how to make his inner child feel safe, so he does not so desperately need to be liked. Feeling safe within himself, he learns the power of transparency and teamwork over control. And how to stand his ground while remaining open to others' input. He keeps a yellow sticky note on his computer with the quote, "Truth can walk the world unarmed and unharmed," to inspire him.

Now, six months after the initial off-site, Lloyd tells me about a new focus on defining his team's culture. It includes the values of radical honesty, respect, craftsmanship, beauty, attention to detail, and fun. He's also opening up to input from the entire company, not just the executives, on their mission, vision, strategy, and values statements. With greater alignment around these values, he cultivates a growing sense of community, which will lead to higher morale, productivity, collaboration, and support for recruiting the right talent at all levels.

Several months later, having successfully recruited another senior executive into his team, Lloyd reported, "Now there is a hive intelligence present on our team that stretches beyond my individual mind or anyone else's." Lloyd also began practicing a modified version of the Buddhist Loving Kindness meditation,[9] which I amended for him to focus on encouraging a collaborative workplace culture.

Research shows that culture has an enormous impact on employee motivation and productivity, especially when it fosters intrinsic motivation through shared purpose, play, and development.[10] In the words of Peter Drucker, "Culture eats strategy for breakfast."

YOUR TURN: THE BENEFITS OF WORKING TOGETHER

Find a comfortable seated position with your spine upright, feeling a sense of alertness as well as one of relaxation. Take a few deep breaths, feel the support of the ground underneath your feet and of the cushion under your pelvis. Let your hands rest. Feel their weight on your lap.

Bring your thumb and pinky finger together in each hand, feeling their contact point. With your eyes closed, imagine yourself seated within the center of your chest and silently recite the following words, substituting with any other qualities you might prefer:

May I be happy and healthy.

May I be safe and free from suffering.

May I actualize and bring my unique gifts to the world.

May I be successful and prosperous in my endeavors.

Take another deep breath, sensing into the center of your chest and your heart area.

Next, recall one of your teammates who is making an important contribution to your efforts, someone toward whom you readily feel gratitude and appreciation. Imagine them seated across from you. Touch your thumb and your ring finger in each hand, once again pausing to feel the contact. Imagine sending out positive energy from your heart and saying to them:

May you be happy and healthy.

May you be safe and free from suffering.

May you actualize and bring your unique gifts to the world.

May you be successful and prosperous in your endeavors.

Again, sense into the center of your chest, your heart area, and the connection you feel with the other person.

Now shifting your thumb to touch your middle finger, bring to mind someone on your team toward whom you have neutral feelings. Again, imagine them seated in front of you and send them positive energy from the center of your chest as you repeat the same affirmations:

May you be happy and healthy.

May you be safe and free from suffering.

May you actualize and bring your unique gifts to the world.

May you be successful and prosperous in your endeavors.

Next, shift your thumb to touch your index finger and repeat the exercise with someone you experience as being difficult to work with. You might notice some resistance to sending them good wishes, which is normal, but you can still choose to do so anyway.

May you be happy and healthy.

May you be safe and free from suffering.

May you actualize and bring your unique gifts to the world.

May all of us be safe and free from suffering.

May all of us actualize and bring our unique gifts to
the world.

May all of us be successful and prosperous in our endeavors.

Continue breathing, sensing into the space at the center of your chest.

What does it feel like now? Has your attitude toward working and collaborating with these people shifted? Do appreciative and benevolent feelings toward all help you alleviate your sense of isolation and engender warm feelings that lift you up? If so, how?

FINDING COMPASSION: THE CASE OF DIONE

Dione, the founder and CEO of a supply chain software company, laments having had to go through a painful layoff process two years into the pandemic. Then, as the company began to recover, Russia invaded Ukraine, interest rates rose, and the economy started heading into a recession, forcing her to cut expenses again. "I guess it's just my bad luck or something," she says, defeated.

I ask Dione how her team is processing it all.

"They're bummed. It's painful and they hate to have to lay off people."

I also ask if she knows of any other companies facing a similar predicament. She tells me that, in fact, most of the portfolio companies her VCs are invested in seem to be in similar circumstances. "I hear pretty much everyone is on shaky ground," she answers with some consolation in her voice.

I invite Dione to think of at least one other CEO dealing with challenging circumstances like hers, and imagine they, along with her executive staff, seated in front of her. Then I describe a Buddhist practice called Tonglen,[11] meaning "giving and receiving," in which she imagines her suffering, her staff's suffering, and the other CEO's suffering as gray smoke, which she inhales directly into her heart. There, it transmutes into the clear, bright energy of compassion. Then to exhale that compassionate loving energy from the middle of her chest back out—imagining herself and those in similar circumstances receiving it.

Dione imagines the outflowing energy as greenish golden light. After only a few moments of practice, her face lights up and she sits more upright. With a sense of wonder, she describes feeling more expansive and open, with a glowing warmth in her chest. She's up for handling the difficulties ahead and feels more connected to her team as well as to others sharing a similar predicament.

Our hearts have amazing capacities. As if by magic, they can transform painful suffering into heartwarming compassion and connection. Indeed, the etymology of the word *compassion* comes from the Latin word meaning "to suffer with." Somehow, opening our heart to care for our own or others' suffering softens our armoring, puts us in touch with the tenderness of our own hearts, and connects us to our loving essence and to that of others. To quote Ralph Waldo Emerson, "It is one of the most beautiful compensations of this life that no man can sincerely try to help another without helping himself."

In this way, compassion activates the two foundational qualities of SI—our inner- and inter-connectedness—which inherently feel good. Indeed, studies show that practicing compassion calms us by activating our parasympathetic nervous system through the vagus nerve.[12]

YOUR TURN: CULTIVATING COMPASSION

Take a moment to get centered and INSPIRED (see page 14).

Now, bring your attention into the center of your chest feeling the sensations, temperature, and density of your heart area, and notice whether you perceive any colors appearing.

Recall a difficult issue you are facing. Notice the impact this has on your energy, your mood, and your body's physiology. Do you feel heavier or lighter? More or less tense? What happens to your breathing?

Now, consider whether anyone else you know is facing a similar challenge, be they family, friends, colleagues, members of your community, or just another person you've heard or read about in the news. Imagine yourself as well as one or more of the others facing a similar problem sitting in front of you.

Take a deep breath and inhale your suffering and theirs into your heart as if it were a thick smoky substance. If it helps, you can imagine a compassionate being such as Jesus, Kwan Yin, the Dalai Lama, or a favorite grandparent abiding in the middle of your chest. Call on their capacity to meet that difficulty with kindness and transmute it into compassion, then exhale the love outward toward yourself and the person or people seated together in front of you.

Continue this practice for a few minutes, inhaling the suffering as dark gray smoke, transmuting it into compassion, and exhaling it as golden light.

What do you notice now? What has shifted for you? How do you relate to your own difficulties now?

Much of our suffering comes from our sense of isolation, that we are in some way special or unique in our pain. Yet, pain and suffering are an inevitable part of human existence. Fortunately, compassion is an alchemical, nearly magical power in our hearts that turns painful suffering into a warm, open sense of connectedness.

In the words of the Buddha, "Resolve to be tender with the young, compassionate with the aged, sympathetic with the striving, and tolerant with the weak and wrong. Some time in your life, you will have been all of these." When you find yourself in one of those situations, remember not only to be compassionate toward yourself, but also that you are not the only one suffering under such conditions. Thus, the practice of Tonglen can be also used as an antidote for loneliness.

By invoking our compassion toward our own and everyone else's suffering, we reintegrate ourselves in the web of life.

SYNTHESIS

FIERCE COMPASSION: THE CASE OF CHARLES

Charles, the founder and CEO of a start-up that is developing an app for the smart home, is hoping to accelerate his company's growth through an initiative to adopt next-generation machine learning technology. Jason, an expert in the field, has agreed to leave the security of his previous job to join Charles's start-up in exchange for a large stock package.

Unfortunately, after nearly a year, Jason has not met expectations, and Charles is continually nudging him to improve his performance. But without success in that regard, the board is accusing Charles of being too soft on Jason. They have been pressuring him to immediately terminate Jason and initiate a search for a replacement.

During our session, Charles seems conflicted. On the one hand, he says, "I convinced Jason to leave a secure job and take a pay cut. I would feel terrible about letting him go." But, on the other hand, "This is a critical initiative, and I just don't see Jason delivering."

I ask him how direct he has been with Jason about his performance. He reluctantly admits that he usually backs off quickly with Jason, as when he brings up his performance, Jason gets defensive and counters with his own list of complaints and criticisms about the company. Charles knows he has to do something but feels torn between being hard-nosed or continuing hope for improvement.

I invite Charles into a Gestalt therapy empty chair exercise to elicit a dialogue between the two parts of himself: the part that wants to let Jason go and the part that wants to give him more time. Charles sits in one chair, embodying one side of the argument while talking to an empty chair, which represents the counterargument. Then Charles changes seats and talks to the other chair, taking on a new posture and persona to talk to his opposing perspective.

As he sits in the chair representing firing Charles, his posture is upright, and he speaks with clarity and authority. He declares, "Enough is enough, we have no time to waste." When he moves to the seat representing being compassionate, his voice becomes gentle, his body softens, and his presence shrinks as if occupying less space in the room. He expresses, "I feel bad about letting Jason go, which will be a big blow for him financially and emotionally."

As he goes back and forth the two sides become more refined as the stricter part of Charles challenges the softer part, questioning if staying on the current track is really the responsible thing to do, given how many other team members rely on the business's success. It is at this point that compassionate Charles says, "At the very least, Jason deserves a fair warning."

By listening to both perspectives, he realizes that they are not irreconcilable opposites, but that both can contribute to a more integrated and balanced perspective through which he can be both kind and firm. He recognizes that Jason needs direct feedback and that avoiding it is not the kind thing to do. But rather the kindest way is to express both perspectives.

Charles says he is now ready to speak to Jason directly about specific objectives he expects him to complete within sixty days, and how, if he can't do so, he will offer him a three-month severance package, which is ample time to find another job.

As it turned out, before the end of the sixty-day period, Jason found another job that better suited him. Charles looked back on the whole experience knowing he acted attentively and thoughtfully. This empowered him to keep moving forward, and eventually he found someone who delivered what was needed.

The Gestalt empty chair exercise is just one method for working with conflicting priorities and values. You can also utilize another approach in which you imagine putting one of the values in each of your hands, alternating your attention between the two to get familiar with each until you're ready to step back and include both in your awareness. (For more on this exercise, please see Chapter 4, section on Freedom.) Giving voice to both sides of a polarity, then listening to and valuing them can lead to a synthesis of the two into a new perspective, which in the case of Charles meant compassion and strength together—or what might be termed fierce compassion.

Life and leadership are complex. Sometimes it can feel like leaders are being tasked with juggling seemingly conflicting qualities like confidence and humility, assertiveness and receptivity, power and vulnerability, or discipline and spontaneity. Such qualities may appear to be mutually exclusive on the surface but can, in fact, be balanced and integrated. In the words of F. Scott Fitzgerald, "The test of a first-rate intelligence is the ability to hold two opposed ideas in the mind at the same time, and still retain the ability to function." Though to do this takes making the shift from an "either-or thinking" to what's referred to as a "both-and mindset."

It's not a new idea. Several human development theories have highlight-ed progressing beyond either-or thinking toward a more inclusive both-and orientation. The nineteenth century German philosopher G. W. F. Hegel proposed a dialectical method and logic in which contradictory propositions, a thesis and its antithesis, can be resolved at a higher lev-el of truth—a synthesis. More recently in 1977, the philosopher Ken Wilber's integral theory posits that human development moves from prerational (childhood), to rational (adulthood), to transrational (sage hood) consciousness.[1] And other developmental theorists, such as Jenny Wade in 1996, hypothesized that human development goes through various stages of consciousness, from the reactive to the authentic, to the transcendent, and then ultimately to the unity consciousness, whereby in the latter two, opposites and dualities are transcended.[2]

In the leadership domain, several modern theories highlight a similar framing of growth and development, such as in 2005 David Rooke and William Torbert's hypothesis on Seven Transformations of Leader-ship.[3] Paralleling the Wade model, they have created a range of lead-ership types, from the Opportunist to the Alchemist, a standout leader who "has an extraordinary capacity to deal simultaneously with many situations at multiple levels. . . . He can deal with immediate priorities yet never lose sight of long-term goals." Lastly, one more leadership the-orist and researcher, Jim Collins, in 2001 found that leaders who com-bine humility and fierce resolve, which he calls "Level 5 Leadership," produce the best financial results for their organizations.[4]

THE SI RESEARCH: FROM EITHER-OR
TO BOTH-AND

In my research, most of my spiritual intelligence interviewees described synthesizing seemingly disparate conflicting qualities into more integra-tive wholes. They spoke of blending confidence with humility, strength with gentleness, power with receptivity, masculinity with femininity. And of accepting these polarities about themselves. As Eli Siegel said, "Beauty is a making of one of opposites."

Many of my subjects also spoke of the importance of honoring multiple perspectives within a community. They mentioned how supporting this diversity increases both overall creativity and a sense of belonging within a team. Those SI subjects in business contexts spoke of values in terms of quality control, risk-taking, speed, reliability, customer service, and engineering, all coexisting in dynamic tension for greater innovation and excellence.

Their comments included the following:

"Spirit to me is the wholeness, the unity, that encompasses polarity. It holds together opposing forces and creates harmony. So, if I want to walk in the world as a person in peace and harmony or harmonious force, I must be big. I need to contain opposites, which means making room for my opinion and its opposite while knowing that truth is the unity of opposites."

"Everything I can analyze or assess about you is included in my consideration. I want to be polite yet irreverent. I need to be humble but simultaneously powerful in our encounter."

"Being in a body yet being a part of the universe puts us into a paradoxical state of existence. And we are born with these two opposing yet influential drives: one is to be acknowledged as being unique and special, and the other is to experience connection and unity. What's most important is actually to enjoy the dance between both perspectives."

As might be expected, we found the capacity of Synthesis to contribute significantly to spiritual intelligence and to leadership effectiveness.

Wisdom and compassion are both essential qualities of awakening, and one cannot have one without the other. They are the two wings we need to fly. As the Indian nondual teacher Swami Maharaj Nisargadatta said, "Compassion tells me I'm everything. Wisdom tells me I'm nothing. Between these two banks, my life flows." This is true individually, societally, and of course for teams and organizations.

For nearly every business in which I have been involved, there has been tension between departments: between marketing and sales, customer service and engineering, speedy product development and quality control, sales and finance. But for businesses to succeed, they need to be able to do it all; *every* department must somehow be prioritized and optimized. So, what does that mean for those in charge? It means leaders need to allow for natural pressures, engage with multiple points of view, and help every role and every department feel heard and valued.

This capacity to reconcile seemingly conflicting positions, whether internal or external, is a recurring theme throughout this book, as it is with SILeadership in general. In Chapter 3, I discuss how Farooq reconciled his need for speedy new feature development in his product with his head of engineering's appeals for reliability and predictability. The synthesis of these needs produced an innovative solution they both liked. And in Chapter 5, I discuss Lloyd's increasing ability to create a safe environment for open and respectful disagreement among his staff to support greater innovation, team cohesion, and the emergence of hive intelligence.

As a leader, rather than feeling pressured to be prematurely decisive, you might often benefit from offering time and space for the full expression of views and facilitating a dialogue about them—to allow them to coexist in a constructive relationship and see what happens. By channeling the energy of this creative tension, holistic solutions informed by the wisdom of the whole can emerge.

YOUR TURN: EXPANDING AND RECONCILING

What you need: two chairs, a journal, and two different colored pens or a recorder.

Centering yourself, taking a few deep breaths, and extending your exhale, let your feet lie flat on the ground and your body sink into your seat cushion, feeling the gravitational pull toward the ground.

Bring to mind a business situation you are facing in which there are competing values, whether within your own mind, between your team members, or amid departments you interact with. Try to personify each value and give it a name, for example, Ms. Profitability Advocate or Mr. Morale Champion. Find names that capture the essence of each position.

Now place two chairs so they're facing each other. Sit in one of them, associating it with one of the characters you've identified. Let yourself feel what it's like to be that character. As you embody them, what happens to your posture and facial expression? Does your body tense or relax? Lean forward or back?

Once you have settled into being this character, allow them to make their case. You can speak out loud as them into your recorder or write out the dialogue using one pen color for each voice.

Once that character makes their case, stand up, shake it off, take a few deep breaths, stretch, and make space for the second character as you switch to the other chair.

Feel this second character's posture and attitude in your body. Notice what they feel like energetically and physiologically. Now let them make their case in response.

After this second character finishes, return to the first chair where you will once again inhabit the perspective and physical and emotional posture of the first character. Continue to go back and forth, letting each character have their say and seeing what emerges.

While inhabiting different characters and speaking out loud may seem awkward at first, stay with it. It's normal to experience conflicting voices within when moving from black-and-white thinking to seeing different shades in between.

After the exercise, reflect on what you've discussed with yourself. Is there some new point of view that has arisen? Is there some insight that has been revealed?

As mentioned earlier, Hegel put forth that for every thesis there is an antithesis, and from the two a synthesis emerges. He describes this process as a dialectic spiral, which impels evolution into ever-greater richness, depth, and wholeness. While Hegel was speaking mainly at the macro-historical level, a similar process can be seen occurring in each of us individually. As you reconcile the polarities within your own psyche, you too develop into a more complex, rich, and nuanced person. May we all enjoy this endless journey of growth as we release our fixation on any one point of view and open ourselves to a greater spectrum of possibilities.

HOLISM

GAINING PERSPECTIVE: THE CASE OF FATIMAH

Fatimah, the founder and CEO of a modeling software company that helps small manufacturers optimize their operations, is struggling with scaling her sales and customer service deployments. Many of the sales professionals she's hired have not been able to attain their quotas and have either been let go or have resigned. At the same time, the engineering team has been having difficulty keeping the software reliably working and responding to customer bug fixes and feature requests. She feels trapped in a frustrating cycle.

In order to analyze and then optimize each customer's operations, the software has to be integrated properly with their Inventory Management Software (IMS), which can be a lengthy process. Plus, every time Fatimah's engineers make headway with adapting their code to a particular IMS brand, any IMS software update undoes all the work they did before.

Meanwhile, the sales and support teams are facing issues of their own. Since the market of IMS providers is so fragmented, Fatimah's software is incompatible with most IMSs in use. One result is the sales team wastes time pursuing customers who won't even be able to use their product.

The customer service team is overwhelmed dealing with unhappy customers as they experience bugs arising from new incompatibilities with new IMS software releases, knowing that the engineering team will most likely be unable to help. And, of course, the engineering team is demoralized from forever chasing a moving target.

During our session, Fatimah diagrams on a whiteboard these departments, the relationships between them, and the problems they face. It quickly becomes apparent that the IMS companies, though outside Fatimah's control, are critical to how her system functions and significantly impact her company's internal dynamics. It also becomes clear that something has to change.

Fatimah comes up with a big-picture idea. She's going to approach an IMS company she is friendly with and offer them a revenue-share incentive in exchange for greater support with integrating her software. She says she's also going to offer an even greater percentage of ongoing revenues if they'll advertise her software to their current base. Following this holistic systems dynamics perspective, she reasons that her company and theirs can collaborate on closing sales leads, reduce customer problems with each new release, and make their engineering team's lives easier.

In the words of Buddha, "Nothing ever exists entirely alone; everything is in relation to everything else." Fatimah's new partnership turned out to be so successful that other IMS providers started approaching *her* hoping to engage in the same deal. This put her company on track as the de facto standard in the market and was a win-win-win for everyone. Of course, it wasn't all smooth sailing. The new system took time to implement and required internal reorganization with some team members ending up being dedicated to the joint venture. But the realignment resulted in greater collaboration among Fatimah's teams and across company boundaries with her partners.

I first encountered the importance of systems thinking myself during my junior year at MIT in a class taught by Peter Senge. "Systems thinking is a discipline for seeing wholes. It is a framework for seeing inter-relationships rather than things, for seeing patterns of change rather than static snapshots," is how Peter describes it. He also introduced me to Jay Forrester, the founder of the systems and industrial dynamics lab at MIT.[1] Peter and I spent time in Jay's lab discussing a potential dissertation research project in systems dynamics. It wasn't widely known at the time, but now systems thinking is used for industrial, business, and urban planning, and in understanding how economic, biological, and ecological systems interact. Just to give one example, in his prescient *World Dynamics*,[2] first published in 1971, Professor Forrester predicted major environmental problems and warned that, without making a combination of social, economic, and technical changes to sustain "world equilibrium," the world would face grave dangers.

Though I ended up choosing a different topic for my thesis, a decade later while at Individual, I would encounter Peter and systems dynamics as a powerful concept once again when I bought his then newly released book and bestseller, *The Fifth Discipline: The Art & Practice of the Learning Organization*.[3] I ended up purchasing a copy for each employee at my company, which led to making "a learning organization" as one of our values. Since then, I have only become more convinced of the importance of using a systems-based approach to address situations holistically.

Here's a primer: systems consist of two fundamental dynamics—positive and negative feedback loops. Positive and negative here do not necessarily mean "good" and "bad." Negative feedback loops generate equilibrium, while positive feedback loops generate a snowball effect. Thus, a system that wisely utilizes both enables equilibrium and growth together. In a negative feedback loop, an increase in one variable brings about a decrease in another. For example, a rise in temperature inside a building activates the air conditioner to go on, while a lowering of the temperature activates the heater to go on.

In contrast, in a positive feedback loop, an increase in part A causes an increase in part B, which in turn causes an increase in part A. In short, success begets success begets success. But a positive feedback system can also have detrimental consequences with exponential out-of-control growth and negative side effects. For example, addiction can give momentary relief from pain, which can lead to requiring even greater and heavier dosages, with a downward spiral of destructive addictive behaviors.

THE SI RESEARCH: ONE COSMIC ORGANISM

Nearly every one of my spiritually intelligent research participants described themselves as both an individual and as part of a larger whole. They thought of themselves as cells in an organ essential to the life of a larger body. Their perception of interconnectedness provides them with support and nourishment as well as a sense of responsibility, as some of their comments indicated:

"A systems approach means seeing the interconnectedness of everything I am a part of. My action has an impact on you, and your action has an impact on me. For me, spirituality is a sense of oneness."

"Holism is the earth's teachings toward a way of wholeness that in my native tradition is called the Beauty Way. It starts with the premise that we are whole, that we are born as whole beings, and that we are part of the wholeness of the life around us, part of the wholeness of the earth. It affects how I see the dynamics within my family, within the nonprofit that I run, and within the ecology of my garden."

"As I see it, God or Reality or Total Being—however we call it—is the ocean, and I am a drop in that ocean. I am as much a part of that ocean, held and carried by it, as all the other drops are. It only makes sense for me to then take the perspective of the entire ocean that I am a part of. If the ocean becomes polluted, so will I as an individual."

We found Holism to contribute significantly to spiritual intelligence and to effectiveness as SILeaders.

YOUR TURN: REFLECTING ON DYNAMIC SYSTEMS WITHIN YOUR TEAM

Find a comfortable, quiet place.

Observe this diagram of the relationship between you and one of your team members, whom we'll call Person A.

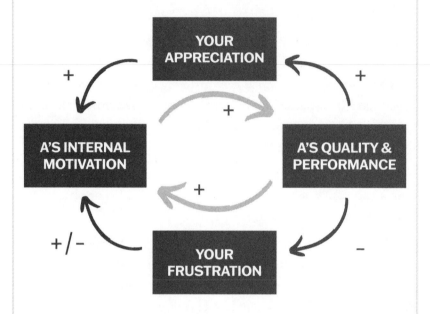

The gray arrows with adjacent plus (+) signs circulating the image represent a positive feedback loop. As their work quality and performance increase, so does their inner motivation to keep up the good work.

The boxes above and below this loop and the black arrows on the top right accompanied by a plus sign represent how *you* fit in: as A's quality of work increases, so does your appreciation for it. And, as you express this appreciation, their motivation increases even further, represented as another black arrow with a plus sign from "Your Appreciation" to "A's Internal Motivation."

Of course, when A's performance decreases, it can increase your frustration. To represent this negative feedback loop, there is a minus (–) sign signaling how these variables move in opposite directions.

So, what to do when your frustration with them increases? If you express your frustration in an overly judgmental or harsh way, you risk reducing their motivation, which will probably weaken their performance further. And if this continues for too long, they might resign or be let go. But, if you offer well-intentioned constructive criticism delivered with kindness, you can increase their motivation and performance. This kind of feedback sets them back on track for greater potential. Thus, the arrow between your "Frustration" box and their "Motivation" box has both a plus and minus sign next to it (+/–). It's up to you whether your feedback works constructively or destructively.

Now, recreate this diagram in your notes using your name and a relevant team member's. Add in your own motivation and/or that of other players on the team, drawing arrows to show the impact of Person A's motivation and performance on your own motivation and performance, independent of any feedback you or they give. Then, create boxes to represent the inner motivation and performance of other colleagues, drawing arrows for people who interact with one another.

As you add more team members, you can begin to see the relational web in your system, and the overall community in which everyone's motivation and performance, frustration, and satisfaction affects everyone else's. Many of your arrows will crisscross and your diagram might start to look like an overly intricate three-dimensional spider's web, in which every person and node is interconnected to every other explicitly and implicitly every day. Considering your actual team members, what do you see? Take some notes in your journal.

Experiment in the coming days with expressing more appreciation and kindness to the team members mapped. Try utilizing small acts of encouragement and notice how those ripple throughout the team.

Most resources in the world are finite. If you share your money or food with others, you are left with less. Except for love. When you share your love through acts of generosity and kindness, your heart's capacity for love grows. The more you express your heart's capacity for love, the more it's likely to spread to others, who will then likely spread it to others you may never know. Whether the kindness or generosity directly returns to you or not, exercising yourself in this way results in you having even more love to give and more to enjoy.

CHAPTER 6

SHOWING UP WITH AUTHENTIC PRESENCE

The greatest gift we can offer is our presence.
—Thich Nhat Hanh

THE PRESENCE DIMENSION OF SILEADERSHIP involves bringing your full attention, focus, clarity of intention, and embodied power to your engagements and interactions. It is built on four competencies: Attention, Intention, Empowerment, and Passion.

■ *Attention*: Being focused on and present with who and what is in front of as well as within you.

■ *Intention*: Bringing awareness and clarity of purpose to your engagements.

■ *Empowerment*: Sourcing, embodying, and expressing grounded personal power.

■ *Passion*: Emanating vigor, aliveness, and wholehearted devotion to your purpose.

ATTENTION

GIVING AND RECEIVING THE MANY GIFTS OF PRESENCE: THE CASE OF NOACH

Noach is the CEO of a rapidly growing enterprise software company. Arriving at our session late, his eyes dart around as he settles in. He then launches into a rapid-fire description of his frustration with the meeting he's just come from. And the next moment he changes the topic. Pretty soon, I notice that my own attention is beginning to wander. I interrupt him, asking, "Where are you? And where am I?"

Puzzled, he responds, "I'm here, and you're here."

I counter, "It hasn't felt like that to me. I know your body is here, but where's your attention?"

"Well, I was thinking and telling you about a product review meeting."

"I know, but it felt like you were gone, reliving the meeting, not here with me." I added, "And how present were you in that meeting?"

"I've been running around all day—hardly catching my breath," he says with a big exhale.

"Can you feel your feet on the ground?" I ask.

"Now I can," he responds.

"Can you feel and wiggle the big toe in your left foot?"

Noach taps his big toe lightly on the floor. Then, following my direction, he taps the pinky of his right hand on his lap, then the pinky of his left hand, and then the big toe on his right foot. He continues grounding himself in the present moment by sensing his feet, hands, arms, and legs, then extending his awareness to his spine. At that point, Noach shifts his posture, sitting up straight with an air of dignity.

I ask what he's experiencing, and he tells me, "Strangely, I feel as large as the room."

I ask, "Do you mean your presence fills the room, and your body is within that presence?"

"I suppose so," he replies.

Noach also describes feeling more confident, energized, powerful, and optimistic. Rooted in this presence, Noach and I review his overpacked schedule. He realizes that he and the company would benefit from him taking a fifteen-minute break between meetings, giving him time to review notes from the last meeting and organize his thoughts for the next one.

We also discuss the benefits of a daily meditation practice. Slowly but surely over the coming months, Noach establishes a new meditation practice and unlearns his bad habits of being distracted and not present in his interactions. Not only does this benefit his presence in meetings at work, but it also improves his relationship with his partner and kids at home.

Abundant research is now available on the many benefits of a meditation practice, from the effect it has on the brain's neuroplasticity, to its impact on our physical and emotional well-being, to how it can help us develop the capacity for focused attention.[1,2,3] Though it is unfortunately difficult for many to maintain a regular discipline, mindfulness and meditation practices are effective treatments for a variety of conditions, including attention deficit hyperactivity disorder (ADHD), which is becoming ever more prevalent in our world.[4,5,6]

THE SI RESEARCH—THIS MOMENT IS ALL YOU EVER HAVE

*Live the actual moment. Only this
actual moment is life.*
—Thich Nhat Hanh

Virtually every one of the spiritual intelligence subjects I interviewed for my research spoke of the importance of slowing down, becoming mindful, and paying attention to what is happening within and around them. They mentioned how only by being attuned to the present moment could they respond appropriately and wisely to the situation. Their comments included the following:

"I cultivate a sense of presence so that when I am with somebody, I can be fully present with myself and with that person. It means that the whole time I can be aware of what's going on in myself, which, given our mirror neurons and our interconnectedness, actually also helps me tune in to what's happening with them."

"When I am more relaxed and present, I am more available—available to life energies as they flow through me. I am also much more resourced, efficient, effective, and creative."

"It is my commitment to 'know thyself' by paying attention to what I am experiencing in the moment. That's how I can access my resources, power, and whatever wisdom is available within and in turn use it to be of service."

"It is my practice of Shabbat, slowing down, stopping the busy habitual doing of life, to notice and reflect. And it's a model for not only one out of seven days in the week, but for each meeting, each hour, each day—pausing, reflecting, and noticing what is within and around me intermittently. Sensing the ever-present presence of the divine that permeates and envelopes all. It is from that place that I am resourced and can choose to respond powerfully and wisely."

We found Attention to contribute significantly to spiritual intelligence and to effectiveness as SILeaders.

THE VALUE OF DEEP LISTENING WITH PRESENCE: NOACH A YEAR LATER

In youth, one learns to talk; in maturity, one learns to be silent. This is man's problem: that he learns to talk before he learns to be silent.
—Rabbi Nachman of Breslov

Over the following year, Noach not only became a faithful meditator but also practiced what he referred to as 50-50, putting half of his attention outward on his interactions with others and half inward on his responses and inner signals. This practice became particularly helpful a year later when his business declined with the economy and new competitors entered the market, forcing his company to go through the unfortunate and painful process of laying off some employees.

During one meeting about the layoffs, the vice president of marketing lamented how they had just hired some of the talented people they would be laying off. She tearfully said, "I just can't see how we can let them go." Noach noticed an impulse arising within himself to defend the layoff, to reiterate that it could save the company. He also noticed his own sadness as he watched his colleague cry. After some reflection, he chose to stay quiet and listen to her, simply remaining present. And he also remained present to his own sadness and didn't attempt to hide it from showing on his face. Not long after, the VP regained her composure. Without needing any further justification, she sighed and said, "I suppose we have to do this." Noach agreed, "Sadly we do. I wish it were otherwise."

Feeling seen, understood, and empathized with are vital human needs. That's why the practice of reflective listening is such a crucial skill in relationships—be they business or personal.[7] You can sense when someone is merely waiting for their turn to speak or is half- present, instead of listening. True listening requires our full attention and presence as

Noach embodied despite his quietness. Indeed, research by two prominent Harvard Business School faculty has highlighted that what companies want most in a CEO is a good listener.[8]

YOUR TURN: HARNESSING THE POWER AND WISDOM OF YOUR PRESENCE

Practice #1

Take a moment to notice right now the state of your mind, emotions, and body. Simply notice.

Bring your attention to the big toe of your left foot and tap it gently
on the floor.

Now wiggle the pinky in your right hand.

Now wiggle the pinky in your left hand.

Now tap the big toe of your right foot.

Next sense and tap all ten toes.

Now sense your ten fingers.

After including your hands, feet, arms, and legs in your field of
awareness, include the verticality of your spine as you are seated
or standing.

Once again, check in on your state of mind, heart, and body.
Simply notice.

How would you describe your state? Are you more present than
before? Are you more relaxed and expanded or more tense and contracted? How has this exercise affected how centered and grounded
you feel, and how strong and stable?

Once again, check in on your state of mind, heart, and body.
Simply notice.

Practice #2

In the coming week, at various times when you can take a momentary break either in between or during meetings, follow this brief attention exercise routine:

Time out: Pause whatever you're doing.

Observe: Your own and others' emotional, mental, and physical state.

Presence: Bring your attention to your presence following the practice detailed above, the INSPIRED protocol (see page 14), or with some other method.

Intention: Recall your highest intention for the meeting or interaction and notice what arises for you as the right action or response.

Confirmation: Notice if you sense a confirmation—a yes or no—to what you are contemplating. As covered in the chapter on Integrity, an inner yes when something resonates as true often feels like a softening, relaxing, opening, and sense of expansion. An inner no often feels like a tensioning and contracting.

Continue repeating steps 3, 4, and 5 until you get a yes so you can act upon it with the full power and alignment of your being and presence.

While there are many approaches to reconnecting to presence, often involving bringing attention to the breath and feet on the ground, I find the above method particularly effective in clearing the busy mind, opening the field of awareness, and bringing both left and right hemispheres of the brain online simultaneously. If it helps, you can use the acronym TOPIC to remember: Time out—Observe—Presence—Intention—Confirmation.

Research indicates that acting with presence is often more effective at supporting goal attainment and promoting wholeness and well-being with increased calm and focus in comparison to acting with a lack of presence.[9, 10] Some, such as Walt Whitman, would argue that "we convince by our presence."

THE SCARCEST RESOURCE: YOUR PRESENCE, TIME, AND ATTENTION

With so many sources of information available at our fingertips and competing for our attention, it is ever easier and more tempting to jump from one thing to another—a text, notification, email, video clip, electronic game, or YouTube video. In some way, many if not most of us are adopting more and more ADHD-like habits. Thus, learning to focus and manage our attention is ever more challenging, yet critically important.

At each moment we choose where to put our attention, and we can never get that moment back. It is gone, lost forever—we can never relive that lost moment. And, as much as we don't like to think about it, eventually our time runs out. In a very real sense then, our attention is our life. Our attention and our presence are the greatest gifts we can give anybody, or any cause. And our full presence with whatever is occurring in our lives is the greatest gift we can give ourselves.

All too often, we ruminate about the past, judging, rejecting, or pushing away our current experience in the moment. Or we fixate upon some experience in the future, only when that desired moment finally arrives, we try to grasp and hold onto it, which never really works. We can never hold onto the moment since the river of life continues to flow downstream. We are at our wisest when we embrace this river's flow, paying attention to the terrain, the landscape, rocks, boulders, and rapids, skillfully navigating our way to enjoy the ride.

It is also wisest to be thankful for the gift of your time and attention. Gratitude helps you use your time and attention even more wisely to maximize the gift of your presence to live each moment as fully as you can, to lead you to the deepest desires in your heart.

INTENTION

INTENTION GETS YOU TO YOUR DESTINATION: THE CASE OF SAM

In Chapter 2 I described Sam, a visionary leader who grew his company from a start-up to a near-billion-dollar business with hundreds of employees around the world. Sam could see the big picture, but sometimes he would become a little too attentive to the details, even to the point of micromanaging his team. He wanted to curb this habit, as his controlling style of leadership left his team feeling frustrated and disempowered.

So I invited him to imagine himself at a future off-site alongside his team, having already cultivated a new approach toward management. He visualized an atmosphere of blameless accountability, vulnerability, openness to learning from mistakes, and one in which his directors could feel uplifted about their responsibilities.

While this vision provided Sam with a compelling North Star, he didn't find the technique easy to follow in the years after. In fact, he was still being overly controlling toward his employees, particularly during meetings. We refined the process for him some and found that what helps him the most is the clarity and strength of his intention to change his behavior. Because no matter how strong his vision may be, it is only through a steadfast commitment to his intention that he is able to address the roots of his reactive patterns and gradually change them.

Sam and I often discuss the meetings that trigger his domineering behavior. What has been unearthed is his realization about how it reflects his relationship with his father, who throughout Sam's childhood would debate and argue with him, at times even blatantly denying the truth. It was crazymaking, and young Sam would feel unsafe, seeing the world as unintelligible and unpredictable. So he learned to vehemently fight back, which conditioned him to stay vigilant, eroding his ability to trust people in general, and specifically resulting in an unproductive dynamic with his team.

Inspiring visions can motivate our journey, energizing us toward beautiful destinations. But overcoming the inevitable obstacles on the way, such as in Sam's case a behavioral pattern stemming from childhood trauma, is no small task. What makes it possible though is the power of our *intention*.

Throughout our work together on this issue, Sam at times gets down on himself for failing to meet his goal of being less argumentative during meetings. At such times, I remind him of the difference between resolutions, goals, and intentions. Then I invite him to imagine a goal of better managing his behavior during meetings, and asking how that phrasing feels to him. He often says he feels his body tighten, as if gearing up for a fight. Next we try different wording, and when he formulates his intention to conduct meetings as a facilitator rather than as an auditor, he feels a greater sense of flow and ease.

Of course, this isn't to say that setting goals isn't helpful or necessary. We often need to set specific milestones for ourselves or our teams such as revenue goals, on-time arrival percentage goals, or specific customer satisfaction metrics. Goals offer a necessary yardstick for measuring performance and progress, but it is also important to not forget that they lead us toward a success versus failure mindset; we either meet our goal or not. Furthermore, goals focus our attention on a future outcome, not on how to observe and apply our efforts in the moment.

Resolutions have their occasional place as well, though best reserved for situations such as grappling with a life-threatening drug addiction, when we know that even a single misstep can lead us down a dangerous, slippery slope. Unfortunately, resolutions can also lead to the same all-or-nothing mentality when it comes to changing our behaviors. We see it every New Year's Eve. For instance, we might resolve to never again eat pizza late at night. And then when we take that first bite, it seems much easier to give up altogether and indulge even more. Seeing ourselves failing saps our power and motivation to get back on track. *After all*, we tell ourselves, *what's the point of holding back when I've already started in?*

Intentions, however, keep us in the game. They are not all-or-nothing propositions. As Derek Rydall says, "Your intention is like the rudder on a boat, giving direction to your life force." Intentions help us navigate the turbulent waters of life and remind us how each moment is an opportunity to start afresh. Over the following months, reminding himself of his intention, exploring and healing the root causes of his argumentative and domineering style, Sam was able to heal and develop a new style of engagement in meetings. Like Sam, we too can return to our true intentions, learning and growing as we form new habits. As Brendon Burchard says, "First, it is an intention. Then behavior. Then habit. Then practice. Then a second nature. Then it is simply who you are."

THE SI RESEARCH—YOUR INTENTIONS ARE YOUR GPS KEEPING YOU ON TRACK

Most of the spiritual intelligence subjects I interviewed in my research spoke of the importance of setting clear intentions and returning to them repeatedly. They set intentions not only to keep themselves on track but also to invite invisible support from the universe. Their comments included the following:

"It's been said that 'The winds of grace are always blowing, but it's up to me to put up the sails.' I always remind myself that the sails are my intentions."

"My intention is my North Star. I always check if I am mindlessly veering off the road, and, when I do, I return to the path and what I am aiming for."

"Whenever I work in a team, it is vital that we align our intentions and synch our aim. When we do, our energies are multiplied manifold.

Otherwise, we would be working at cross- purposes, which is frustrating and wasteful to everyone."

We found Intention to contribute significantly to spiritual intelligence and to effectiveness as SILeaders.

INTENTION SUPPORTS OUR PRESENCE AND EFFECTIVENESS

Sam utilized the power of intention to support him in realizing his vision of learning to lead from behind, a relatively large endeavor that took several years to attain. Chapter 2 also included the case of Ted, who started practicing visualization as a tool to help him develop and command presence before important gatherings, including family dinners. Like Sam, Ted has been using the combined powers of vision and intention before each interaction to get in the right state of mind so he can show up in a way that is most conducive to his desired outcome, be it building rapport with an important client or sharing a relaxing outing with his family. Once clear on his intention, he can consider his words more carefully before speaking and then gauge how supportive they are of his intention.

Of course, like all of us, Ted is far from perfect. Despite his best intentions, he still checks his phone during conversations, goes off on tangents, and lets his ego take the wheel, instead of actively listening. Yet, by returning to his intention again and again, he has learned from each setback and become better able to restrain those impulses.

Our intentions especially impact our interactions when giving feedback. Most people brace themselves when receiving critical feedback, even when it's done with the best intentions. But just the mere awareness of our intention can create a world of difference in our energy and tone, which itself has a greater impact on others than our words. And that's the difference that makes a difference. This means it's critical to carefully consider your intention, to regard it with utmost sincerity, before offering any feedback. If you're not quite sure how to do that, this next exercise might be of some help.

YOUR TURN: CLARIFYING YOUR INTENTION IN GIVING FEEDBACK

Take a moment to tune into yourself using the INSPIRED protocol (see page 14) or any of the techniques from previous chapters. Taking a few deep breaths as you sense your presence, think of someone you would like to give critical feedback to.

Explore your intention in giving them that feedback by reflecting on these prompts:

What do you want to feel as a result?

What do you want them to feel as a result?

Is there any part of you that feels judgmental and wants to somehow show them how inadequate, bad, or wrong they've been?

Do you simply want to help them avoid similar mistakes in the future, or do you need them to know how wrong they were? If so, to what end, and, without judgment, ask yourself where it comes from—perhaps you've been disappointed by that person, or their performance negatively impacted your ability to get your own work done?

Bring compassionate awareness to the part of you that may have been hurt or annoyed. Ask yourself what else you need so you can relax and open.

Attend to the hurt, then let it go so you can let your caring side lead.

Once you feel motivated to provide your feedback from a place of support, rehearse it in your mind. Look for the place in your heart that sees the person's beauty and trusts in their potential to give them feedback in a way that is kind and constructive. Then, in your mind's eye, visualize them receiving it graciously.

When you're ready, create the best conditions possible for the interaction to go well. Here's a basic structure that helps:

Invite the person to meet with you at a time that feels unhurried and without distractions.

Open the meeting by offering a few words of appreciation and stating your intention to give them constructive feedback.

After this introduction, ask them if they're willing to receive the feedback.

For example, "I appreciate all the ways you support our team like last week when you stayed late to finish your report. I'd love to see you continue to advance. I have some feedback that might support your growth. Would you like to hear it?"

The above is an ideal scenario. But of course, there are going to be times when we may need to give feedback to someone who isn't open to receiving it. Giving critical feedback is never easy. Plus, it's important to remember that even with the best intention, sometimes our impact may be different than we imagined. In those cases, it's best to be curious about what might be going on for you and for that person. Was it your delivery or might it be their life experience, or both? In any case, practicing compassion and developing greater attunement will lead to more successful interactions for the two of you in the future. It is up to us to take on the responsibility of keeping our intentions clear and clean to maximize those opportunities.

PRACTICING PRESENCE IN MEDITATION: DIRECTING OUR ATTENTION WITH INTENTION

Meditation is one of my favorite practices for cultivating presence. It involves both attention and intention. Except for the very advanced practices of letting go of all intentions and simply resting in pure being, most meditation practices center on picking an object of concentration, such as a mantra or the breath, and setting an intention to focus awareness on it. Unfailingly, our attention will drift away as thoughts, sounds, memories, fantasies, and emotions arise. Thus, the practice of remembering our intention and using it to redirect our attention back to the object of concentration helps us deepen our sense of presence. In this way, meditation exercises both our intention and attention capacities, among many other benefits.

THE EXPONENTIAL BENEFITS OF
SHARED INTENTIONS

Intentions are vital not only for us individually, but also for our relationships and communities. An organizational mission and values statement defines a shared intention to reinforce and multiply people's energy and motivation. It keeps everyone on board and rowing in the same direction.

A large body of research highlights these benefits, particularly when each individual's tasks and roles cannot be entirely scripted, thus requiring more discernment and improvisation.[1] Other research shows how shared intentions enable collective agency among interdependent actors to drive the emergence of a larger cohesive service ecosystem.[2] An additional study found there was synchronization in the brain activities of individual group participants when they acted with a shared intention, which then led to greater team cohesion and improved performance.[3] Without a shared intention, groups can waste an enormous amount of time.

INTENTIONS: BIG AND SMALL

We can set intentions for any span of time. Sam's intention to learn to lead from behind required several years of concentrated effort, while Ted set distinct intentions for each important encounter, some of which only lasted a few moments. Regardless of size, intentions can remain effective and relevant for years, decades, or a lifetime.

In addition, they can be hierarchically organized and/or mutually reinforcing. For example, you might cultivate an intention to grow spiritually. To that end, you may intend to find a teacher or a guide, join a supportive spiritual community, or engage in a regular spiritual practice, all of which support your primary intention. Or you might set an intention to live a healthy lifestyle, which may involve several supportive intentions such as getting quality sleep, exercising, and eating well. These interrelated intentions all reinforce the primary intention of greater health and well-being.

YOUR TURN: SETTING AN INTENTION

Pick a time frame in which you wish to consider and clarify your main intention. It could be limited to a specific upcoming encounter, or applicable to the next week, month, or year. You might feel inspired to focus on your highest intention for life, such as showing up with authentic presence, giving and receiving love, embodying peace, realizing your fullest potential, or living in service to name a few.

In reflecting on this, you may wish to revisit your notes from the Chapter 1 sentence-completion exercises. As you reflect, notice your current priorities, accepting without judgment that your highest intentions to address those priorities may remain constant or change over time. Either way can be healthy and natural.

That said, you can only have one highest intention at any given time, and the clearer you are about it and the more consistency with which you return to it, the more likely it will become a powerful North Star to guide you. So, for your intention to be effective, it must represent a true priority for you at this time in your life, something that you're willing to put the time, effort, and discipline into, and return to time and again. Once you establish habits that support your intention, it will require less conscious effort, thus freeing up the space to focus on and set intentions in other areas.

Several spiritual traditions suggest contemplating your highest intention as the first thing upon waking up and as the last thing before falling asleep. Those are the moments when your mind is most open and relaxed, making it possible to touch into your essential nature and align it with your subconscious mind.

In those liminal moments, recall your intention, and let it fill your heart as your deepest prayer and yearning. As you do, you'll find forces beyond your imagination, the winds of grace as some might call them, aligning to support you toward your aspiration.

EMPOWERMENT

THE POWER AND WISDOM OF OUR BEING: THE CASE OF TED

Ted, CEO of an enterprise software start-up, is visibly distraught as he comes into my office. Shaking his head, he collapses into the chair and unloads:

"I can't believe it. The company that offered to acquire us a year ago just announced a new product that looks very competitive with ours. What was I thinking when I turned down their offer? If I'd just accepted it, I'd have met all of my long-term financial goals and walked away a winner. Now, I'm not sure if we can compete with such big players—I might lose everything." After he's done, his body goes limp. He musters, "Everyone is waiting for my response to the competitor, but I just want to hide."

I invite him to take a deep breath and simply tune in to what's happening. He describes sensing a ball of tension in the pit of his stomach, shallowness in his breath, and stress throughout his body. "What are you feeling?" I continue to inquire.

He thinks, then responds, "I'm scared and second-guessing my decision."

I then guide Ted in a process I use with many clients. "Let's start by exploring your fear." Ted's face scrunches with distaste. I follow up,

"You don't have to like it, but try treating your fear with respect by just allowing it to be there."

Then, following the Allow and Include method, I invite Ted to feel his feet on the ground—his whole body held by Mother Earth, supporting him exactly as he is. Ted takes a deeper breath and reports that, while the fear is still there, it is less overwhelming, and the tension he felt has softened a little.

We continue drawing from the breath and begin a sequence of statements starting with, "I am here, now, aware of my fear." With these words, Ted's face softens a bit. On the next exhale, I invite him to shorten the sentence to, "I am here now aware." After a few more breaths, I suggest he shorten the sentence to "I am here now," then to "I am here," and finally to simply, "I am."

After this sequence, Ted says his whole body is softened, and his presence feels much larger. He tells me that, while he can still sense some fear, it, and everything else "just is." As he describes it, "There is an 'is-ness' to everything, if that's even a word."

While he is present to his fear, rather than being consumed by it, I invite him to listen to any messages his fear has for him. First, he says it tells him that he needs to be more vigilant, to up his game, and to accelerate product innovation at the company to stay ahead of the competition. Then, his fear proceeds to list all the improvements he should make: enhancing customer support, offering more complete solutions, forming partnerships, and considering acquisitions, all of which make sense to him. But now, rather than feeling overwhelmed by the decisions before him, he feels energized. He feels called to action.

The week that followed our session, Ted rallied his team around these new initiatives. Still, staying ahead in an increasingly competitive market is no small feat, and over the next few months and years, he found himself growing quite familiar with fear. But, when he practiced acknowledging and learned to simply be with his fear, it no longer paralyzed him.

Ted's company managed to remain a leader in the industry, ultimately becoming a stand-alone public company. This, however, would bring its own set of even greater hurdles. Playing a bigger game invariably means facing bigger challenges. And whether we meet those challenges or not, our work is to always continue to grow and evolve.

It's easy to view fear as a sign of weakness—something to avoid, suppress, or run away from. The fear of fear can paralyze us more than the fear itself. We need not be fearless, rather we need be courageous—the capacity to move forward in the face of fear. In the words of Martin Luther King, Jr. "First, we must unflinchingly face our fears and honestly ask ourselves why we are afraid. This confrontation will, to some measure, grant us power. We shall never be cured of fear by escapism or repression, for the more we attempt to ignore and repress our fears, the more we multiply our inner conflicts."

We couldn't survive without fear. It alerts us to threats and heightens our senses so we can quickly flee or fight. Although our nervous system's response to fear is based on evolutionary adaptation to physical threats, more often than not the fear we experience isn't a sign of imminent mortal danger. What gets us is the worry that we can't handle the situation at hand emotionally and will end up experiencing some ugly feeling we weren't able to tolerate earlier in life.

We need to understand our fears and develop the capacity to distinguish between ones that represent a real threat to our physical survival versus ones that threaten our psychic comfort or egoic identity. We can only do so by turning toward the fear with curiosity. As the Buddhist teacher Chögyam Trungpa instructs, "Smile at Fear."[1] When we do, we become present to the truth of our experience, which is the source and expression of our power.

While fear happened to be what Ted felt most averse to, he, like most of us, tended to resist feeling any difficult emotion, whether it was fear, anger, hate, sadness, grief, confusion, or despair. But whatever the feeling, there is power in being willing to face it head on and containing it within our field of presence so that we can listen to and learn from its messages.

THE SI RESEARCH—THE IMMANENT POWER WITHIN

Nearly every spiritual intelligence research participant I interviewed described the importance of tuning into themselves, opening up to their experience, and grounding themselves in embodied presence. This provides them with the courage and strength to meet challenges. They elaborated:

"When I'm in a challenging situation at work—like trying to solve a tough problem—I try to be aware of what's going on in my body. What is the tightness in my neck telling me? What about the way my breathing has changed? I can reconnect to my power and my strength first by contacting myself as an enfleshed, living, and breathing being. The answers are nowhere to be found outside myself. Finding them always starts with reconnecting with myself in my grounded embodied presence."

"A key practice for me is finding God in all things, including my body, my pain, and my so-called negative emotions. And when I open to whatever is within me and treat it with reverence, then even the 'negative' is experienced as beautiful and sacred."

"I can't imagine a universe where some parts of it are divine and other parts aren't. It just doesn't make sense to me . . . it would be putting a limit on God. So, I believe that there is nothing that isn't divine, that the very substance that we are made up of is divinity, and that if I want to be in touch with the divine, all I have to do is be in touch with what is. Of course, that includes horrifying things like jealousy, financial problems, and issues with relationships, even bodily fluids—all the stuff of being human. This means I don't need to reject or run away from anything. It empowers me to turn toward life and whatever life brings."

We found Empowerment to contribute significantly to both spiritual intelligence and to SILeadership.

YOUR TURN: FINDING THE POWER AND WISDOM OF YOUR PRESENCE

Sit in a posture that is both alert and relaxed—back straight, with your feet flat on the ground. Take a moment to feel the weight of your body and the force of gravity pulling you in.

Take a few deep breaths, letting out a sigh on the exhale. Now, bring your attention inward and simply notice what it is like to be with yourself right here and now.

Notice where you feel your strength, pleasure, and well-being, and where you feel their absence. Notice what feeling you wish wasn't there and touch it gently with your awareness, letting it be just as it is, knowing there is nothing to fix, no problem to solve. Notice the sensations in your body. Perhaps there's agitation, tension, or heaviness. Check your jaw, chest, and belly. However they are, simply allow it to be. At the same time, include awareness of your feet, legs, and the support of the ground. Be here now as you are.

Ask yourself what it's like to be exactly as you are. If you are aware of only ease and well-being, marinate in it. See how this changes as you maintain your awareness. If you feel some discomfort, turn toward that as well.

Take a few full breaths and on the exhales say to yourself, "I am here now, aware of X." Then take another breath in silence. And, on the next breath, shorten the statement to "I am here now aware." After another breath, "I am here now." Then, "I am here." And finally, simply "I am." Notice what it's like to simply affirm your existence, your being.

If the negative experience persists, without resistance enter a dialogue with it, inviting it to express itself in words. Ask what it wants you to know and if there are any actions it wants you to take. For example, anxiety may say, "I'm worried about your presentation tomorrow. I want you to spend more time preparing and mastering the material." Sadness might say, "I'm sad about the loss of XYZ. I really loved it."

Take the time to listen, then acknowledge the message you receive and thank that part of you for communicating. You can choose which actions to take to honor that part's wisdom, such as honoring fear by channeling it toward achieving your visions.

If you're curious about why this "shortening the sentence" technique works, it's because our being, our presence, our existence, is what's primary. In fact, Descartes's "I think therefore I am" got it backward. Regardless of any thought or feeling or their absence, we are, I am, and you are. Tuning into this immutable truth of our being empowers us. It gives us unshakable ground to stand on, and from there we can face whatever confronts us.

USING EMOTIONS TO TAP INTO THE INTELLIGENCE OF YOUR BEING

When rooted in the depth of our being, we can observe our emotions and listen to their wisdom rather than letting them define us. When we can simply sit with them and receive their messages, we expand our sense of self to contain them. We can include emotions within our being—within our field of presence, which has no beginning and no end. In this way, they are a part of us, yet they don't consume us. Rather than trying to suppress or ignore our emotions, which divide us by putting us at war with ourselves and reality, we can tap the vast resource of our unbounded awareness.

For example, anger alerts us that something we value is being threatened. In this way, it activates our strength so we can defend and protect what we value, perhaps by setting healthy boundaries. This requires entering into a conscious relationship with our anger, receiving its messages, and then skillfully and assertively responding to the situation. When we do, empowerment comes from neither bottling up our anger, nor from acting out in a fit of rage, both of which only create further problems.

Sadness, to use another example, invites us to connect with what we value and love so we may grieve its loss. After all, we wouldn't be honoring our sadness over the things we love if we didn't care about losing them. In this way, sadness and grief remind us of some value we've lost so that we can let go and create space for new things to enter.

As Karla McLaren explained in her book *The Language of Emotions*, "With the help of your emotions . . . you can learn to focus and work honorably with the incredible information inside each of your feeling states . . . you can become intimately connected to the source of your intelligence."[2] However, we can only listen to our feelings' messages by becoming present to them. It is only within our presence that our emotions arise, and only through them can we tap into our grounded personal power and inner wisdom.

PASSION

REKINDLING YOUR FIRE, RECOMMITTING TO YOUR PURPOSE: THE CASE OF NANCY

Nancy is a mother and entrepreneur who started an education technology company to help improve the educational experience for students, teachers, and parents. Charismatic and energetic, she's assembled a dynamic and seasoned team and raised money from prominent investors. While feedback from early customers has been positive, getting schools to adopt a new platform is proving difficult. With slow customer adoption and revenue growth, Nancy is struggling to keep the company afloat. She's already implemented two rounds of layoffs and is feeling pained and demoralized. Determined to succeed, she's been white-knuckling it for months and is on the brink of burnout.

In our session, she laments her difficulties with investors, explaining how "they get excited by the concept, mission, and vision, but then seem to move very slowly. With only two months of runway, things are very stressful."

I suggest that some self-compassion might help, so she puts her hands on her heart and sends herself some care. As she begins to relax, she tells me that she's feeling a vortex of tension the size of a tennis ball in her lower belly. After putting some attention on it, she notices that this tension is fear—a fear of failure and of disappointing her employees, investors, and customers, all of whom appreciate the product's benefits.

I ask Nancy if this fear of disappointing others is familiar. Her eyebrows furrow as she recounts the numerous times as a teenager when her mother was disappointed by her not following teachers' instructions. She painfully remembers the disapproving look on her mother's face after meetings with the principal. I suggest she ask her teenage self what that part of her needs. The response is a clear: "I need to be seen and understood, to be myself and follow my own interests and passions!" The frustration behind this unmet need makes her want to scream. Sensitive to our neighbors, instead of inviting Nancy to scream out loud, I suggest she imagine herself unleashing the most satisfying scream possible. She takes a few deep breaths and opens her mouth wide with an imaginary scream.

A few moments later, she sits up straight and describes how there's now a lot of energy in her lower belly where the tension used to be. Acknowledging her fear of disappointing others and expressing her frustration and imagining herself screaming feeling unappreciated for who she is, connects her to the potent life force that needs to be acknowledged, actualized, and expressed as her true passion. As an adult, her passion has evolved to be a provider of learning environments that support others' interests and passions in schools and in her company's culture. Now, connected to her life force, she reports the area in her lower belly feels hot, fiery, and energetic. And with color returning to her face, she looks radiantly enlivened and vibrant. With a sparkle in her eye, she tells me, "It's so good to remember why I'm doing this. I feel energized and committed. We're going to make this happen, I don't care what it takes."

As may have become clear through these case studies, a recurring theme and foundational element for SI work is that it is only by embracing and opening to the totality of our experience, including our pain, discouragement, and fear, and shining the light of our awareness on it, that we can become integrated and whole. It is this state of integration and wholeness from which our aliveness most powerfully flows. Turning away from any aspect of our experience dampens our energy, while turning toward it unlocks often hidden or suppressed energies. Peering into those dark shadowy places requires our confidence and trust in life and in our ability to handle that darkness. It is there that we rediscover our light, as it expresses itself and flows through us. It is often only in the dark that we can liberate the light so that the spark of our passion illuminates the way for ourselves and others.

Through repeating this process with Nancy several times, each time reconnecting her to her source of inspiration, she was better able to get through the dark and difficult moments. With the benefit of her burning passion, as well as with her regular rejuvenation from spending time in nature, she was able to convince her existing investors to continue funding the company while she and her team reached several new milestones over the coming months. In time, and after meeting additional financial milestones, Nancy's passion enabled her to gain a large round of additional funding from several new investors. As Robert Kiyosaki says, "True passion attracts. If you have passion in your business, the right people will be attracted to your team."

THE SI RESEARCH—PASSION CAN MOVE MOUNTAINS

While Passion was not a quality I specifically called out in my spiritual intelligence research, it was both implied and explicitly mentioned by those I interviewed. Indeed, passion is naturally associated with and is the outgrowth of other SI qualities such as Purpose, Service, Joy, Sacredness, and a general love of life. Some of the interviewee comments included the following:

"I orient my life toward the truth, and that's truth with small t and Truth with capital T, the latter being one of the names of God in some traditions. After all, reality is an expression of the truth. And the more I open and am in love with the truth, the more the truth reveals itself to me. Like when a lover who is passionately in love with their beloved, the beloved naturally unveils and reveals herself. And if it sounds a little erotic, it's because it is. That's the nature of Rumi's poetry or the 'Song of Songs.' A passionate love affair—passionately loving the truth for its own sake. And in that passionate fire of love the ego is consumed."

"As I look at my life and my work, the more I love what I do, the more fired up I am about realizing my vision, the more passionate, empowered, strong, and powerful I feel. And people are just drawn in to help realize it."

"It's touching into my life force, my inner fire, and from there naturally arises passion, engagement, and full-on playing without being attached to outcome."

"My true passion for the divine—its best antidote for my ego."

PASSION FUELS LIFE AND NATURALLY GROWS OUT OF SPIRITUAL INTELLIGENCE

While we didn't include Passion explicitly in our model and scale for spiritual intelligence, it correlates closely with and naturally emerges out of many other SI qualities. These include Purpose, Service, Vision, Trust, Beauty, Joy, Inner-Wholeness, Integrity, and Devotion. Further, we can tap into the life force that's integral to SILeadership when we feel:

- devoted to a Purpose
- called to be of Service
- pulled by our Vision
- comforted by Trust in life

- drawn by Beauty
- enlivened with Joy
- invested in Inner-Wholeness
- aligned with Integrity

It is by unleashing and focusing the primal life force of passion that we can become inspired SILeaders. Meaning, the same boundless, steamy energy that pulsates through our veins during all-consuming lovemaking, is also available to us when we are wholeheartedly and selflessly devoted to our calling. It is a true blessing to discover and follow our passions. And indeed, in our research, Passion turned out to be an important contributor to effective SILeadership.

YOUR TURN: WHAT MAKES YOU COME ALIVE?

Complete the following sentence with five to ten variations without editing or judging your responses. As you do, notice your posture, breathing, energy, and mood.

I feel alive when _____.

Review your list. What difference would it make if you brought the same quality of energy you feel now doing this exercise into the rest of your life? Your work? Your relationships? Take some notes.

Complete the following sentence with five to ten variations without editing or judging your responses. As you do, notice your posture, breathing, energy, and mood.

I am passionate about _____.

Review your list. When you engage in these activities that are aligned with your deeply held values, do you feel passionately enlivened? About your work? About your relationships? Take some notes.

How does this exercise shed light on your living a more passionate life?

DISCERNING SPIRITUALLY INTELLIGENT PASSION FROM OBSESSION OR COMPULSION

At a recent gathering I was chatting with an acquaintance. We were sadly reflecting on the loss of someone we both knew, who died from a drug overdose. Speaking about the dangers of drug addiction, which, tragically, some people fall into because of the intensity of aliveness it gives them, this acquaintance started to raise his voice ranting about someone else he knew of who'd sold his car to get money for heroin. "What a f— idiot!" he nearly shouted. As he was continuing on with his righteous anger, I noticed my body was tensing up and I was having a hard time hearing and comprehending what he was saying. I knew my nervous system had gone on alert from his vexation. I pointed this out to him, to which he exclaimed, "This is who I am! I'm just a passionate man!"

More truthfully, I suspect his behavior reflects poor self-regulation around anger rather than passion. I would have been delighted to hear him speak passionately about whatever work he was doing to help battle drug addiction. While outbursts of anger can give a sense of aliveness, can awaken us from a sense of numbness, they usually lead to destructive behaviors. Obsessions, compulsions, addictions, including workaholism, sometimes even whole-hearted blind commitments, fanaticisms, all may provide a sense of intensity and aliveness, but are ultimately dysfunctional.

YOUR TURN: DISCERNING YOUR SPIRITUALLY INTELLIGENT PASSIONS

Ask yourself what makes you feel alive. Perhaps look over the prior exercise for a jumpstart. What are you are passionate about? Are there some ways in which you seek a sense of aliveness that are counterproductive?

Fanning your spiritually intelligent passion will naturally lead you away from poor imitations and draw you toward following your authentic calling to contribute your unique gifts to the world, while drawing resonant others with your infectious vibrant aliveness.

CHAPTER 7

MOTIVATING BASED ON TRUTH

Pride is concerned with who is right; humility is concerned with what is right.
—Ezra Taft Benson

THE TRUTH DIMENSION OF SILEADERSHIP involves shifting your overall focus from ego to truth. It is built on two competencies:

- *Openness*: Embracing yourself and other people with receptive curiosity and wonder.

- *Egolessness*: Cultivating humility and devotion to the truth.

OPENNESS

OPENING TO AND LEARNING FROM WHAT IS: THE CASE OF DHARVESH

Dharvesh, the CEO and cofounder of his company, shakes his head, wiping sweat from his brow. The night before he learned that an early investor was badmouthing the company. He tells me that there'd been some conflict with this person from back when they were working together, but he'd believed the issues were largely resolved, and even thought they had parted on good terms. He'd given the investor a generous return on their investment, and both had signed a mutual non-disparagement agreement.

Dharvesh's face is flushed. "How could this happen?" he asks. He tells me he feels anxious and angry.

When I ask how he feels about these emotions, he looks at me in disbelief, "I want to get rid of them, thank you."

So, I invite him to try. He focuses for a moment, and then tells me that the tension he's feeling has only intensified, gripping him more and more tightly. He seems even more upset than before. I invite him instead to consider the full measure of his resistance to his anxiety with curiosity and interest. "What might this resistance be trying to do?" I say.

"It's trying to keep me from feeling bad," he snaps, as if this were obvious. "And how does resisting feel?" I ask, undeterred. He takes a minute before answering, "It feels tight, bad, exhausting." By the time he's finished the sentence, Dharvesh has let go of the resistance.

Then, he starts to explore his anxiety, opening himself up to it. He's worried that the old investor's vilification will make it harder for him to raise money now. Facing his concern head on, he realizes that he needs to research the nature of the rumors openly and prepare a response. With this plan in mind, he begins to relax.

Next, I ask about his anger. This prompts Dharvesh to erupt again, "It's not fair! Our company treated him well, and he signed a non-disparagement agreement!"

I validate his anger as a natural, healthy response to this injustice and violation of boundaries. We explore how the anger feels physically. He says he senses red fiery energy and strength throughout his whole body. It's urging him to leap into action, to enforce the contract, and to defend his company. Ultimately, he decides to write the old investor a polite yet direct email, reminding him of the non-disparagement agreement.

When Dharvesh stopped resisting and opened himself up to his emotions, both his anxiety and anger provided important guidance. Furthermore, he told me he found the experience to be empowering and freeing.

Our capacity to respond skillfully and adequately to any situation is only possible to the extent that we are open to the truth of what's happening, both within ourselves and externally. Full engagement with truth in and of itself requires openness. According to the contemporary spiritual teacher Adyashanti, "When we are completely open—even if it is difficult—we have stopped fighting against life, we have stopped moving against whatever situation we find ourselves in, and there is a possibility for discovery. This is where a great movement of grace can occur."

Paradoxically, opening toward the truth starts with acknowledging our resistance to it, since our resistance is also part of the truth. Resisting our resistance only tightens the knots. Opening to our feelings, however uncomfortable that may be, liberates them. Neuroscientist Jill Bolte Taylor notes that when we pay attention and are fully present to an emotion, its intensity tends to last for about ninety seconds in our body and brain before naturally dissipating, thus enabling the natural flow of life's river to continue unimpeded.[1] An important exception to this is when we get stuck in a looping thought track or a trauma vortex, which requires further work to liberate our life force energy.

Dharvesh's case also highlights how we can learn from the totality of our experience. Had he not consciously explored his anxiety and anger, he might have lashed out and threatened to sue the former investor without ever investigating or preparing a more thoughtful first response. Opening with curiosity to the totality of his experience enabled him to discern the truth and respond effectively.

While staying curious about our own experience is a critical initial step, it's not enough. We also need feedback from our customers, coworkers, investors, friends, and everyone else whose opinions we value. As the ancient text of Jewish sages in the Mishnah states, "Who is wise? One who learns from every human being."

THE SI RESEARCH—AN OPEN EMBRACE OF REALITY

Virtually everyone I interviewed in my spiritual intelligence research observed the importance of opening to reality, to life, to themselves, and to other people. When coupled with curiosity, this openness empowers them to learn what is true and real. Opening to their own experience brings insight, guidance, and confidence, while opening to others engenders vulnerability, deeper trust, and more authentic connections. Their comments on this included the following:

"I practice opening to life itself, to whatever circumstances, person, or situation is in front of me. And with that greater openness to life, every moment and every experience becomes richer, more creative, and full of possibilities for discovery."

"I am actively cultivating feedback from my community on what I can do better as their leader. It sets an example, a tone, and a culture for mutual feedback. It breeds trust and fosters an open atmosphere for interpersonal learning and growth."

"I welcome everything that comes, instead of worrying about what I might think could be a threat. After all, how could reality or truth be a threat?"

"We have been instructed to love God, with all our heart, with all our soul, and with all our might. That's why I love inquiry and discovery. And since all is an expression of the One or of God, then I practice opening to everything as I want to know what is real, what is true— Truth being one of the names of God. Opening to everything includes opening to other people in particular, as all humans are made in the image and likeness of God. This way I open to and accept everything and everyone, myself included, with all our limitations and imperfections. And it brings more reverence, ease, and peace into my life—I am not at war with reality."

We found Openness to contribute significantly to spiritual intelligence and to effectiveness as inspired leaders.

YOUR TURN: GETTING CURIOUS

Practice 1: Turning Inward—Opening to Yourself

Without making any adjustments to your posture or position, simply notice your experience. Allow your body to move toward greater comfort naturally and spontaneously until you've settled into stillness. What are you aware of physically and emotionally now? Is anything surfacing that you were not aware of before? How do you feel about the experience you're having? Are you judging and resisting it or welcoming it with curiosity? Simply notice. If your experience is neutral or positive, open to it further and allow it to deepen, spread, and unfold naturally.

If you're feeling resistance, welcome that too. Try expressing how you feel toward the emotion you're trying to avoid (e.g., "I don't like you," "I wish you weren't here," or "I want you to go away"). Stay with the resistance and notice how your experience shifts. Notice the amount of tightness in your body, as well as any letting go, distractions, emotions, or images that bubble up.

Is the underlying emotion still there? If so, as an experiment, give yourself permission to allow it to be just as it is. With a sense of wonder, you might say something like, "Hello, Sadness. I'm curious to see what you feel like. I'm interested in any messages you have for me. You're welcome to stay here as long as you wish." What happens as you open with wonderment to exploring this, or any other so-called negative emotion? What messages do you receive?

Or if you become aware of a so-called positive emotion such as peace, joy, or pleasure, notice your orientation to it. Do you welcome and allow it fully? How long can you stay open to it? Is there some part of you that believes feeling joy for more than a second is indulgent or that you have more productive things to do?

Continue to track your experience, aware that by its very nature, the ego is threatened whenever you are open and tries to keep control, pushing or pulling, judging or denying—otherwise, it would be out of a job. Also notice how certain emotions are revealed as you find more ease in your body. And notice as you become more present, the more life naturally unfolds with a greater sense of wonderment.

Practice 2: Opening to Others' Feedback

Call to mind a relationship with a team member. Reflect on how it's working for each of you. How do you think the other person feels about your relationship? How much support, guidance, or coaching do they need? How much are they receiving? How much do you care about their perspective and experience?

Notice how it feels to reflect on these questions. Does it strike any nerves you'd rather avoid? Are you open and curious? Disinterested and distracted? Simply notice.

Experiment during your next one-on-one with the person. Once you've connected and established some rapport, express your interest in their perspective on your working relationship. Ask what they feel is working well and what might be improved upon, then sit back in silence and wait for their response. Offer to resume the conversation later if they need more time to reflect. Listen intently to their responses and ask questions as needed to help clarify your understanding. Notice how it feels to hear their feedback. Are you able to remain open and curious, or do you become closed and defensive? If the latter, as most of us do at times, how much are you able to allow the discomfort without trying to control it? How much are you able to disarm it in the moment knowing you can explore it later on your own?

Following the meeting, notice what relational changes may have unfolded between the two of you, such as issues previously kept under the surface that have now been brought to light. Perhaps both of you have learned to work better together. Or a new channel of communication has opened up.

Continue to track your experience. Who knows what other truths might be revealed?

EGOLESSNESS

LETTING GO OF OUR EGOIC IDENTITIES: THE CASE OF JACOB

Jacob's head and shoulders are slumped. "I don't know where to go next with our product," he groans. After successfully selling his first company, Jacob is now facing a dilemma running his second one. Nearly a year after launch, his product's user engagement is minimal despite his world-class team and millions of dollars in investor backing. "I thought I knew how to do this," he laments.

I ask, "Who and what are you if you're not the successful designer with the Midas touch?" Jacob slides down his chair and sighs heavily. I repeat the question. "What do you mean?" he says, sincerely perplexed. I clarify that I'm asking him about his identities. He lists a few, "I'm a father. I'm a husband. I'm a Latin American." After a pause, he adds, "Underneath it all and common to all these is, I'm just a human being."

I suggest he imagine each of his many identities as if they were objects he could hold, then place a few in each hand. "What's that like?" I ask. "It feels good," Jacob responds. "At least I know who I am." After a moment, I invite him to open his hands and toss those identities into the air behind him. He hesitates, takes a deep breath, and, with a sigh and a smile, flings them into the air. We pause for a moment, letting it sink in. Then, I ask, "What remains here now?" He says, "Well, I'm still just here . . . and you are too. We're here together." After another moment, he describes, "There is just this presence, this awareness here. Maybe that's what I really am."

He sits up and makes direct eye contact with me, realizing he's been stuck trying to reconcile his identity as a successful designer with the fact that his product was failing. Once he stopped a preoccupation with his identity, he had more energy and creativity available to help him tackle his product dilemma.

Indeed, when our energy isn't absorbed in maintaining our identities or feeding our ego, desperately shoring up our sense of self-worth, we're far more available to respond to circumstances in fresh, unencumbered ways.[1] Of course, when we shed our identities, they don't vanish permanently. They come back. When we need to show up as a parent or partner or manager, we can honor those roles without merging with them, like putting on certain clothes for an occasion and taking them off when we don't need to wear them. In fact, the word personality comes from the Greek *persona*, meaning "a face mask used to denote a character or a social role." Though any mask, even a positive one, can become limiting. For example, if you're attached to the identity of being smart, you may be reluctant to ask questions you might consider dumb, which will limit what you can learn.

After peeling away our identities, if only for a moment, it becomes clear that the "I am" we can experience as our essential nature is a pure, radiantly alive, and loving consciousness.

THE SI RESEARCH—SURRENDERING TO TRUTH

Every spiritual intelligence research participant I interviewed mentioned the practice of letting go of ego by opening, surrendering, and devoting themselves to a higher calling, which some called the truth, the divine, or their purpose. They reported that the humbler and more spacious they became, the more that greater force flowed through them and guided their lives. In other words, relaxing their identification with their smaller self enables them to expand into their larger self where they can access vastly more resources of energy, creativity, compassion, and wisdom. Their comments on this included the following:

"Part of egolessness means allowing myself to 'not know' in a profound way. I let go of the constant grasping of my egoic conditioned mind, relaxing 'my' self into the greater self. What follows from there is a pure state of immense creativity."

"The word Muslim comes from the root of 'someone who surrendered.' Surrendering my ego, I become a devoted servant, rather than the emperor, a servant of the truth. And paradoxically it empowers me and gives me greater freedom and courage to do what needs to be done as I become less preoccupied with my personal payoff and with what others think of me."

"All the inner work I've done has helped me to get myself out of the way, emptying myself, so that the light can come through me. The light is not mine. I am just a channel, a vehicle. I become humble without giving away my power, surrendering without submitting. That's the source and nature of true power, which enables me to be humble and strong at the same time—surrendered to truth yet not resigned nor passive—proactively doing what needs to be done."

"I just watch when I get contracted, when I'm holding onto my ego, wanting to be right, or wanting something to be different from what it is. And I suffer and I'm dissatisfied. And the faster I can see and release that egoic grip, the more aliveness, ease, and peace there is."

We found Egolessness contributes significantly to spiritual intelligence and to effectiveness as inspired leaders.

BLENDING HUMILITY WITH CONFIDENCE AND DEVOTION

Clients often ask how they can be humble while also remaining confident. To be clear, humility does not imply meekness nor poor self-esteem. C. S. Lewis said it beautifully: "Humility is not thinking less of yourself, but thinking of yourself less." When we're less self-absorbed, it's possible to be wholeheartedly devoted to something larger than ourselves. As Gandhi said, "There comes a time when an individual becomes irresistible, and his action becomes all-pervasive in its effect. This comes when he reduces himself to zero."

Research shows how humility enhances leadership. Surveying over 1,500 workers across the world, leadership researchers Jeanine Prime and Elizabeth Salib published in the *Harvard Business Review* their report "The Best Leaders are Humble Leaders."[2] Furthermore, they found that altruistic leadership predicts employee innovation and responsible team citizenship. Similarly, leadership expert Jim Collins found that leaders who combine humility and fierce resolve, which he calls "Level 5 Leadership," produce the best long-term financial results.[3]

Humility enables holy audacity—or, as some call it, holy chutzpah. Indeed, the Bible considers Moses, who led the Israelites out of Egypt, the humblest human on earth. Yet, he had the courage to confront the pharaoh, the ruler of the greatest empire in the ancient world. Devoted to his mission, Moses even had the audacity to confront God, demanding his people be forgiven, "Forgive their sin—and if not, blot me . . . out of thy book" (Exodus 32:32). No wonder the Israelites followed him.

YOUR TURN: YOUR ESSENTIAL SELF, BEYOND IDENTITIES

Have a pen and notebook ready. Set a timer for four minutes.

Find a comfortable seated position following the INSPIRED protocol (see page 14). Continue breathing naturally with your attention turned inward.

Silently or aloud ask yourself, "Who am I?" Allow all responses to bubble up without censoring or judging them. This might evoke your various identities, such as gender, age, race, or nationality. Or the roles you play: engineer, leader, parent, partner. Give yourself space to be truly authentic and write down your answers.

Repeat the question, "Who am I?" Keep repeating the question and writing your responses until the timer rings.

Now review your list and notice how it feels. Does your list capture who you feel you are, or does it leave something out? Or include something you wish wasn't there? Whatever it is, just let it be.

Next, imagine taking half of the items on your list and placing them in one hand while placing the second half in the other. Let your hands rest on your lap. Simply notice what it feels like to hold all these identities in your hands. Notice your breathing, tension level, and sensations in your chest, throat, arms, and legs. Stay with it for a moment or two, even if it's uncomfortable.

Then take a deep breath, and as you exhale, open your hands and toss all these identities over your shoulder behind you. Notice how light or heavy you feel now? How open or closed? Look around. How has your visual perception changed, if at all? How has your sense of time shifted, if at all? Welcome and be with whatever shows up.

Ask, "Who am I now?" You may have a sense of an essential self that precedes any identities. If so, dwell in the experience of that essential you as long as you can, knowing that your identities will likely return soon enough, and that it's important to be aware of them when they do.

Trying to eliminate the ego entirely is an unrealistic and even undesirable goal. In fact, doing so is yet another egoic ambition—this one to proudly wear a badge of enlightenment. All we need to do is simply notice our ego. In fact, we can even hold it in the embrace of our loving awareness. After all, it is only trying to help us feel good about ourselves, albeit somewhat unskillfully. We naturally disidentify from our ego when we come to see it as but a small part of ourselves and instead recognize the larger field of our loving consciousness. With practice, the ego will relax its grip, and you can remove it as the dominant driver of your life.[4]

SURRENDER AND HUMILITY: DO THEY REALLY CONTRIBUTE TO LEADERSHIP?

Many people I've worked with confuse the idea of resignation with surrender. Resignation comes with a sense of deflation and collapse, often leaving us feeling like we are being held captive by a diminished ego and less available to live to the fullest. In contrast, when we surrender, we submit our ego to something larger than ourselves (e.g., a higher self, the truth, the divine). Released from the cage of self-preoccupation, we feel freer, more open, and available to the fullest life.

By surrendering, we align ourselves with truth, strength, peace, and ease. In fact, holding onto our limited, separate self is a direct denial of our essential and higher self. It disconnects us from our essence, it divides and misaligns us with our higher self, which invariably weakens us.

You may be wondering though why so many successful leaders appear to have oversized egos. The short answer is that successful leaders are still flawed leaders. I've never met one who excels in every dimension—all of us are flawed human beings with our unique mixture of virtues, strengths, as well as shortcomings and opportunities for further growth. For example, Steve Jobs,[5] a powerful and inspirational leader, was notoriously domineering and abusive—not exactly signs of spiritual intelligence. He displayed little regard for others and let nothing stand in the way of his vision. People found him difficult to work with, and in that way, he failed to bring out the best in others. Yet, he was also a passionate, single-minded visionary with a keen eye and appreciation for beauty. Those qualities reflected his spiritual intelligence capacities that were key to his success. The compelling beauty of his vision, along with his devotion to it, inspired and drew others to stick around despite the shadowy aspects of his personality.

It is also worth remembering that sometimes success can go to our heads, inflating our ego and overshadowing some of our SI qualities that got us to be inspirational leaders in the first place. As Bill Gates puts it, "Success is a lousy teacher. It seduces smart people into thinking they can't lose."

YOUR TURN: REFLECTING ON YOUR NONDUAL SELF

First read this exercise from beginning to end.

Next, find a comfortable seated position with your spine straight. Let your feet rest flat on the ground and feel the weight of your body supported by the cushion and the floor under you.

Take a few deep breaths. As you inhale, imagine drawing in each breath from the center of the earth through your feet, legs, pelvis, and up your spine to the crown of your head. On your exhale, imagine releasing it back down into the center of the earth. Repeat this cycle for four to five breaths.

Now, as you inhale, bring the breath only up to the level of your heart, and exhale out through the side of your arms and hands. Repeat this a few times.

Notice how your body feels. Where do you feel relatively relaxed and open? Let your attention gently rest on this sensation. For a moment or two, explore this relative relaxation and openness. Breathe into it and simply feel what it's like. Do you feel a familiar sense of yourself—a "you" that is separate from the openness? Or has that familiar sense of yourself receded? If the latter, what is present instead? What else are you experiencing?

When we're fully absorbed in an experience, even if only for a moment, the sense of a separate self disappears, and we're no longer living in a duality in which we, as subjects, are separate from the object of our awareness. Nondual experiences are often the aim of spiritual practices, yet most people experience them in their everyday lives. Watching a beautiful sunset, reading a captivating book, playing a game, or sensing a flow can captivate us to the point where we feel we disappear and return only as we reflect on the "I" having had the experience.

While most of us do everything possible to preserve and bolster our sense of self, we are in fact most powerful and happy when we allow that self to be absorbed and dissolve into the larger, more encompassing connection to everything else. This may also be happening during flow states in which you are absorbed into your activity and thereby experience the natural well-being of your nondual nature.[6,7] Savor and marinate in it. Because when you do, you're getting a glimpse into your essential being and the source of your power as a leader who can inspire those around you.

CHAPTER 8

UTILIZING YOUR INNER WISDOM

*Listen to the wind, it talks. Listen to
the silence, it speaks. Listen to your
heart, it knows.*
—Native American Proverb

THE WISDOM DIMENSION OF SILEADERSHIP involves
the ability to access your inner knowing and intuitive guidance for insight and enlightened action. It is built on four competencies: Intuition,
Higher-Self, Devotion, and Practice.

- *Intuition*: Utilizing your gut sense and its insights.

- *Higher-Self*: Connecting with and receiving guidance from
  your inner wisdom.

- *Devotion*: Harnessing the power of loyalty for a cause
  greater than yourself.

- *Practice*: Setting times for rejuvenation, self-reflection, and
  the cultivation of desired SI qualities.

INTUITION

LISTENING TO YOUR INTUITION: THE CASE OF ALDO

Aldo, the founder and CEO of a rapidly growing mobile app, takes a seat across from me, his hands trembling. "My depression and muscle spasms have been getting worse this past week, and the doctors can't find anything," he says. "They don't agree, but I think it must be MS."

Aldo has suffered from depression for most of his adult life. As an only child, he was close to his mother, but lived in fear of his father, who would physically abuse them both. His father would tell him he'd never amount to anything while his mother would say he was gifted and destined for greatness. Consequently, he grew up alternating between a sense of worthlessness and grandiosity. Much of his ambition can be traced back to a mostly unconscious desire to prove his father wrong and make his mother proud.

After years of working over eighty hours a week, Aldo has built a billion-dollar company with thousands of employees. Yet, working nonstop has taken a serious toll on him physically and emotionally. To help Aldo relax, I invite him to slow his breath and bring gentle awareness to the tremors he's feeling. Once they subside, I guide him in scanning his body part by part to release more tension. Then, I invite him to open his awareness to sense his body as a whole and the space within and around it.

Once he has found this expanded field of awareness, I invite Aldo to tune into what we might call his intuition. This intuitive part, an "inner doctor," tells him his physical symptoms are likely the result of stress, and that he should see a physician and take a month-long medical leave to recharge.

After repeating this guidance out loud, he tells me he is experiencing an affirming spaciousness in his chest. But, immediately after comes a fear that his business will suffer. I invite his fear to enter a dialogue with his intuition, sharing his concerns and objections so his inner doctor can respond. Eventually, though reluctantly, he musters the courage to follow his intuitive guidance.

Though he had difficulty unplugging completely from work, Aldo took good care of himself during his month off, spending time in nature, exercising regularly, maintaining a healthy diet, and getting plenty of sleep. He also consulted numerous medical experts, but none could find a physical cause for his symptoms. Nonetheless, his mood and symptoms improved, and when he returned to work, he maintained better self-care than before. In addition, while he was away, his team stepped up, and the company performed well. This inspired him to delegate more. Grateful, Aldo continued to practice listening to and developing a rapport with his intuition.

Of course, his muscle spasms didn't alleviate instantly. However, over time, and alongside routine medical checkups, he was able to observe more evidence that his tremors increased with stress, and that with proper rest and healthy habits, they all but disappeared.

While reason has its place, intuition has informed many of the world's greatest discoveries and creations. According to Einstein, "I never came upon any of my discoveries through the process of rational thinking. . . . The intuitive mind is a sacred gift and the rational mind a faithful servant. We have created a society that honors the servant and has forgotten the gift." Steve Jobs concurred, "Intuition is a very powerful thing, more powerful than intellect." And Picasso liked to describe his intuition as a carrier pigeon, never appearing without a message for him.[1]

In my own life, I have found intuition tremendously helpful during the hiring process. Virtually every time I ignored my gut sense about turning away an applicant and proceeded to hire them based on their résumés or strong references, I came to regret it. If nothing else, that gut sense was a powerful warning that merited my further investigation. In this way, intuition is not a substitute for analysis but rather a powerful complementary partner to analytical thinking.

How does intuition work? It's *transrational*, meaning it goes beyond the thinking mind, drawing from the intelligence of the unconscious.[2] In *Blink: The Power of Thinking Without Thinking*, Malcolm Gladwell discusses how our mental processes, even while unconscious, work rapidly and automatically, sometimes with very little visible information. These "blink-of-an-eye" intuitions are routinely used by brilliant decision-makers.[3] Furthermore, the idea of having a gut sense is now supported by scientific discoveries showing that the average gut contains over one hundred million neurons. This makes your stomach a small brain unto itself, constantly in communication with your other two brains: the main brain inside the skull, and the heart-brain, which utilizes over forty thousand neurons itself. In fact, modern research has corroborated the important role the heart plays in receiving, processing, and responding to intuitive information.[4] In that regard, it is no wonder that intuition as a valid decision-making tool is finding more and more prominence and legitimacy in management.[5]

THE SI RESEARCH—TRANSRATIONAL INNER KNOWING

Most of the spiritual intelligence participants I interviewed in my research reported regular use of transrational modes of knowing. To develop their individual intuition, many practiced emptying their narrative mind, which made them receptive to different methods of knowing. They observed that intuition tended to show up as a gut sense and/or a feeling in their chest:

"I can tap into my intuition by stilling and quieting the noise in my mind and emptying myself of all the things I think I know. But I must become an open, receptive channel."

"My intuition comes from my heart, my head, my womb . . . the places in my body that carry the wisdom of my ancestors. It's a deeper, broader knowing than that of my academic degrees. It's more complete knowing because it's informed by various sources of wisdom."

"There is just an inner 'yes' that is beyond thought. I can use my rational mind to explore and investigate it. I find that both contribute in complementary ways."

"One of the ways I tap into the wisdom of my intuition is to listen to my dreams. If there is an issue I am wrestling with, I invite my mind to give me insights through my dreams before I fall asleep. Often, it will result in intriguing dreams that I can then use my intuition to interpret."

We found Intuition contributes significantly to spiritual intelligence and to effectiveness as SILeaders.

YOUR TURN: ACCESSING YOUR INTUITIVE KNOWING

Sit with your spine vertically aligned, feet resting flat on the ground hip-width apart, in a comfortable position that supports both your alertness and relaxation. Take a few deep breaths, letting go of tension as you exhale.

Recall an issue or decision you're wrestling with. Next, without any further analysis nor expectation of an immediate response, gently invite your intuition to shed some light on it.

Then let go of the issue. Then, begin scanning your body from your toes up to your head. Sense your toes while breathing into them, silently stating the words "sensing toes" on your exhale. On your next exhale, silently repeat "toes are relaxing." (Avoid using pronouns or possessive terms, such as "I" or "my," which can activate your egoic mind.)

Next, move your attention to the entirety of your feet and exhale with the statement, "sensing feet." On the following exhale, "feet are relaxing." Repeat this process for each of the following: ankles, knees, hip joints, pelvis, lower belly, diaphragm, chest, shoulders, elbows, wrists, hands, throat, jaws, cheeks, eyes, and brain.

Breathe normally as you focus your attention imagining a blue star of light in the area between your temples, about an inch up from the bridge of your nose. Next, shift your attention to explore the space in the center of your chest. Imagine a tiny North Star there as you tune into that space. Next, sense into your lower belly, imagining a small orange ball of light below your navel. Then feel into the space between your knees. And then into the space between your big toes. Now sense your entire body. Lastly, feel into the space around your body, allowing it all to be there, as much as is in your awareness without strain. Simply notice, listen, and allow.

Now, reconsider the issue you contemplated at the beginning of this exercise. As you do, you might receive some insight into the path forward or the nature of the issue itself. If not, review some possibilities that come to mind, checking in with your body for any sense of a yes or no. A yes usually comes with feeling a softening, relaxing, opening, and sense of expansion. A no often feels like a tensioning and contracting.

If you have questions or feel uncertain, ask your intuition how and why it reached its conclusion. Like exercising a muscle, the more you engage your intuition, the more you get to know how to listen to and trust it.

Over the next few minutes, hours, or days, sit with whatever your intuition did or didn't reveal. Notice whether you're any closer to some sense of clarity or have gained new perspectives or insights. At night, before falling asleep, invite your intuition to provide further insights through your dreams.

This is just one of many techniques to help your body and mind become relaxed, open, and receptive. If you have other methods that you prefer to help you empty your mind, feel free to use them instead. Don't worry if you don't connect to your intuition right away. Like any relationship, it can take time, commitment, and practice. And like any relationship, it can bring immense richness, reward, and guidance.[6]

HIGHER-SELF

TAPPING INTO THE WISDOM OF YOUR FUTURE SELF: THE CASE OF BATYA

Batya taps her foot nervously as she sits facing me in my office. Looking at the ground, she wastes no time explaining her dilemma. "I'm the CEO of my own company! How could I be so intimidated by my own Chief Marketing Officer [CMO]?" Batya's consumer app company had begun to grow rapidly and just recently attracted a large round of financing. Until this point, the company could only afford to give the CMO a part-time contract position, so now that the funding is available, he's been making the pitch to expand his hours at the current relatively high contract rate or to come on full-time with an expensive package. Batya still needs his services at this critical juncture, yet she is not impressed with how he's been performing.

This would have been challenging enough for anyone, but for Batya, who is all of thirty something years, it has an extra charge. She had grown up with an authoritarian father whose angry outbursts scared her. The CMO also bears an uncanny resemblance to her father, which makes her feel even more intimidated and weak.

I invite her to call to mind someone strong and kind. It could be someone she knew personally, a historical figure, or a fictional character. Batya's brow furrows as she tells me no one comes to mind. So, I suggest one of my favorite options—that she connect to her own future aspirational self.

I explain to her how a sense of connection to our future self, a being who has traveled our path longer, ripened with wisdom, and who knows us intimately, can be an immense resource for wisdom and guidance. I start the meditation with the get INSPIRED protocol, then guide Batya in a visualization through a lush meadow, a mysterious forest path, and into a clearing where she meets an older, wiser version of herself.

She drops into the visualization deeply and meets a woman fifteen to twenty years older than her, whom she recognizes as her own future self, and sits across from her on a log. After a moment of silent eye contact, Batya asks this wise woman for advice on how to deal with the intimidating CMO. She learns from her future self that the best thing to do is to tell him that so far, he has not proven himself eligible for the full-time position, and that if he wants to be considered, he needs to demonstrate more capacity and commitment. In the meantime, she needs to be working with a recruiter to search for the best person.

Coming out of this guided meditation, Batya is sitting upright, smiling softly, and filling the room with a warm, calm presence. She describes how inspired and calm she felt around the peaceful, loving, wise, kind, grounded, and strong presence of her future self. Toward the end of our meeting, Batya and I practice informing her current part-time CMO of her stance.

While she still felt some anxiety, she found the courage to confront the man she found so intimidating. The conversation was challenging emotionally, but it ultimately helped Batya claim her power and authority as a leader. In the end, the CMO stepped up his game, but after a thorough search, Batya found a better person for the position.

Batya's relationship with her future self didn't end with that. Having painted this image in her psyche, Batya began calling on her future self periodically whenever she needed some sage advice. As the seed of this vision was already planted in her soul, invoking its image and dialoging with it was like watering the soil to grow and bear fruit. After about six months, Batya told me "the more I call on this powerful, wise, successful future Batya, the more readily accessible she is and the more I start to feel like her now."

JUNGIAN ARCHETYPES AND OUR WISE SELF

The meditation I guided Batya through draws on a practice developed by renowned psychologist Carl G. Jung called active imagination. Through it, you can access what Jung described as the "wise-self" archetypes of the wise old woman and the wise old man. Archetypes are a recurrent character pattern or motif that is universally recognized by people all over the world, regardless of their geography or culture, because it's part of humanity's collective unconscious and hence exists in the psyche of all humans.[1] (Another archetype might be the innocent playful child.) Jung identified the archetype of the wise old woman or the wise old man, who draw their wisdom from the "higher Self"—(Jung capitalized the S). The wise old being shows up in Greek mythology as Athena, in Hindu mythology as Krishna and Saraswati, and more recently as the character of Yoda in *Star Wars*. These energies of the wise person, like all archetypes, dwell in the unconscious until they surface spontaneously in dreams or when we intentionally invite them into the light of consciousness where we can engage their energy and draw on them directly.

With some training and cultivation of the wisdom of this higher self, we can all learn to tap into the force, as Yoda points out. Our higher self is none other than that aspect of our being that it is intimately connected with our divinity, which permeates all existence. Connected to our higher self, we can naturally tap into a vast evolutionary power and intelligence that animates and sustains all of life.

While we can access this inspiration and wisdom through guided meditations, people often find it themselves by spending quiet time in nature. It's readily available whenever our habitual mind can rest, allowing us to openly receive inspiration from the beauty and mystery of life—the sheer creative intelligence that underlies all of existence. Encountering this source, we can access wisdom far greater than our own.

Or, as shown with Batya, the practical and readily available method for accessing the wisdom of our higher self is possible by connecting with our future self. Indeed, research has shown that simply entering a dialogue with the best imagined self we aspire to become increases our resourcefulness, competence, and confidence in the present with a lasting effect, thus helping us realize that future self we envision.[2, 3]

THE SI RESEARCH—TRANSRATIONAL INNER KNOWING

Most of the spiritual intelligence subjects I interviewed for my research spoke of tuning into and calling on the wisdom of their higher self. Like accessing the qualities of Intuition discussed in the previous chapter, these individuals access this wisdom either by quieting their mind and/or by shifting their identity to the larger self through intentional practices. For some, this is achieved by entering an imaginary dialogue with someone they consider wise, like a spiritually mature figure such as the Buddha, Jesus, or the Dalai Lama. Or by asking a divine being they might call God for guidance, even though they can't define nor describe what God is. Their comments included the following:

"I receive wisdom from my higher self by quieting my habitual thinking mind and listening to the whisper of the small, still voice in my heart."

"In difficult moments to gain guidance, I used to imagine a conversation with one of my spiritual teachers, my 'guru.' Over time, I have internalized their wisdom and absorbed their energetic transmission, so I can just tune into that channel, that frequency, which has become my inner guru. It is always alive, present, and available within me."

"My greatest wisdom comes from my 'higher self,' which is my deepest self. It is that sacred spark of the divine that lives in and animates all of us. And it is the intelligence that is responsible for the evolution of our universe and of life. This intelligence is far greater than my own. When I listen and follow it, I am swimming down in the flow of the river of life, as I am aligned with divine will."

"When I can shift my identity from the small egoic self, the separate me, to the larger cosmic organism of which I am but a cell, that some refer to as the capital S Self or God, I naturally take the widest holistic perspective. That is the wisest and best way to serve the greater whole and fulfill the mission and contribute the gifts of my unique individual cell."

We found a deep connection to a higher self contributes significantly to spiritual intelligence and to effectiveness as SILeaders.

YOUR TURN: ACCESSING YOUR WISE-SELF ARCHETYPE THROUGH THE WISDOM OF YOUR FUTURE SELF

Find a comfortable seated position with back support. Leaning back, feel the pressure of the seat cushion behind your spine and heart area. Let yourself release into this support.

Close your eyes and take a couple of moments to get INSPIRED (page 14).

Now, recall a challenge you're facing. Then imagine yourself in a beautiful, lush meadow. As you explore this meadow, notice the plants and animals all around you, the colors, smells, sounds, and temperature and texture of the air on your skin. Meandering to the edge of the meadow, you find a grove of trees and a path through the woods. As you walk down a path, the trees are getting thicker and taller, blocking out the sunlight. Let yourself smell the bark of the trees and hear the crackling of the leaves under your steps. Listen to the birds chirping and the tree branches swaying in the breeze.

Eventually the path leads you to a circular clearing filled with bright sunlight. At the other end of the circle, you see someone across from you approaching the center. It is you, the future person you aspire to become fifteen or twenty years from now. Notice their grounded confidence, strength, and the loving qualities emanating from them. As they get closer, notice the familiar features of your own face and that knowing look in their eyes.

Imagine greeting this future self in a way that feels right to you, making eye contact and acknowledging mutual recognition. Dwell in their presence and feel its impact on you. What is it like? How does your body respond?

Take a seat across from this wise person, perhaps on some rocks, a tree stump, or on the earth, and enter a dialogue with them. You might talk about how it feels to be together. Then, when you're ready, explain your dilemma and ask for their advice. Then simply wait silently for their response.

As they respond, tune in closely and notice how listening feels; perhaps it's like being with an intimate friend. If they can't offer specific solutions, ask them what values and principles to follow as you deal with the situation.

When your conversation comes to a natural end, acknowledge each other, perhaps with a nod or a hug.

As you part ways, imagine each of you walking back to where you came from, tracing your steps, returning on the path through the woods to the meadow where you began.

When you're ready, open your eyes and take notes. What happened for you? What did you hear or feel? How is the experience affecting you now? What might be possible for you with their readily available guidance? How would you like to cultivate this relationship with your future self?

While this may feel like a simple exercise, your relationship to your wise, future self is real because the seed is clearly already planted within you, and your outstanding qualities, at least to some measure, already live inside you. If it's difficult to visualize your future self, pick any person, living or dead, historical or fictional, who embodies the wisdom you aspire to. Over the coming weeks and months, you might want to test this connection further by reaching out. Every encounter you have with your higher self not only provides guidance in the moment, but also supports you in developing wonderful aspects of your nature.

DEVOTION

PLUGGING INTO THE POWER GRID: THE CASE OF DAVE

Dave is the general manager of a business that designs tools for developers to help them work easily across different smartphone platforms. When Apple announced new changes to their platform that would render his product obsolete on the iPhone, it wiped out half of his business overnight. Now, he and his company are facing drastic layoffs, and potentially even closing.

But Dave isn't giving up yet. He recently gathered his executive team at a retreat and, together, they were able to figure out a new direction for their business. Describing it to me during our session, he exclaims, "Apple did us a favor! We now have a much more exciting future than we would've ever had without this crisis." Sweeping his arms open, a radiant smile on his face, he adds, "It's our time to shine."

Before he can continue, I invite Dave to repeat this gesture slowly, asking him to tell me how it feels. He describes his commitment to this new direction and the excitement that arises in him as he envisions their future. When I ask what he feels in his body, he describes energy flowing up his torso and radiating out his chest. After a quiet moment, he says it seems to be coming up from his lower belly, an energetic center martial artists call the "hara."

Focusing on this area, Dave describes how it's filled with brilliant light, growing brighter every moment. Then, he sits up straight and states, "This light seems connected to some kind of larger energy field. They arise together and reinforce each other. It feels like what I imagine 'the Force' from *Star Wars* would be." Plugged into such an immense force field of energy and power, he feels wholeheartedly devoted to actualizing his unit's new vision, giving him a strong sense of meaning and purpose.

Over the next few months, he and his team encountered many roadblocks while implementing their new strategy. At times, his confidence wavered, and he was overtaken with doubt. But eventually, he would recall the compelling power of his vision, imagining potential users enjoying all the benefits of their efforts, and that kept him going. As Dave put it, "I feel a sense of responsibility, like I must go for it, giving it my all. At least I'll never wonder if I did my best. And after all, that's all I can do."

THE SI RESEARCH—LIVING WITH WHOLEHEARTED DEVOTION

Most spiritual intelligence participants I interviewed for my research spoke of the immense power and liberating freedom of living in wholehearted devotion to their purpose, cause, higher self, or to the divine. Their wholeness and alignment with the larger self gives them access to a source of power and wisdom much greater than their individual self. Their comments on this included the following:

"To me, devotion means opening one's heart to feel and express love and commitment to the force of love—which to me is divine. It can also mean loving those around you, like your family. But it really entails maintaining that fundamentally loving approach to all life and ultimately everything in creation. It is a giving of oneself to love. And there is a sense of freedom and liberation that comes with that."

"My yogic Bhakti path of devotion to God involves seeing all reality as an expression of God. And from that perspective, all reality is knit together—made of one sacred fabric. And I naturally want to act, dance, and sing in service to all of it. It is ecstasy."

"'Devotion' means complete dedication to my mission and my work, but without attachment to the outcome. So, I can be wholehearted in my actions while still remaining free and lighthearted in my interactions."

"As my Aikido teacher used to say, when I am connected and in alignment with the center of the universe, then anything that comes at me doesn't stand a chance, because I have the power of the whole universe behind me."

We found Devotion contributes significantly to spiritual intelligence and to effectiveness as inspired leaders.

THE POWER OF DEVOTION: THE CASE OF JAMES

James is a second-time entrepreneur. The first time he was pushed out of his company by the board. He started this one hoping to redeem himself and restore his reputation. For seven years, the strategies he's been applying have worked. The company has grown rapidly, giving him a measure of confidence and financial success.

Unfortunately, a recent tech market meltdown stalled the company's growth, and he's had to defer its IPO. Though still committed to running his business, he's also become enticed by other ideas, including writing a book on leadership.

I invite him to explore what's motivating him to write such a book. He blurts out, "Maybe it's my ego, but I want to use the book to build my personal brand, to tell my story of what happened in my first company and how I was able to do what many thought was impossible with my current company."

When I ask how that motivation feels inside, James reports a sense of contraction and smallness. As we dig deeper into this, he says he also wants to spread his ideas about leadership to help build the kind of world he wants to live in—a free world that rewards entrepreneurship, effort, and skill, and one that encourages responsibility. Then, sitting upright, he adds, "I'd be willing to risk and probably give my life for that world." James's commanding presence now fills the room, a sharp contrast to how small he felt when expressing his first motivation.

The difference between these two sources of motivation was clear: the first came from James's ego, which is inherently small, while the second came from a deeper presence that aligns his essence to the larger force that sustains life. I describe to him how when we tap into that force, we feel strong, grounded, and expanded, imbuing our lives with meaning. And to his comment about being willing to risk his life for his beliefs, I tell him a quote by transformational leadership author Robert E. Quinn: "Until we have something worth dying for, we have nothing worth living for."[1] Next, I invite James to elaborate on what he means by "responsibility."

"I'd like everyone at my company to take on more responsibility and show more initiative in support of our mission," he explains. "After all, we're all part of one company, one community, with a shared mission. Ideally, we all care and feel responsible as part of it."

James's desire to write a book about leadership and to promote responsibility among his employees reflected his own desire to take responsibility for the larger human community we are all a part of. His devotion to this worthy cause was aligned with his highest purpose. This is a clear example of when we are more attuned to what is near and dear to our heart, we feel more aligned and wholesome in our motivations.

In the end, James prioritized seeing his company through to a successful outcome to fulfill his own responsibilities. But with his new clarity about what writing a book could mean to him, he resolved to start taking notes for it along the way, realizing that both seeing his company through and writing his book would fit into his larger purpose.

Staying the course was no easy journey, but his vision of a better world meant so much to him that he was willing to endure the pain and make the sacrifices for what he loved deeply. When we do the same in our own lives, we make that bond sacred. It's interesting that "sacred" and "sacrifice" share a common Latin root: *sacrificium* (sacrifice); *sacr-*, *sacer* (sacred).

YOUR TURN: WHAT IS WORTHY OF YOUR WHOLEHEARTED DEVOTION?

Note that the word "devotion" means "loyalty, love, or care for someone or something," according to the Cambridge dictionary.

Now, take a moment to become INSPIRED (see page 14), quieting your mind and dropping into your presence.

Contemplate the word "devotion." Observe any thoughts, feelings, sensations, or associations, without judgment or censorship, that come to you.

Call to mind an example of someone you think of as devoted, whether to a cause, another person, or a group. What arises in you when you think of them?

Now, think of times when you have experienced devotion. What did it feel like? How did it affect your sense of purpose, energy, clarity, strength, and vision?

Ask yourself if there's anything in your life currently that you love or value enough to be worthy of the pain that your devotion to it may cause you? Anything you might risk your life for?

To consider some possibilities, complete this statement with at least three different answers:

I am devoted to _____.

Notice any differences in how you feel toward certain answers. Do you see any patterns when you feel more contracted versus when you feel more expanded?

While devoting oneself to a cause or a person may sound idealistic, it is also highly practical. In the words of Pedro Arrupe, "Nothing is more practical than finding God, that is, than falling in love in a quite absolute, final way. What you are in love with, what seizes your imagination, will affect everything. It will decide what will get you out of bed in the morning, what you will do with your evenings, how you will spend your weekends, what you read, who you know, what breaks your heart, and what amazes you with joy and gratitude. Fall in love, stay in love and it will decide everything."

PRACTICE

RECHARGED AND ENERGIZED: THE CASE OF ENZO

Enzo arrives in my office with his shoulders pulled up practically to his ears and dark bags under his eyes. He has been working tirelessly for three years, and it shows. Over the past year, his company started running out of money and had to face the prospect of layoffs and possibly shutting down. However, at the last minute, he managed to secure some funding. While he's enormously relieved, he's also under immense pressure to deliver on the projections in his business plan.

Knowing he hasn't taken more than three consecutive days off in years, I encourage Enzo to push the pause button now, post the close of funding and the new sales team kickoff, and then take a vacation. Despite his reluctance, he rents a vacation home on the beach for his family and spends two weeks relaxing and surfing with his daughter.

Fresh from time off, the bags under his eyes are gone. Enzo beams describing the wonderful time he had with his family. With a sparkle in his eyes, he says the sales results for the quarter are better than expected. I invite him to check in with how his body feels: "My lower belly feels full and grounded—like ocean waves." I suggest he apply his surfing skills to those waves. His smile widens. "Not only did the team do great in my absence, I also had some exciting new ideas for how we expand our market footprint and accelerate growth in very cost-effective ways." He continues, "And the last

company all-hands meeting went incredibly well. I was energized
and inspired, and everyone seemed to get jazzed up as well. Hard to
believe, given where we were less than a quarter ago."

Taking time to reflect and renew ourselves has numerous benefits,
including better health, more happiness and creativity, greater problem-solving and visioning skills, and more ability to inspire ourselves
and others. Since research shows how closely creativity is linked to a relaxed, open, and spacious mind, it is no surprise that the vacation helped
Enzo's ingenuity flow. In fact, many successful leaders know the value of
taking time off and changing context. Bill Gates ritualized taking one
week off twice a year to escape to a cabin in the woods. No one visited
him except to deliver food.[1] During his "think week," he read, reflected,
and thought strategically about Microsoft's future.

It's possible to step back and quiet the mind without taking a two-week
vacation or a retreat in the woods. Just spend time outdoors. A Stanford
study comparing sitting inside, walking on a treadmill inside, walking
outside, or being rolled outside in a wheelchair, showed that walking
outside produced the highest level of creativity.[2] Indeed, spending time
in nature not only benefits overall health, but also cognitive and working memory performance.[3] And in *Invent and Wander*,[4] Jeff Bezos, Am-
azon's founder, spoke to how rest and prioritizing sleep were critical to
his ability to make high-quality decisions, adding, "I need eight hours. I
think better. I have more energy. My mood is better."

Abundant research shows that regular breaks don't just support leadership, they also generate performance benefits, including greater productivity and effectiveness at all levels in the organization,[5] not only
for knowledge workers,[6] but also across a wide spectrum of other jobs.[7]
Regular breaks have been shown to improve job satisfaction, life satisfaction, and mental health.[8] Doing so is even more practical when you
see your primary role as an SILeader is to inspire others, and that's
directly tied to the quality of the energy, vigor, vision, and passionate
devotion you radiate.

THE SI RESEARCH—PRACTICE AS A WAY
OF LIFE

Virtually every spiritual intelligence participant I interviewed for my research reported they engaged in practices to develop their consciousness and embodiment of spiritual qualities. They described taking time to open to and align with the sacred through a wide range of activities, including setting aside daily and weekly periods for meditation, prayer, contemplation, silence, study, yoga or tai chi, and being in nature. Their comments on this included the following:

"Every single day, rain or shine, I do my meditation practice. . . . I sometimes meditate indoors or hike with my partner, as a walking awareness meditation. And at the end we sit on the grass and share our appreciation for the beautiful world around us. Seated there supported by Mother Earth, appreciating the beauty of nature that I'm surrounded by, there's a devotional loving energy that spontaneously arises in my heart."

"There were periods of intensive three-month meditation retreats, then integrating them with my life, then going back in for another three months. That was in the early years. Now it's much more a part of my life and less like something special. So, life is my main practice—seeing the divine in all."

"I regularly stop and experience the sun setting, and I contemplate it in its beauty and all different aspects of its colors as it shines through the horizon, the sky, and the clouds. It deepens my experience of beauty and awe, which nourishes my spirit and opens me up."

"It's an ongoing practice of coming into presence—asking where am I now, what's happening within and around me, and what am I doing with myself? How does it help, how does it align with my intention, or what purpose does it serve? Am I making the world a little safer, a little kinder? Am I having a positive impact on those I encounter, be it in big or small ways?"

We found Practice contributes significantly to spiritual intelligence and to effectiveness as SILeaders.

WE ARE WHAT WE PRACTICE

The English word *practice* has two main dictionary definitions: a rehearsal for a future performance, or our work or a vocation, as, for example, a doctor who practices family medicine, is also performing such. In this sense practice, work, and life are one and the same, an art form that expresses our unique, authentic self.

Interestingly in Hebrew, the word for practice is *emun*, which shares a root with *emuna*, meaning faith or trust, and *eomanute* (art). This highlights the connection between practice and the cultivation of faith since building and maintaining trust is not a one-time event but an ongoing practice and a way of living, which is an art form. It reminds us that all is okay since we have survived whatever challenges the universe has presented so far, and thus gives us hope things will be okay in the future, regardless of any difficulties we may be experiencing in the moment. Indeed, the practice of seeing all as expression of one divine reality leads to the cultivation of trust.

Though it may seem more complex than, say, practicing to develop your basketball or public speaking skills, developing your SILeadership qualities uses the same process. After all, we become what we practice. Practice kindness, and we become kind; practice generosity and gratitude, and we become generous and grateful. So, if you want to know what you practice at, look at who you are. The trick is to be intentional about what we practice so we may become the person we aspire to be.

For example, ever since I started spending at least two hours a day doing physical and spiritual exercises, I've experienced vast improvements in my health, well-being, productivity, and creativity, as well as in my spiritual growth, which further supports my wellness. When I am tempted to skip my meditation practice, I remind myself of Gandhi's words, "I'm so busy today, that I'm going to meditate two hours instead of one." Productivity and effectiveness, especially for leaders, has less to do with the number of hours we work than with the quality of our presence and inspiration.

WHAT SHALL WE PRACTICE?

In addition to the INSPIRED protocol that I use at various times during the day, I have a daily routine that almost always includes physical exercise, energy work like yoga and qigong, prayer, and meditation. The benefits of physical exercise are self-evident. Yoga and qigong help me feel centered, open, and balanced, harmonizing the polarities of the yin and yang, the sky and earth energies within me. The benefits of meditation are backed by an exploding body of research for health, well-being, and spiritual development.[9] And a smaller yet growing body of research highlights the benefits of prayer.[10, 11, 12, 13]

In my own prayer practice, as in any relationship, I find it important to start with gratitude for what I've been given. I also include reverence for the beauty and mystery of existence, which invokes the experience of awe with its many benefits.[14, 15, 16] Then I might petition for peace or healing for myself and/or others. Whether my requests are granted or not, the very act of prayer facilitates peace and healing in my heart. And it nourishes my soul by connecting me to the mystery and benevolent presence much greater than my individual self.

After praying I shift into silent meditation and simply listen, receiving anything the divine communicates back. This opens me to recognize and receive every expression of reality as sacred. And rather than making me feel passive, this receptivity gives me a greater sense that I am a part of the One Infinite Life, along with a responsibility to play my unique instrument in the greater symphony of creation.

In addition to open and receptive listening described above, I also practice other meditation techniques that focus on cultivating specific qualities, like compassion, peace, and joy—though many of these qualities overlap since embodying one will naturally invoke and support the others. It is also worth noting that the qualities I have focused on have tended to shift over time. For example, finding my true calling was a major focus at one point in my life, while now I feel clear and devoted to that purpose, so I have shifted greater attention to cultivating my devotional love, joyful service, humility, and patience.

Maintaining a regular practice requires strong motivation, steadfast intention, and ongoing commitment and discipline. But the payoffs are well worth it. In addition to whatever specific qualities we want to develop, practicing in and of itself cultivates the essentials of intention, commitment, and discipline for application to other aspects of our life.

YOUR TURN: WHAT IS YOUR PRACTICE?

Reflect on and write down a list of what you are currently practicing in your life physically, mentally, emotionally, and/or spiritually—both deliberately and unconsciously. Consider what impact each has on your life. Reflect on how you feel before and after your deliberate practices.

Use the INSPIRED practice on page 14 and recall your highest aspiration and/or deepest longing. Accept that your answer may naturally shift over time. Is it the same now as when you asked yourself this question before in a previous chapter, or has it shifted?

Next, consider what you could practice to get you closer to who you would like to be. Notice what it's like to simply be with and feel your deepest heart's desire in this moment. How does the energy of this yearning move within you? What does it call forth?

How devoted do you feel toward this aspiration? How strong or passionate is your desire? How loyal or committed are you?

What are you willing to do to realize your deepest yearning? What daily, weekly, monthly, or annual practices would support your journey of reaching for this aspiration?

It is important to start small so you can enjoy the rewards of your practice and build confidence in staying the course, slowly moving toward greater commitment and building new habits as you go. Even just pausing and meditating for two minutes a day can have a profound impact over time. Or, one of the most powerful practices I've found and that you can try, is daily gratitude—listing five things you're grateful for before going to sleep. You might also try following the INSPIRED protocol once or twice during your day between meetings. Whatever you choose, try it for a week and notice how it affects you.

As you practice and develop your spiritual intelligence and SILeadership capacities, you and your world will gradually change. In the words of Vivienne Westwood, "It's a philosophy of life. A practice. If you do this, something will change, what will change is that you will change, your life will change, and if you can change you, you can perhaps change the world."

May you reach for the summit of your highest aspirations and the fulfillment of your heart's deepest desires, and may you enjoy your journey and all the practices along the way. Thank you for including me along your path. I hope our time together has in some measure inspired you. For when you're inspired, you invariably inspire others, which further feeds your spirit and uplifts the world. There is no greater lasting fulfillment, power, privilege, or joy.

THE JOURNEY IS THE REWARD

If there is righteousness in the heart, there is beauty in the character. If there is beauty in the character, there will be harmony in the home. If there is harmony in the home, there will be order in the nations. When there is order in the nations, there will be peace in the world.
—Confucius

LEADERSHIP AS A CRUCIBLE FOR HEALING AND GROWTH: THE CASE OF TED

WHEN TED AND I FIRST met nearly nine years ago, he was bordering on clinical depression. After raising millions of dollars from investors, his company had failed to meet their expectations, and he was forced to lay off 20 percent of the workforce. Ted believed he had failed everyone, and the shame weighed on him heavily, affecting his productivity, his family life, and his sense of self-worth.

Now, all these years later, I see a changed man. He is beaming with pride and gratification during our session, having just returned from visiting his kids at college, where he was excited to see them doing so well on their own. He describes how he has, most recently, finally grown comfortable proclaiming to his employees that he loves them at company-wide meetings. And he tells me how, while they might have found it a little odd at first, they have learned to appreciate and receive his sincerity.

Ted has even more good news. He shares that he is ready to move on from his role as CEO now that his company has been public for over three years. He's just celebrated his fifty-second birthday and wants to travel for a while with his wife. Ted is unsure of what he'll do when he returns. It could be launching another start-up, or finding a new CEO gig, or even focusing his energy on the public sector. He recalls how nine years ago his goal was to reach a net worth of $20 million, which he felt would allow him to focus on nonprofit work. Now, with a net worth several times over that mark, he tells me, "I have more than enough, and I'm ready to give back."

He also tells me how, despite the stress he'd faced at the time, he is happy that he didn't sell his company a few years before when he had the opportunity. He says it was a hard decision, especially since he could have cashed out and achieved his financial target much sooner. But he adds that he'd grown a deep fondness for his team and building a company culture aligned with his values, and that was more important than selling his stake at that time. He recalls how frightening it was when he wasn't sure if his company would even survive after that. Yet he learned to find his power by confronting those fears, listening to their messages, and moving forward with courage.

Ted and I start to reflect on his journey from the first day we met and how he went from feeling like an abject failure to becoming a confident SILeader. How listing five specific things he's grateful for at the end of each day and how resuming his daily exercise routine, slowly but surely, has helped him deal with depression and have a foothold in some well-being. And how this success gave him the inner resources to delve more substantively into the feelings of inadequacy he'd had since he was a boy.

As our session ends, he recounts, "My friends often say to me, 'I have known you for ten or more years, and you feel so different now. What's changed?' I never know how to answer. It hasn't been a momentary epiphany, though I've had a few of those, but more of a slow, gradual, and consistent growth, which has really been the best part . . . though certainly challenging and scary at times. It's impacted all aspects of my life—not just my work, my leadership, and my company, but also all my relationships, including with my family, my wife, and my kids. While I'm far from perfect and have a long way to go, there's just a lot more openness, connection, and love."

In Chapter 2 we also discussed how Ted had visualized his company hitting all their targets for the year and reporting on their success at a company-wide celebration. And that after experiencing the power of his process, how Ted had started visioning with his team to help them fulfill their potential as well. The power of intention also played a significant role in his journey. As discussed in Chapter 6, before each important meeting, Ted would clarify his intention to be present and deliberate in his interactions. He found this to be impactful in his business dealings, as well as at family dinners. He also started to meditate—first only occasionally, but, over time, as he learned to enjoy its effect on his ability to be present, his practice became more consistent. This strongly supported our work together, helping him be in touch with himself and with the core of his being where his true source of power and strength ultimately lies.

Through it all, Ted practiced and developed trust in himself and in the unfolding of life. "Most importantly, it's been a journey of personal growth," he told me. Indeed, throughout our years of working together, not only did he cultivate SILeadership qualities, he did so while facing his demons.

One of those demons revealed itself about eighteen months into our work together, when he was recounting a difficult interaction with a loud, aggressive board member. As I listened, I felt as if the Ted I knew had disappeared. His breathing became shallow. He paused mid-sentence and started gasping for air. He suddenly looked like a young boy holding back tears. The confrontation with the board member had triggered a memory of being molested as a young boy by a priest—an event Ted had never shared with anyone before. I referred him to a specialist in early childhood sexual abuse, and, with the specialist's support, he was able to finally face many layers of his trauma. Simultaneously, he and I continued to work on ways to maintain healthy boundaries with the aggressive board member, and to cultivate an environment where disagreements could be aired with respect.

The work of becoming an SILeader will reveal anything in our way, which inevitably includes our deepest, most buried wounds and secrets. Nearly everyone I have met and worked with carries some trauma. We might have experienced a disturbing event like a fire, a car accident, or an attack. Or the trauma may have been chronic like from poverty, bullying, neglect, parental alcoholism, or poor parental boundaries. We may even hold trauma from our ancestors who were refugees or survivors of genocide. And we are all exposed to the collective traumas of sexism, racism, ageism, homophobia, ecocide, and our disconnection from nature and from our sense of the sacred.

Often our natural responses to these are to put up walls and shut down the sensitivity of our hearts to avoid danger and pain. Such survival strategies, as essential as they may have been at the time, can end up stifling our life force and limiting our access to human connection and love.

Ted is typical of many of the leaders I have worked with. Their journeys are crucibles for transformation, with every apparent obstacle providing an opportunity for healing and growth. The journey is never a walk in the park. It requires a growth mindset that relies on and supports resilience and perseverance. To quote Lord Jonathan Sacks, "Leadership at its highest level transforms those who exercise it and those who are influenced by it. The great leaders make people better, kinder, nobler than they would otherwise be. That was the achievement of Washington, Lincoln, Churchill, Gandhi and Mandela."

Such exemplars all practiced the art of leadership—taking responsibility first for their own growth, and then for realizing their purpose, mission, and vision through others. For without actualizing our own higher potential, we have no hope of inspiring others to actualize theirs. And, as the Talmud says, "Greater is one who causes others to do good than one who does good himself." Fortunately, as SILeaders, we are called to do both.

Like Ted's, like yours, and like mine, all our journeys are not complete until the moment of our death. As you continue on your path, remember that your life and journey, like every human life and journey, is a sacred hero's journey—a journey of your soul's essence trying to express its highest potential for the good, the true, and the beautiful. May you enjoy the travels. And, while holding your highest potential in mind, please also remember to be kind and patient with yourself. As the renowned spiritual teacher Ram Dass once said, "I've been on the path fifty years and experienced spiritual highs and spiritual lows. But I always returned to the only effective means to bring love and peace into this world: Serve others as you would yourself."

SUMMARY OF SILEADERSHIP COMPETENCIES

1. MOBILIZING MEANING:

- *Purpose*: Identify and maintain focus on the deeper values and mission that drive you and your organization.

- *Service*: Answer the question, "Why are we here?" Articulate how your work and organization serve needs and add value to those around you and to the world.

- *Vision*: Painting a detailed and compelling picture of the future.

- *Reframing Difficulties into Opportunities*: Finding meaning in adversity and setbacks. Relating to them as opportunities for growth and learning.

2. INTERACTING WITH GRACE:

- *Trust*: Inspiring confidence, optimism, and hope for the future in yourself and in others.

- *Beauty*: Recognizing the sparkle of life's creative intelligence that shines through, in, and around us.

- *Joy*: Radiating delight and bringing lighthearted playfulness, humor, and celebration to your engagements.

- *Gratitude*: Appreciating ourselves, the people, the learning, and all the gifts we receive along the way.

3. BECOMING INNER-DIRECTED:

- *Centeredness*: Staying grounded and openhearted amid chaos.

- *Integrity*: Standing firmly in alignment with your values.

- *Confidence*: Expressing your unique whole self with ease.

- *Freedom*: Playing in the realm of limitless possibilities.

4. CULTIVATING COMMUNITY:

- *Connectedness*: Fostering a web of relationships based on mutual empathy, compassion, and shared values and purpose.

- *Synthesis*: Finding common ground and integration among conflicting viewpoints by adopting a wider, more inclusive view.

- *Holism*: Viewing situations through a holistic "systems perspective."

5. SHOWING UP WITH AUTHENTIC PRESENCE:

- *Attention*: Being focused on and present with who and what is in front of as well as within you.

■ *Intention*: Bringing awareness and clarity of purpose to your engagements.

■ *Empowerment*: Sourcing, embodying, and expressing grounded personal power.

■ *Passion*: Emanating vigor, aliveness, and wholehearted devotion to your purpose.

6. MOTIVATING BASED ON TRUTH:

■ *Openness*: Embracing yourself and other people with receptive curiosity and wonder.

■ *Egolessness*: Cultivating humility and devotion to the truth.

7. UTILIZING YOUR INNER WISDOM:

■ *Intuition*: Utilizing your gut sense and its insights.

■ *Higher-Self*: Connecting with and receiving guidance from your inner wisdom.

■ *Devotion*: Harnessing the power of loyalty for a cause greater than yourself.

■ *Practice*: Setting times for rejuvenation, self-reflection, and the cultivation of SI qualities.

EMOTIONAL INTELLIGENCE AND SPIRITUAL INTELLIGENCE: WHAT'S THE DIFFERENCE?

WHILE THERE IS SOME OVERLAP between emotional intelligence (EI) and spiritual intelligence (SI), they are distinct, as both contribute to our functioning and well-being in complementary and unique ways. Emotional intelligence is usually understood as the ability to draw on emotional resources, be aware of and regulate our emotions, and accurately perceive and modulate the effect we have on others. Paralleling EI, SI is the ability to draw on spiritual resources and embody qualities from the world's spiritual and wisdom traditions to enhance functioning and well-being.

We can expect some overlap between the two based purely on how they are defined. For example, EI involves awareness of one's feelings and emotions, which relates to the SI capacity for mindfulness. Like EI, mindfulness as an SI capacity requires awareness of thoughts, feelings, and bodily sensations, but it goes farther than EI to include the desire to discover all of oneself—both the light and the dark aspects of our psyche. Similarly, EI's emotional self-regulation overlaps SI's capacity for equanimity. Yet equanimity goes deeper than emotional self-regulation by including the capacity for maintaining inner peace in the face of chaos.

Indeed, SI encompasses capacities far beyond the strictly interpersonal range of emotional intelligence. SI includes the capacity for transcendence and holism, experiences of oneness, and the ability to utilize post-rational modes of consciousness such as intuition and synthesis, among others. However, some EI competencies such as the capacity to influence emotions in others sit more squarely in its domain.

Although EI and SI may have some unique domains, some correlation between the two can occur, depending on the definitions, models, and measures used. For example, some authors include resilience and optimism in their EI models, capacities that can be closely aligned with the SI capacity of trust.[1, 2, 3, 4, 5] In my research, self-reported EI and SI showed a moderate correlation: R-Squared=0.27, which means that 27 percent of the variance of each may be explained by the other.[6] Other research, using different models and measures, also found a moderate correlation (R-Squared=0.4).[7]

SI has demonstrated incremental predictive validity relative to EI and other constructs, contributing to positive outcomes beyond what can be accounted for by emotional intelligence alone.[8, 9] Specifically, SI provides incremental predictive validity for leader effectiveness even after controlling for EI. Conversely, EI provides incremental predictive validity after controlling for SI. Incremental predictive validity going both ways suggests that the two constructs are distinct and complementary—both discretely contributing to work performance.[10, 11] While controlling for one, the other makes a distinct and valuable contribution to well-being, functioning, and leadership effectiveness.[10, 11]

SPIRITUAL INTELLIGENCE DOMAINS AND CAPACITIES

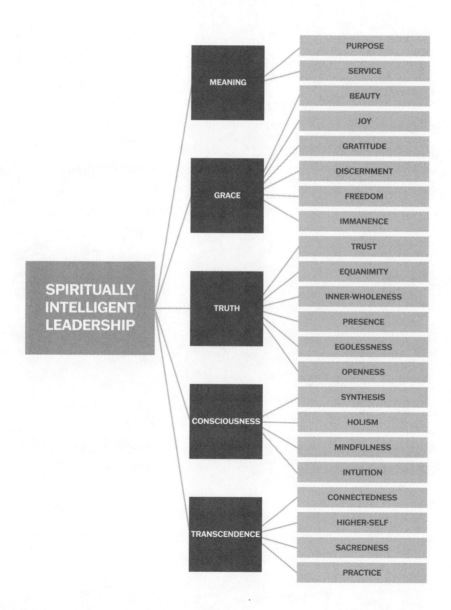

SPIRITUAL INTELLIGENCE AND HOW IT TRANSLATES INTO LEADERSHIP

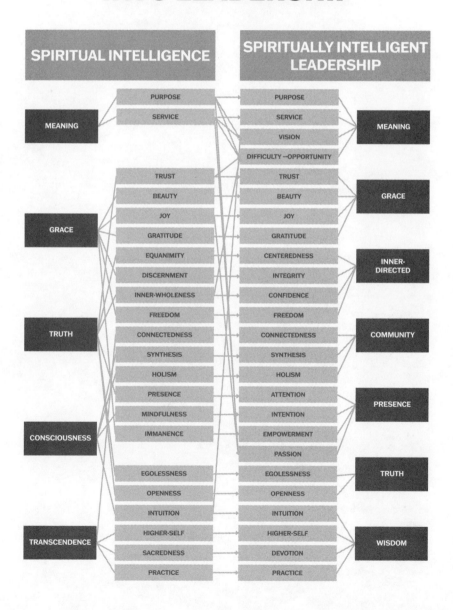

ENDNOTES

INTRODUCTION

1. *The Self-Aware Universe: How Consciousness Creates the Material World* by Amit Goswami (1993). NY, New York, Penguin Group.

2. *A First-Rate Madness: Uncovering the Links Between Leadership and Mental Illness* by Nassir Ghaemi (2012). NY, New York, Penguin Group.

3. *Rewiring the Corporate Brain: Using the New Science to Rethink How We Structure and Lead Organizations* by Danah Zohar (1997). Oakland, CA, Berrett-Koehler.

4. The Seven Dimensions of Spiritual Intelligence: An Ecumenical Grounded Theory by Yosi Amram. Paper published at the 115th Annual (August 2007) Conference of the American Psychological Association, San Francisco, CA. Available at Intelligensi.com/spiritual_intelligence/.

5. Effects of Top Turkish Managers' Emotional and Spiritual Intelligences on Their Organizational Financial Performance by Evren Ayranci (2012). *Business Intelligence Journal, 4*(1), 9–36.

CHAPTER 1: IGNITING YOUR SPARK, MAPPING YOUR JOURNEY

1. An Invented Life: Reflections on Leadership and Change by Warren Bennis (1994). Cambridge, MA: Basic Books.

2. Authentic Leadership: Rediscovering the Secrets to Creating Lasting Value by Bill George (2003). San Francisco, CA: Jossey-Bass.

3. The Seven Transformations of Leadership by Rooke, D., & Torbert, W.R. (2005). *Harvard Business Review*, 83(4): 66–76.

4. Level 5 Leadership: The Triumph of Humility and Fierce Resolve by Jim Collins (2001). *Harvard Business Review*, 79(1), 66–76.

5. *Primal Leadership: Unleashing the Power of Emotional Intelligence* by Daniel Goleman, Richard Boyatzis, & Annie McKee (2013). Boston, MA: Harvard Business Review Press.

6. *Conscious Leadership: Elevating Humanity Through Business* by John Mackey, Steve McIntosh& Carter Phipps (2020). New York: NY: Penguin Random House.

7. *Servant Leadership: A Journey into the Nature of Legitimate Power and Greatness* by Robert Greenleaf (2002). Mahwah, New Jersey: Mattist Press.

8. How Leaders Inspire: Cracking the Code by Bain & Company (2016). Available at: https://www.bain.com/insights/how-leaders-inspire-cracking-the-code/.

9. Among the main spiritual traditions and paths I draw on are the Diamond Approach, mystical Judaism and Kabbalah, Buddhism, Christianity, Sufism, Kundalini Yoga, Advaita Vedanta, and the indigenous earth-based traditions.

10. The main schools of therapy I use in my practice are psychodynamic object relations theory, Jungian psychology, Psychosynthesis, Gestalt therapy, Internal Family Systems, Hakomi, Somatic Experiencing, Acceptance and Commitment Therapy, Existential Humanistic psychology, and the field of positive psychology.

11. *The 8th Habit: From Effectiveness to Greatness* by Stephen Covey (2004). New York, NY: Simon and Schuster (p. 53).

12. The Contribution of Emotional and Spiritual Intelligences to Effective Business Leadership by Yosi Amram (2009). (Doctoral dissertation, Institute of Transpersonal Psychology (Sophia University), Palo Alto, CA. Available at Intelligensi.com/inspirational_leadership/.

13. Validating the Persian Integrated Spiritual Intelligence Scale Within and Islamic Context by Khodadady, E., Taheryan, A., & Tavakoli, A. (2012). *Ilahiyat Studies: Journal on Islamic and Religious Studies, 3(2)*.

14. Adaptation of the Integrated Spiritual Intelligence Scale into Turkish by Soylemez, A., Koc, M., & Soylemez, B. (2016). *Journal of Family Counseling, and Education, 1(1)*, 18–24.

15. The Impact of Spiritual Intelligence, Gender and Educational Background on Mental Health Among College Students by Pant, N. & Srivastava, S. K. (2019). *Journal of Religion & Health* (58), 87–108.

16. What is the Relationship Between Spiritual Intelligence and Job Satisfaction Among MA and BA Teachers? by Yahyazadeh-Jeloudar, S., & Lotfi-Goodarzi, F. (2012). *International Journal of Business and Social Science*, 3(8).

17. The Relationship Between Spiritual Intelligence and Work Satisfaction Among Leaders and Employees by Koražija, M., Žižek, S. Š., & Mumel, D. (2016). *Our economy*, 62(2), 51–60.

18. The Impact of Spiritual Intelligence on Work Performance: Case Studies in Government Hospitals of East Coast of Malaysia by Rani, A. A., Abidin, I., & Hamid, M. R. (2013). *The Macrotheme Review*, 2(3), 46–59.

19. Spiritual Intelligence and Resilience Among Christian Youth in Kerala by Narayanan, A., & Jose, T. P. (2011). *Journal of the Indian Academy of Applied Psychology*, 37(2), 263–268.

20. Effects of Ethnicity and Spiritual Intelligence in the Relationship Between Awe and Life Satisfaction Among Chinese Primary School Teachers by Liu, Z., Li, X., Jin, T., Xiao, Q., & Wuyun, T. (2021). *Frontiers in Psychology*, 12, 2719.

21. Malik, M. S., & Tariq, S. (2016). Impact of Spiritual Intelligence on Organizational Performance. *International Review of Management and Marketing*, 6(2), 289–297.

22. Effects of top Turkish managers' emotional and spiritual intelligences on their organizational financial performance by Evren Ayranci (2012). *Business Intelligence Journal*, 4(1), 9–36.

23. The Intelligence of Spiritual Intelligence: Making the Case by Yosi Amram (2022). *Religions*, 13:1140. Available at: https://www.mdpi.com/2077-1444/13/12/1140.

CHAPTER 2: MOBILIZING MEANING

INSPIRING SERVICE

1. Connecting Prosocial Behavior to Improved Physical Health: Contributions for the Neurobiology of Parenting by Stephanie Brown & Michael Brown (2015). *Neuroscience & Behavioral Reviews 15*, 1–17.

2. Volunteering is Associated with Delayed Mortality in Older People: Analysis of the Longitudinal Study of Aging by Alex H. S. Harris, & Carl E. Thoresen (2005). *Journal of Health Psychology*, 10(6), 739–752.

3. Rudimentary Sympathy in Preverbal Infants: Preference for Others in Distress by Yasuhiro Kanakogi , Yuko Okumura, Yasuyuki Inoue, Michiteru Kitazaki, & Shoji Itakura (2013). *PLOS ONE, 8*(6).

4. *The Origin of Virtue: Human Instincts and the Evolution of Cooperation by* Matt Ridley (1998). New York, NY: Penguin Books.

5. Ethics + Stakeholder Focus = Long-Run Shareholder Profits: Torrey Project's Evaluation of the Financial Performance of Highly Ethical Companies and Stakeholder-Focused Companies by David J. Ferran and Kathy Sperry. (2019). https://www.torreyproject.org/post/ethics-stake-holder-focus-greater-long-run-shareholder-profits.

ARTICULATING VISION

1. Representation, Pattern Information, and Brain Signatures: From Neurons to Neuroimaging by Philip A. Kragel, Leonie Koban, Lisa Feldman Barrett, & Tor D. Wager (2018). *Neuron 99*(2), 257–273.

CHAPTER 3: INTERACTING WITH GRACE

TRUST

1. Putting Feelings Into Words: Affect Labeling As Implicit Emotion Regulation by Jared B. Torre & Matthew D. Lieberman (2018). *Emotion Review, 10*(2), 116–124.

2. *Your Resonant Self: Guided Meditations and Exercises to Engage Your Brain's Capacity for Healing* by Sarah Peyton (2017). New York, NY: W.W. Norton & Company.

3. The Neuroscience of Trust by Zak, P.J. (2017). *Harvard Business Review, 95*(1), 84–90.

BEAUTY

1. Shinrin-Yoku (Forest Bathing) and Nature Therapy: A State-of-the-Art Review by Margaret M. Hansen, Reo Jones, & Kirsten Tocchini(2017). *International Journal of Environmental Research and Public Health,* 14(8), 851.

JOY

1. Ideas Are Born in Fields of Play: Toward a Theory of Play and Creativity in Organizational Settings by Charalampos Mainemelis, & Sarah Ronson (2006). *Research in Organizational Behavior, 27,*81–131.

2. *The Book of Doing: Everyday Activities to Unlock Your Creativity and Joy* by Allison Arden (2012). New York, NY: Penguin Group.

3. *The Progress Principle: Using Small Wins to Ignite Joy, Engagement, and Creativity at Work* by Steven Kramer, & Teresa Amabile (2011). Boston, MA: Harvard Business Review Press.

4. *Playfulness: Its Relationship to Imagination and Creativity* by Nina Liberman (1977). New York, NY: Academic Press.

5. Consequences of Play Deprivation by Stuart L. Brown (2014), *Scholarpedia, 9*(5).

6. Well Played: The Origins and Future of Playfulness by Gwen Gordon (2014). *American Journal of Play, 6*(2), 234–266.

7. The Adult Playfulness Scale: An Initial Assessment by Mary Ann Glynn & Jane Webster (1992). *Psychological Reports, 71*,83–103.

8. Ideas Are Born in Fields of Play: Toward a Theory of Play and Creativity in Organizational Settings by Andrea B. Horn, Andrea C. Samson, Anik Debrot, & Meinrad Perrez (2019). *Journal of Social and Personal Relationships 36*(8): 2376–2396.

9. A Short Humorous Intervention Protects Against Subsequent Psychological Stress and Attenuates Cortisol Levels Without Affecting Attention by Eva Froehlich, Apoorva R. Madipakkam, Barbara Craffonaraet, al (2021). *Scientific Reports 7284*(11).

10. *Why Humor Enhances Creativity From Theoretical Explanations to an Empirical Humor Training Program: Effective "Ha-Ha" Helps People to "A-Ha,"* by Ching-Hui Chen, Hsueh-Chih Chen, & Anne M Roberts (2019). In *Creativity and Humor: A volume in Explorations in Creativity Research*, edited by Sarah R. Luria, John Baer, and James C. Kaufman (pp. 83–108). Cambridge, MA: Academic Press.

11. Psychological Studies of the Relationship of Sense of Humor to Creativity and Intelligence: A review by Graeme Galloway (2006). *European Journal of High Ability 5*(2), 133–144.

GRATITUDE

1. Extending the Tradition of Giving Thanks: Recognizing the Health Benefits of Gratitude by Grif Alspach (2009). *Critical Care Nurse, 29*(6): 12–18.

2. Exploring Neural Mechanisms of the Health Benefits of Gratitude in Women: A Randomized Controlled Trial by Laura I. Hazlett, Mona Moieni, Michael R. Irwin, et al. (2021). *Brain, Behavior, and Immunity,* 95: 444–453.

3. The Relationship Between Gratitude and Loneliness: The Potential Benefits of Gratitude for Promoting Social Bonds by Andrea Caputo (2015). *Europe's Journal of Psychology,* 11(2): 323–334.

4. Gratitude as a Psychotherapeutic Intervention by Robert A. Emmons, & Robin Stern (2013). *Journal of Clinical Psychology,* 69(8): 846–855.

5. Thank You for Voting: Gratitude Expression and Voter Mobilization by Costas Panagopoulos (2011). *The Journal of Politics*, 73(3): 707–717.

CHAPTER 4: BECOMING INNER-DIRECTED
CENTEREDNESS

1. *How Leaders Inspire: Cracking the Code* by Bain & Company (2016). Available at: https://www.bain.com/insights/how-leaders-inspire-cracking-the-code

INTEGRITY

1. Integrity and Leadership: A Multi-Level Conceptual Framework by Michael E. Palanski & Francis J. Yammarino (2009). *The Leadership Quarterly*, 20, 405–420.

2. How Leadership and Integrity Affect Employee Performance With Organizational Commitment by Sabil Sabil, Lukman Hakim, Andi Martias, et al (2021). *Journal of Industrial Engineering & Management Research*, 2(5), 164–172.

3. How Leaders Inspire: Cracking the Code by Bain & Company (2016). Available at: https://www.bain.com/insights/how-leaders-inspire-cracking-the-code/.

CONFIDENCE

1. *Radical Acceptance: Embracing Your Life with the Heart of a Buddha* by Tara Brach (2004). New York, NY: Bantam Books.

2. *Psychosynthesis: A Collection of Basic Writings* by Roberto Assagioli (1965). Amherst, MA: Hobbs Dorman & Co.

3. *Subpersonalities: The People Inside Us* by John Rowan (1990). New York, NY: Routledge.

4. *Somatic Internal Family Systems Therapy: Awareness, Breath, Resonance, Movement, and Touch in Practice* by Susan McConnell, & Richard Schwartz (2020). Berkeley, CA: North Atlantic Books.

5. From Reality to Morality: Spirituality and the Role of Our SuperEgo by Yosi Amram (2022). Available on Medium: https://medium.com/@jyamram/from-reality-to-morality-spirituality-and-the-role-of-our-superego-a942fd2dd80a.

6. *The Courage to Be* by Paul Tillich (2000, second edition). New Heaven, CT: Yale University Press, custodians.

FREEDOM

1. Edison Was Right: Waking Up Right After Drifting Off To Sleep Can Boost Creativity: The State Between Wakefulness and Sleep Is a Sweet Spot for Problem-Solving by Sofia Moutinho (2021). *Science*, December 2021.

2. The Inspiration Paradox: Your Best Creative Time Is Not When You Think by Cindy May (2012). *Scientific American*, March 6.

3. Hacking Creativity: Unlocking the Jujitsu of Innovation by Steven Kotler (2012). *Psychology Today*, July.

4. REM, Not Incubation, Improves Creativity by Priming Associative Networks by Denise J Cai, Sarnoff Mednick, Elizabeth M. Harrison, et al., (2009). *Proceedings of the National Academy of Sciences* 106(25), 10130-10134.

5. *Dreamworking: How to Use Your Dreams for Creative Problem Solving* by Stanly Krippner and Joseph Dillard (1988). Buffalo, NY: Bearly Ltd.

CHAPTER 5: CULTIVATING COMMUNITY
CONNECTEDNESS

1. Student Elaborations in Cooperative Learning Dyads by Jeroen Janssen, Karen Krol, & Simon Veenman (2003). Paper presented at the 10th Biennial Conference of the European Association for Research In Learning and Instruction.

2. *Social: Why Our Brains Are Wired to Connect* by Matthew Lieberman (2014). New York, NY: Crown Publishers.

3. *Wired to Connect: The Surprising Link Between Brain Science and Strong, Healthy, Relationships* by Amy Banks (2016). New York, NY: Penguin Random House.

4. *Aging Well: Surprising Guideposts to a Happier Life from the Landmark Harvard Study of Adult Development* by George Vaillant (2003). New York, NY: Hachette.

5. Loneliness and the Workplace. CIGNA (2020). Available at: https://www.cigna.com/static/www-cigna-com/docs/about-us/newsroom/studies-and-reports/combatting-loneliness/cigna-2020-loneliness-factsheet.pdf.

6. Myeloid Differentiation Architecture of Leukocyte Transcriptome Dynamics in Perceived Social Isolation by Steven W. Cole, John P. Capitanio, Katie Chun, Jesusa M. G. Arevalo, et al. (2015). *Proceedings of the National Academy of Sciences*, 112(49), 15142–15147.

7. Census Bureau Releases New Estimates on America's Families and Living Arrangements. US Census (2021). Available at: https://www.census.gov/newsroom/press-releases/2021/families-and-living-arrangements.html.

8. *I and Thou* by Martin Buber (translation by Walter Kaufmann) (1970). New York, NY: Simon & Schuster.

9. *Loving-Kindness: The Revolutionary Art of Happiness* by Sharon Salzberg (2018). Boulder, CO: Shambhala.

10. How Company Culture Shapes Employee Motivation by Lindsay McGregor and Neel Doshi (2015). *Harvard Business Review, 11,* 1–13.

11. *Love on Every Breath: Tonglen Meditation for Transforming Pain into Joy* by Lama Palden Drolma (2019). Novato, CA: New World Library.

12. Affective and Physiological Responses to the Suffering of Others: Compassion and Vagal Activity by J.E. Stellar, A. Cohen, C. Oveis, & D. Keltner (2015). *Journal of Personality* and Social Psychology 108(4), 572.

SYNTHESIS

1. *The Spectrum of Consciousness* by Ken Wilber (1993). Wheaton, IL: Quest Books.

2. *Changes of Mind: A Holonomic Theory of the Evolution of Consciousness* by Jenny Wade (1996). Albany, NY: State University of New York Press.

3. Seven Transformations of Leadership by David Rooke & William Torbert (2005). *Harvard Business Review,* April.

4. Level 5 Leadership: The Triumph of Humility and Fierce Resolve by Jim Collins (2001). *Harvard Business Review,* 79(1), 66–76.

HOLISM

1. *Industrial Dynamics* by Jay Forrester (1961). Cambridge, MA: MIT Press.

2. *World Dynamics* by Jay Forrester (1973). Cambridge: MA, MIT-Wright-Allen Press.

3. *The Fifth Discipline: The Art & Practice of The Learning Organization* by Peter Senge (1990). New York, NY: Crown Publishers.

CHAPTER 6: SHOWING UP WITH AUTHENTIC PRESENCE

ATTENTION

1. Cultivating Well-Being Through the Three Pillars of Mind Training: Understanding How Training the Mind Improves Physiological and

Psychological Well-Being by Andrew Villamil, Talya Vogel, Elli Weisbaum, & Daniel J. Siegel. (2019). *OBM Integrative and Complementary Medicine*, 4(1), 1-1.

2. Neuroplasticity Within and Between Functional Brain Networks in Mental Training Based on Long-Term Meditationby Roberto Guidotti, Cosimo Del Gratta, Mauro Gianni Perrucci, Gian Luca Romani, & Antonino Raffone. (2021). *Brain Sciences*, 11(8), 1086.

3. The Effect of Focused Attention and Open Monitoring Meditation on Attention Network Function in Healthy Volunteers by Ben Ainsworth, Rachael Eddershaw, Daniel Meron, David S. Baldwin, & Matthew Garner. (2013). *Psychiatry Research*, 210(3), 1226–1231.

4. Yoga, Mindfulness, and Meditation Interventions for Youth With ADHD: Systematic Review and Meta-Analysis by Alyssa Chimiklis, Victoria Dahl, Angela Page Spears, Kelly Goss, Katie Fogarty, & Anil Chacko. (2018). *Journal of Child and Family Studies*, 27(10), 3155–3168.

5. Systematic Review of Meditation-Based Interventions for Children With ADHD by Subhadra Evans, Mathew Ling, Briony Hill, Nicole Rinehart, David Austin, & Emma Sciberras. (2018). *European Child & Adolescent Psychiatry*, 27(1), 9–27.

6. Mindfulness Meditation Training for Attention-Deficit/Hyperactivity Disorder in Adulthood: Current Empirical Support, Treatment Overview, and Future Directions by John T. Mitchell, Lidia Zylowska, & Scott H. Kollins. (2015). *Cognitive and Behavioral Practice*, *22*(2), 172–191.

7. Enhancing Couples' Communication Through Systemic-Constructivist Couple Therapy: The Relationship Between Marital Listening and Relationship Quality by Faye K. (2010). York University.

8. What Companies Want Most in a CEO: A Good Listener by Joseph Fuller & Raffaella Sadun (2021). *Harvard Business School Working Knowledge*. Available at: https://hbswk.hbs.edu/item/what-companies-want-most-in-a-ceo-a-good-listener.

9. Presence-Based Coaching: The Practice of Presence in Relation to Goal-Directed Activity by Elizabeth Topp. (2006). Doctoral dissertation, Institute of Transpersonal Psychology/Sofia University, Palo Alto, CA.

10. *Presence-Based Coaching: Cultivating Self-Generative Leaders Through Mind, Body, and Heart* by Doug Silbee. (2008). Jossey-Bass.

CHAPTER 7: MOTIVATING BASED ON TRUTH

INTENTION

1. Emergent Shared Intentions Support Coordination During Collective Musical Improvisations by Goupil, L., Wolf, T., Saint-Germier, P., Aucouturier, J. J., & Canonne, C. (2021). *Cognitive Science*, 45(1), e12932.

2. The Role of Shared Intentions in the Emergence of Service Ecosystems by Taillard, M., Peters, L. D., Pels, J., & Mele, C. (2016). *Journal of Business Research*, 69(8), 2972–2980.

3. Neural Correlates of Observing Joint Actions With Shared Intentions by Eskenazi, T., Rueschemeyer, S. A., de Lange, F. P., Knoblich, G., & Sebanz, N. (2015). *Cortex*, *70*, 90–100.

EMPOWERMENT

1. *Smile at Fear: Awakening the True Heart of Bravery* by Chogyam Trungpa. (2010). Boston: Shambhala.

2. *The Language of Emotions: What Your Feelings are Trying to Tell You* by Karla McLaren. (2010). Boulder, CO: Sounds True.

OPENNESS

1. *My Stroke of Insight: A Brain Scientist's Personal Journey* by Jill Bolte Taylor (2009). New York, NY: Penguin.

EGOLESSNESS

1. *Ego Free Leadership: Ending the Unconscious Habits that Hijack Your Business by Black*, B., & Hughes, Shayne (2017). Austin, TX: Greenleaf.

2. The Best Leaders Are Humble Leaders by Prime, J., & Salib, E. (2014). *Harvard Business Review*, 11(5), 1–5.

3. Level 5 Leadership: The Triumph of Humility and Fierce Resolve by Jim Collins (2001). *Harvard Business Review*, 79(1), 66–76.

4. *The Way of Grace: The Transforming Power of Ego Relaxation* by Miranda Macpherson (2018). Boulder, CO: Sounds True.

5. *Steve Jobs* by Walter Isaacson (2011). New York, NY: Simon & Schuster.

6. *Flow: The Psychology of Optimal Experience* by Csikszentmihali, Mihaly (2008). NewYork, NY: Harper Prennial.

7. *The Role of Nonduality in the Relationship between Flow States and Well-Being* by Lynch, J. & Allison, S. (2021). Mindfulness, 12(7), 1639-1652.

CHAPTER 8: UTILIZING YOUR INNER WISDOM

INTUITION

1. What Artists Have to Say About Intuition by Seed, John (2017). *Huff-Post*. Downloaded from https://www.huffpost.com/entry/artists-intuition _b_1191320 on December 27, 2022.

2. *Gut Feelings: The Intelligence of the Unconscious* by Gigerenzer, G. (2007). New York, NY: Penguin.

3. *Blink: The Power of Thinking Without Thinking* by Malcolm Gladwell (2005). New York, NY: Little, Brown and Company.

4. Electrophysiological Evidence of Intuition: Part 1. The Surprising Role of the Heart by McCraty, R., Atkinson, M., & Bradley, R. T. (2004). *The Journal of Alternative and Complementary Medicine, 10*(1), 133–143.

5. Intuition: Myth or a Decision-Making Tool? by Sinclair, M., & Ashkanasy, N. M. (2005). *Management Learning, 36*(3), 353–370.

6. *Awakening Intuition* by Frances Vaughan (1979). New York, NY: Anchor Random House.

HIGHER-SELF

1. *Archetypes and the Collective Unconscious* by Jung, C.G. (1959). Princeton, NJ: Princeton University Press.

2. Increasing EFL Learner Self-Confidence With Visualization Tasks by Al–Murtadha, M. (2020). *ELT Journal*, 74(2), 166–174.

3. How to Increase and Sustain Positive Emotion: The Effects of Expressing Gratitude and Visualizing Best Possible Selves by Sheldon, K. M., & Lyubomirsky, S. (2006). *The journal of positive psychology*, 1(2), 73–82.

DEVOTION

1. *Change the World: How Ordinary People Can Accomplish Extraordinary Results* by Robert E. Quinn (2000). San Francisco, CA: Jossey-Bass.

PRACTICE

1. Bill Gates Took Solo 'Think Weeks' in a Cabin in the Woods—Why it's a Great Strategy by Catherine Clifford (2019). CNBC available at: https://www.cnbc.com/2019/07/26/bill-gates-took-solo -think-weeks-in-a-cabin-in-the-woods.html.

2. Give Your Ideas Some Legs: The Positive Effect of Walking on Creative Thinking by Oppezzo, M., & Schwartz, D. L. (2014). *Journal of experimental psychology: learning, memory, and cognition*, 40(4), 1142.

3. Understanding Nature and its Cognitive Benefits by Schertz, K. E., & Berman, M. G. (2019). *Current Directions in Psychological Science*, *28*(5), 496–502.

4. Invent and Wander: The Collected Writings of Jeff Bezos by Walter Isaacson and Jeff Bezos (2020). Boston, MA: Harvard Business Review Press and Hachette Book Group.

5. A 4-Day Workweek? A Test Run Shows a Surprising Result by Charlotte Graham-McLay (2018). *The New York Times*, available at: https://www.nytimes.com/2018/07/19/ world/asia/four-day-workweek-new-zealand.html.

6. Role of Work Breaks in Well-Being and Performance: A Systematic Review and Future Research Agenda by Lyubykh, Z., Gulseren, D., Premji, Z., Wingate, T. G., Deng, C., Bélanger, L. J., & Turner, N. (2022). *Journal of Occupational Health Psychology*, 27(5), 470.

7. Give Me a Break!" A Systematic Review and Meta-Analysis on the Efficacy of Micro-Breaks for Increasing Well-Being and Performance by Albulescu, P., Macsinga, I., Rusu, A., Sulea, C., Bodnaru, A., & Tulbure, B. T. (2022). *Plos one*, 17(8), e0272460.

8. Outcomes of Work–Life Balance on Job Satisfaction, Life Satisfaction and Mental Health: A Study Across Seven Cultures by Haar, J. M., Russo, M., Suñe, A., & Ollier-Malaterre, A. (2014). *Journal of vocational behavior*, 85(3), 361–373.

9. Meditation Programs for Psychological Stress and Well-Being: A Systematic Review and Meta-Analysis by Goyal, M., Singh, S., Sibinga, E. M., Gould, N. F., Rowland-Seymour, A., Sharma, R., ... & Haythornthwaite, J. A. (2014). *JAMA internal medicine*, 174(3), 357–368.

10. The Psychological Benefits of Prayer: What Science Says about the Mind-Soul Connection by Kristen Rogers (2020). CNN available at: https://www.cnn.com/2020/06/17/health/benefits-of-prayer -wellness/index.html.

11. Are Prayer-Based Interventions Effective Pain Management Options? A Systematic Review and Meta-analysis of Randomized Controlled Trials by Jarego, M., Ferreira-Valente, A., Queiroz-Garcia, I., Day, M. A., Pais-Ribeiro, J., Costa, R. M., ... & Jensen, M. P. (2022). *Journal of Religion and Health*, 1–30.

12. A Meta-Analysis on the Relationship Between Prayer and Student Outcomes by Jeynes, W. (2020). *Education and Urban Society*, 52(8), 1223–1237.

13. The Benefits of Prayer on Mood and Well-Being of Breast Cancer Survivors by Levine, E. G., Aviv, C., Yoo, G., Ewing, C., & Au, A. (2009). *Supportive Care in Cancer*, 17, 295–306.

14. Awe and The Interconnected Self by Chen, S. K., & Mongrain, M. (2021). *The Journal of Positive Psychology*, 16(6), 770–778.

15. The Proximal Experience of Awe by Nelson-Coffey, S. K., Ruberton, P. M., Chancellor, J., Cornick, J. E., Blascovich, J., & Lyubomirsky, S. (2019). *PloS one*, 14(5), e0216780.

16. Benefits of Awe in the Workplace by Perez, K. A., & Lench, H. C. (2018, October). *Social Functions of Emotion and Talking About Emotion at Work*.

APPENDIX A

1. The Relation between Emotional Intelligence and Resilience in At-Risk Populations by McCrimmon, A. W., Climie, E. A., & Huynh, S. (2018). *Developmental Neurorehabilitation*, 21(5), 326–335.

2. The Bar-On Model of Emotional-Social Intelligence (SCI) by Bar-On, R. (2006). Psicothema, 18, 13–25.

3. Clustering Competence in Emotional Intelligence: Insights from the Emotional Competence Inventory (ECI) by Boyatzis, R. E., Goleman, D., & Rhee, K. (2000). *Handbook of Emotional Intelligence*, 99(6), 343–362.

4. The Effects of Emotional Intelligence on Optimism of University Students by Kumcagiz, H., Celik, S. B., Yilmaz, M., & Eren, Z. (2011). *Procedia-Social and Behavioral Sciences*, 30, 973–977.

5. Resilience as a Mediating Variable between Emotional Intelligence and Optimism-Pessimism among University Students in Spanish Universitiesby Gavín-Chocano, Ó., García-Martínez, I., Pérez-Navío, E., & Molero, D. (2022). *Journal of Further and Higher Education*, 1–14.

6. The Contribution of Emotional and Spiritual Intelligences to Effective Business Leadership by Amram, Yosi (2009). Doctoral dissertation, Institute of Transpersonal Psychology (Sophia University), Palo Alto, CA. Available at Intelligensi.com/inspirational_leadership/.

7. Connecting the Spiritual and Emotional Intelligences: Confirming an Intelligence Criterion and Assessing the Role of Empathy by King, D. B., Mara, C, & DeCicco, T. L. (2012). *The International Journal of Transpersonal Studies*, 31, 11–20.

8. Effect of Spiritual Intelligence, Emotional Intelligence, Psychological Ownership and Burnout on Caring Behavior of Nurses: A

Cross-Sectional Study by Kaur, D., Sambasivan, M., & Kumar, N. (2013). *Journal of Clinical Nursing* (22), 3192–3202.

9. The Roles of Emotional Intelligence and Spiritual Intelligence at the Workplace by Chin, S., Anantharaman, R., & Tong, D. (2011). *Journal of Human Resources Management Research*, (2011).

10. Age as Moderated Influence on the Link of Spiritual and Emotional Intelligence with Mental Health in High School Students by Shabani, J., Hassan, S., Ahmad, A., & Baba, M. (2010). *Journal of American Science*, 6(11), 394–400.

11. A Study of Occupational Adjustment in Relation to Emotional Intelligence and Spiritual Intelligence and among Senior Secondary School Teachers by Sharma, S. (2017). *DVS International Journal of Multi-Disciplinary Research*, 3(2), 30–39.

ACKNOWLEDGMENTS

THE COMPLETION OF THIS BOOK and the entire journey leading up to it would not have been possible without the immense support and assistance from numerous individuals.

First and foremost, I wish to express my heartfelt gratitude to each of my clients who put their trust in me. Bearing witness to the healing, growth, and beauty of the unfoldment of your soul's potential is among the most fulfilling experiences of my life's work. It is an incredible privilege and honor to be doing this work together with you.

I would like to extend my sincere appreciation to the numerous spiritual teachers, organizational leaders, their staff, and other participants in my research on spiritual intelligence (SI) who made this work possible. I also wish to thank my Integrated Spiritual Intelligence Scale research collaborator, Christopher Dryer, and my dissertation committee members Fred Luskin, Barry Posner, and Shauna Shapiro. Their generosity of time and spirit have been invaluable to the insights I have gathered and put forth.

Furthermore, I would like to thank the mentors, therapists, and teachers who have supported my personal growth through my own inner work. Their insights, compassion, wisdom, and loving presence have helped me navigate through challenging times, heal, and grow to become a better version of myself so I may hopefully pass some of those benefits on to others.

I would also like to express my gratitude to my editors, friends, and reviewers who generously provided their valuable insights and feedback on numerous drafts of this manuscript. I extend special thanks to Gwen Gordon, Val Bodurtha, Jenny Wade, Chini Krishnan, Magdalena Yesil, Jackie McGrath, Kristin Cobble, Kenneth Kales, and Josh Freel for their editorial contributions. And to my cover and book designers, Stewart Scott-Curran, and Joel Chamberlain.

Special thanks to my publisher Bill Gladstone, who believed in me and the potential significance of this book.

Finally, I want to bow down in reverence and gratitude to the creative spirit that inspires us all. It is this spirit that has blessed me with the ability to serve as a vessel for any of the work that has come through me in this life. Despite my ego's proclivity to claim ownership, the truth is that none of this is truly mine.

ABOUT THE AUTHOR

YOSI BEGAN HIS LEADERSHIP JOURNEY in the Israeli military where he received numerous awards and garnered the fastest promotion record in his regiment's history. Despite these accomplishments, the military chafed at his soul, eventually inspiring his lifelong quest for more humane approaches to leadership.

After leaving the military, Yosi studied engineering at MIT and earned an MBA from Harvard. He took the leap into leadership experiments of his own as the founder and CEO of two tech start-ups, both of which he led through successful IPOs.

Then, as CEO of a public company with a rising stock price, he experienced a psychospiritual breakdown, a "dark night of the soul," which catapulted him into a spiritual awakening. The epiphany and the manic episode that went with it were both excruciating and exalting, enabling him to see through the illusion of separation to the truth of our interconnectedness. This put his life and value system on a fresh trajectory.

He went back to school for a PhD in clinical psychology, ultimately developing the first research-grounded theory and validated measure of spiritual intelligence (SI) with an associated model he created and named Spiritually Intelligent Leadership (SILeadership). This research has received over a thousand citations to date.

Yosi is devoted to awakening greater spiritual intelligence in himself (a lifelong journey) and in the world. Working as a therapist and leadership coach, he has supported clients as they built organizations, led thousands of employees, and reached annual revenues in the billions, all while increasing their happiness, power, and effectiveness as leaders in their work and personal lives.

He is also the founder of several nonprofits, including trueMASCU-LINITY.org and Engendering-Love.org. Yosi is blessed with two wonderful grown children who are the bright stars of his life. He enjoys nature, hiking, biking, reading, playing chess, meditating, and dancing.

To receive your FREE spiritual intelligence assessment showing a profile of your strengths and areas for development along with customized tips, see intelligensi.com. There you can also receive a self- or 360-profile of your SILeadership competencies. For a 25 percent discount on any of the paid assessments, use code SILeadershipBook during checkout.

To learn more or to connect with Yosi, see: yosiamram.net.